KOREAN YEARBOOK OF INTERNATIONAL LAW

KOREAN YEARBOOK OF INTERNATIONAL LAW

Volume 12
2024

PARKYOUNGSA
THE KOREAN BRANCH OF THE INTERNATIONAL LAW ASSOCIATION

KOREAN YEARBOOK OF
INTERNATIONAL LAW

Published by PARKYOUNG Publishing&company

PARKYOUNG Publishing&company
210-ho, 53, Gasan digital 2-ro, Geumcheon-gu, Seoul, 08588, Korea
Tel 82-2-733-6771
Fax 82-2-736-4818

First published 1 December 2025
Printed in Seoul, Korea
ISBN 979-11-303-9860-0 93360
ISSN 2635-8484
For subscriptions to this Yearbook, please contact the sole distributor, PARKYOUNG Publishing&company
210-ho, 53, Gasan digital 2-ro, Geumcheon-gu, Seoul, 08588, Korea
Tel 82-2-733-6771 Fax 82-2-736-4818 E-mail: pys@pybook.co.kr

THE KOREAN BRANCH OF THE INTERNATIONAL LAW ASSOCIATION

MEMBERS OF EXECUTIVE COUNCIL

All correspondences concerning the Yearbook should be sent to:
Secretary-General, Korean Branch, ILA
#422, Jamsil REZION Officetel, 87, Ogeum-ro, Songpa-gu, Seoul, Korea
E-mail: ilakoreanbranch@gmail.com / Homepage: http://www.ilakorea.or.kr

EDITORIAL ADVISORY BOARD

CONTENTS

EDITORIAL NOTE

It is our great pleasure to present Volume 12 of the Korean Yearbook of International Law. We would like to express our sincere gratitude to the thirteen authors for their insightful contributions regarding the current development of international law in the Republic of Korea. This volume consists of an array of topics including but not limited to the law on cultural and national heritage, judicial decisions regarding both public and private international law, data privacy, law of the sea, artificial intelligence (AI), environmental law, Korea-Japan relations, and Korea-China Investment Treaty.

Professor Gyooho Lee's article on "The Framework Act on National Heritage and Related Laws" covers the most recent law on national heritage enacted in the Republic of Korea on May 16, 2024. The article provides a thorough discussion on the purpose of the Act, keynote provisions, and how the Act aligns with the international standard of the UNSECO system. The author emphasizes the importance of the Act, which purports to transform the cultural heritage system into a national heritage system by changing and expanding the name of cultural property by subdividing it into cultural heritage, natural heritage, and intangible heritage.

Honorable Judge Jung Hwa You provided his insight into the recent judicial decisions in private international law decided in 2024, specifically focusing on three major 2024 Supreme Court decisions in Korea related to private international law, dealing with contract law (Supreme Court decision (2019Da261558)), arbitration matters Supreme Court decision (2024Ma5904)), and insurance law (Supreme Court decision (2019Da256501)), respectively. Honorable Judge Eun Gi Hon covered three landmark decisions held in 2024, focusing on public international law, including the status of same-sex partners under the National Health Insurance system, the reduction of greenhouse gas reduction targets under environmental law, and administrative regulations regarding access to facilities for persons with disabilities.

Considering the progressively development of data protection law and extraterritoriality, Attorney Ju Eun Lee's article on "Application of Korean Data Privacy Regulations to Foreign Business Operators" examines the extraterritorial application of Korea's Personal Information Protection Act (PIPA) to foreign business operators by providing an in-depth analysis of the 2024 Guidelines issues by the Personal Information Protection Commission (PIPC).

Contributing to the Yearbook are renown international scholars, Professor Lucas Carlos Lima, Professor Aziz Tuffi Saliba and Professor Lutiana Valadares Fernandes Barbosa. Professor Lucas Carlos Lima's article on "The International Tribunal for the Law of the Sea's Advisory Opinion on Climate Change: A Rift Among Equals" discusses the most recent landmark ICJ Advisory Opinion on climate change and its implications to the international community.

With the rapid development in AI, Professor Aziz Tuffi Saliba and Professor Lutiana Valadares Fernandes Barbosa's article on "Artificial Intelligence and Human Rights: A Double-Edged Sword" focuses on both the implications of artificial intelligence to the obligations to protect, respect, and fulfill economic, social and cultural rights, and also the challenges of human rights issues in the context of the AI revolution.

Continuously contributing to the historical aspects of international law in the Republic of Korea, Director General See-Hwan Doh's article on "A Review of Sakutaro Tachi's Distortion of the Principles of International Law on Japan's Invasion of Dokdo in 1905" commemorates the 80th anniversary of Korea's liberation from Japanese colonial rule and the 60th anniversary of the normalization of diplomatic relations between Korea and Japan, by historically analyzing the essential problems of the distortion of the principles of international law in Japanese claims to Dokdo raised by mobilizing international law. Professor Jang-Hie Lee contributed to this volume through his analysis of the Korea-Japan's relations focusing on the victims of Japanese forced labor and the recent Korean Supreme Court decision that ruled in favor of the victims of forced labor for the first time, in his article "Victims of Japanese Forced Labor & Its Approach by the Transitional Justice of the UN Human Rights Committee in the B (ICCPR) Covenant of the Human Rights".

Considering the ongoing importance on environmental law and maritime delimitations in international law, Mr. Jinwoong Seo's article on "Ecologically or Biologically Significant Marine Areas (EBSAs) in the Convention on Biological Diversity and the Issue of Dokdo" interprets the Convention on Biological Diversity and its new proposal of the Ecologically or Biologically Significant Marine Areas (EBSAs) by critically examining the current trends in EBSAs and potential issues that may arise.

Dr. Min-Jung Chung provides two contributions on the current developments in legislation in the Republic of Korea, one focusing on the "Resolution Relating to International Law Adopted by the National Assembly in 2024" and the other focusing on "The Possibility of the 2028 Termination of the Korea-Japan Joint Development Agreement on the Continental Shelf and Anticipated Consequences". As the National Assembly of the Republic of Korea expresses its positions in the form of resolutions, Dr. Chung's article on the "Resolutions Relating to International Law Adopted by the National Assembly in 2024" is crucial in this year's volume as there are two resolutions worth noting related to international law, dealing with the dumping of contaminated water from the Fukushima Daiichi Nuclear Power Plant and the call to the Japanese Government to withdraw its reapplication of Sado Gold Mine on the World Heritage

Committee List and implement UNESCO's recommendations. The second piece by Dr. Min-Jung Chung focuses on the Agreement between the Republic of Korea and Japan Concerning the Joint Development of the Southern Part of the Continental Shelf adjacent to the Two Countries (JDZ Agreement) which was signed on January 30, 1974.

With the increase in foreign investment, Attorney Changwan Han's article on "Three Blades of Leverage: A Critical Perspective on the Korea-China Investment Treaty Framework", provides a comprehensive analysis on three coexisting international investment agreements between Korea and China (BIT, TIT, and FTA). Last but not least, Attorney Yunjeong Hwang's article on "International Divorce in Korea: Legal Framework and Practical Issues" examines the legal framework and practice issues of international divorce in Korea, focusing on procedural aspects and private international law by discussing the amendment to Korea's Act on Private International Law in 2022.

Once again, we are grateful to the authors for their invaluable contribution in the field of international law in the Republic of Korea. We look forward to the ongoing contributions to the Yearbook as it continues to cover current developments in international law.

Professor Junha Kang
Editor-in-Chief
Hongik University

Professor Angela Semee Kim
Executive Editor
Handong Global University

ARTICLES

KYIL

A Review of Sakutaro Tachi's Distortion of the Principles of International Law on Japan's Invasion of Dokdo in 1905

See-Hwan DOH
Director General of Office of Dokdo Research and Public Relations
Northeast Asian History Foundation, Seoul, Korea

Abstract

This year marks the 80th anniversary of Korea's liberation from Japanese colonial rule, and the 60th anniversary of the normalization of diplomatic relations between Korea and Japan. Simultaneously, this year marks the 120th anniversary of Japan's invasion of Dokdo and forced Japan-Korea Treaty in 1905.

On February 22, the 120th anniversary of Japan's invasion of Dokdo, Shimane Prefecture, Japan, held an event to commemorate the 20th anniversary of the so-called "Takeshima Day" established in 2005, and the "Territorial Sovereignty Exhibition Hall", which has been stating Japan's claim to Dokdo, is scheduled to reopen in April after undergoing large-scale remodeling with an investment of 10 billion won. The seriousness of the problem exists in that Japan's provocation of Dokdo, a symbol of Korea's territorial sovereignty, is still ongoing.

Under such awareness of the problem, this article analyzes deeply into the essential problem of the distortion of the principles of international law in Japanese claims to Dokdo raised by mobilizing international law. Through this, this article tracked and identified the problems of Japanese colonialism inherent in the study of title of international law at the Japanese Society of International Law, which has established the policy foundation of the Japanese government's claims, and the Japanese "violence and greed" in the Cairo Declaration, which first declared Korea's independence in 1943, are not only being coincident as an essential substance but also leading to result in the distortion of international law.

It is at this point that it is necessary to pay attention to the fact that Japan, a late imperialist country, established the Japanese Society of International Law in March 1897, the first in the world, before and after the 1905 invasion of Dokdo, and distorted the legal principles of international law to mobilize it for the development and implementation of its invasion policy. The 'International Law Journal', a journal published since 1902, contains many articles regarding the Korean invasion policy.

Moreover, the 'Temporary Investigation Committee of the Ministry of Foreign Affairs'(March 1904-February 1906), which the Japanese government has concealed, was composed entirely of international law scholars and was an organization that legally established the colonialist invasion policy of the Japanese Empire. Its duration coincided with the period of the invasion of Dokdo and the forced signing of Korea-Japan Treaty in 1905, and the members even led the subsequent theory of forced annexation. In particular, Sakutaro Tachi who served as an advisor to the Ministry of Foreign Affairs until his death in 1943, is not free from criticism that he distorted the legal basis for Japan's claim to Dokdo by linking the colonial acquisition methods of European imperialism to the theory of occupation of terra nullius.

This article argues that Japan should fulfill its true historical and international legal obligations as a member of the Northeast Asian Peace Community through overcoming the Japanese colonialism inherent in Japan's invasion of Dokdo, which has lasted for 120 years since 1905 and the distortion of International law by the Japanese Society of International Law since Sakutaro Tachi.

Key Words

International Law, Korea's sovereignty over Dokdo, Invasion of Dokdo, Korea-Japan Protective Treaty in 1905, Sakutaro Tachi, Japanese colonialism, Theory of occupation of *terra nullius*, Japanese Society of International Law, Temporary Investigation Committee of the Ministry of Foreign Affairs

1. Introduction

This year marks the 80th anniversary of liberation, when Korea regained its sovereignty after Japan's 1910-45 colonial occupation, and the 60th anniversary of the normalization of diplomatic relations between Korea and Japan. However, Japan's provocation of encroachment on Dokdo, a symbol of Korea's territorial sovereignty, is still ongoing. The Japanese "Takeshima Issue Research Group", which has been sending out Japan's claim to Dokdo, has begun to denigrate the 1877 Daijokan Directive of the Meiji government, which recognized Korea's sovereignty over Dokdo, and the Japanese Territorial Sovereignty Exhibition Hall is currently undergoing a large-scale remodeling project with a budget of 10 billion won.[1]

The background to this situation is that the year 2025 marks the 120th anniversary of Japan's invasion of Dokdo, and the 20th anniversary of the enactment of "Takeshima Day" in Shimane Prefecture, Japan, which was founded to commemorate the 100th anniversary in 2005.[2] Moreover, the seriousness of the problem is revealed in that Japan's attempt to invade Dokdo based on its imperialist aggression in 1905 has been openly expanded and reproduced to the present day, 120 years later, running counter to the establishment of a community of peace in Northeast Asia.

Under such awareness of the problem, this article aims to dive deeply into the essential problem of the distortion of the principles of international law in Japanese claims to Dokdo raised by mobilizing international law. Through this, this article tracked and identified the problems that the Japanese colonialism inherent in the title study of international law at the Japanese Society of International Law, which has established the policy foundation of the Japanese government's claims, and the Japanese "violence and greed" in the Cairo Declaration, which first declared Korea's independence in 1943, are not only being coincident as an essential substance but also leading to result in the distortion of international law.

In previous research, the author of this paper clarified and identified that Japan, a late imperialist state, laid the foundation for distorting the principles of international law to justify and legitimize aggression in its foreign policy before and after the invasion of Korea's sovereignty over Dokdo in 1905, not only by mobilizing the Japanese Society of International Law founded in March 1897 as the world's first, but also by establishing the Temporary Investigation Committee of the Ministry of Foreign Affairs, a confidential organization linked to the Japanese Society of International Law.[3]

Moreover, the author examined the distortion of the principles of international law by focusing on the Temporary Investigation Committee who were composed entirely of international law scholars by Enjiro Yamaza, who planned Japan's continental aggression starting with the invasion of Dokdo in 1905, during his tenure as the Director of the Political Affairs Bureau (1901-1908), and not the "seven doctors of the Tokyo imperial University" who argued for the opening of the war against Russia on June 10, 1903.

In particular, unlike scholars who resigned in June 1905, Sakutaro Tachi examined the essential problems of distortion of international law in that he comprehensively presented legal principles for legalizing aggression based on Japanese colonialism.

Consequently, Sakutaro Tachi, who is evaluated as the only member fulfilling his responsibilities during the temporary investigation committee's duration, could not be free from the responsibility of leading the distortion of international law as the basis for his policy of aggression against Korea as an adviser of the Ministry of Foreign Affairs until his death in 1943.[4]

2. The Role of the Temporary Investigation Committee of the Ministry of Foreign Affairs and Sakutaro Tachi

2.1 Establishment of the Japanese Society of International Law

The Japanese Society of International Law was established to become a major indicator of the development of international law in Japan, and to "contribute to the development of international law research", with members who were foreign affairs officials "taking charge of diplomatic affairs", and some members "submitting their opinions on current issues as members of the Temporary Investigation Committee".[5]

On the surface, the Japanese Society of International Law aims to advance the principles of justice and humanity for human society based on international law, but in reality, its true purpose was to fully utilize international law as a tool to coordinate the interests of imperialist countries in the struggle for colonies, which was confirmed during the process of plundering Korea's sovereignty and invading the continent, starting with the invasion of Dokdo.[6]

2.2 Establishment of the 'Temporary Investigation Committee' of the Ministry of Foreign Affairs

On June 10, 1903, the Temporary Investigation Committee of the Ministry of Foreign Affairs, which consisted entirely of international law scholars instead of the "Seven Doctors of Tokyo Imperial University" who argued for the opening of war against Russia, was secretly operated as a secret organization, but its basis was confirmed when Sakuye Takahashi, a founder of the Japanese Society of International Law, contributed to the Tokyo Nichnich Shinbun.[7]

Sakuye Takahashi stated that Japan's research on international law has made great progress since the Sino-Japanese War and has developed further since the Russo-Japanese War, claiming that international law contributed to the war in which Japan broke out. He emphasized that not only did the Japanese government value international law issues, but also that the Foreign Ministry, especially facing "international issues" in the Russo-Japanese War, established an "investigation department" targeting "international law scholars" and asked them to consult on "big international issues".

And he evaluated that the Ministry of Foreign Affairs' attitude of respecting the opinions of international law scholars and approaching national affairs with serious thought not only raises Japan's status, but also that organizing an 'academic research institute' within the Ministry of Foreign Affairs to carefully study "international issues" is beneficial.[8]

The Temporary Investigation Committee, which became known through Sakuye Takahashi, was ultimately a confidential organization that was linked to the Ministry of Foreign Affairs and international law scholars who desired to resolve international law issues in the Russo-Japanese War in a way that was favorable to Japan. Sakuye Takahashi highly valued the close relationship between the Ministry of Foreign Affairs and international law scholars from the perspective of an international law scholar.[9]

2.3 Temporary Investigation Committee of the Ministry of Foreign Affairs and Sakutaro Tachi

The Temporary Investigation Committee, established by the Ministry of Foreign Affairs on March 5, 1904, was composed mainly of high-ranking officials from the Ministry of Foreign Affairs and international law scholars.[10] Among the members of the Temporary Investigation Committee, international law scholars Toru Terao, Sakuye Takahashi and Shingo Nakamura were absent due to illness and overwork, while Sakutaro Tachi was the only member of the Temporary Investigation Committee to fulfill his responsibility until the expiration of the term.

Sakutaro Tachi decided not to begin his commitment as professor because he wanted to devote his time to the work of the committee. He was also not assigned to teach a course on diplomatic history until April 5, 1906, after the dismemberment of the Temporary Investigation Committee. These circumstances demonstrate that the Ministry of Foreign Affairs valued Sakutaro Tachi's ability as an international scholar and his research on international law. The Ministry of Foreign Affairs assessed Sakutaro Tachi as "a member of the Ministry of Foreign Affairs who is in charge of research and investigation on all matters of international law and who has performed his duties with great dedication and merit".[11]

However, the assessment of Sakutaro Tachi that he was the only member of the Temporary Interrogation Committee who fulfilled his duties until the expiration of the term is paradoxical because he thoroughly mobilized and implemented international law as the basis for the Japan's policy of aggression and it is an urgent task to clarify the problem of distortion of the principles of international law.

3. International Legal Review on the Occupation of Terra Nullius Theory by Sakutaro Tachi

3-1. A Review on the Historical Theory of the Occupation of Terra Nullius by Sakutaro Tachi

3-1-1. Sakutaro Tachi's Claim Regarding the Historical Theory of the Occupation of Terra Nullius

The historical theory of occupation of *terra nullius* from the 15th to the 19th century presented by Sakutaro Tachi is summarized as follows.

In the 15th century, land discoveries became active, but in the previous period, the effectiveness of control seemed to have been important in terms of land acquisition. Under the feudal system, acquisition of land required an oath of obedience from the inhabitants as a subordinate people. And in order for this master-servant relationship to be established, it was essential that the master had the ability to defend against external enemies and protect the people in the land while effective control of the land was established.[12]

In the Middle Ages, the Roman Pope issued a papal decree granting rights to land. While generally acknowledging that the papal decree had some legal effect, it was recognized that it simply confirmed the rights of land already acquired or created an inchoate title to land to be acquired.[13] After the Reformation, the effect of the Roman Pope's license was not recognized by either the Catholic or Protestant nations.

In the late Middle Ages and early modern era, the claim that one acquired territorial rights to a certain land by discovering it was generally not recognized by other countries, and it was thought that only when a discovery was followed by a symbolic act of annexation could one acquire rights to land or an inchoate title to land.[14]

In the mid-16th century, as England and France followed Spain and Portugal into the world as colonial powers, the validity of the preemptive annexation by Spain and Portugal and the sanction of the Roman Pontiff were denied, and the necessity of actual occupation was insisted on.[15]

Looking at the practice of preemptive annexation in Australia in the 17th and 18th centuries, it was recognized that the preemptive annexation was insufficient to grant sufficient territorial rights to newly discovered lands, and that it simply granted inchoate titles, and that titles should be extinguished if actual possession was not achieved within a considerable period of time, that is, a reasonable period of time.[16]

In the 19th century, as the great powers actively carried out colonization and competed to occupy lands, the preemptive annexation gave rise to the issue of granting territorial rights to newly discovered lands. However, during this period, the prevailing view, both in theory and in practice, was that effective control was the only and sufficient legal cause for acquiring territorial rights.[17]

Thus, the historical theory of occupation of *terra nullius* occupation, which Sakutaro Tachi presented with a considerable time difference in relation to Japan's invasion of Dokdo while he was a member of the Ministry of Foreign Affairs' Temporary Investigation Committee, is analyzed as an attempt to distort the principles of international law - that Japan's invasion of Dokdo was legitimate under international law by linking it to the means of acquiring colonies by European imperialist countries.

3-1-2. A Review of Historical Theory of the Occupation of Terra Nullius by Sakutaro Tachis

As is well known, the term "*terra nullius*" was introduced in international law at the end of the 19th century. There are no cases in which the term *terra nullius* was clearly mentioned until the 18th century, and there exists a record of discussions at the International Law Society in 1888-1889 in its yearbook.[18]

The history of occupation of *terra nullius* described by Sakutaro Tachi is a discussion that develops from the necessity of rights that would legitimize the acquisition of territory in the New World following the external expansion of European powers that began in the mid-15th century. The early advancing countries tried to legitimize the spoils through the authority of the Pope,[19] - but as the authority of the Pope gradually declined, European countries began to develop more realistic legal principles.

The theory of occupation later served to legitimize the results of imperialistic colonial acquisition by European countries, while also serving as a basis for expressing mutual respect for the results of colonial development. Specifically, the judgment of the extent to which state actions constitute effective control that completes occupation varies depending on the era and the situation of the target area. In the early stages of colonial development, even symbolic acts such as simple discovery or raising a national flag were given considerable legal meaning, but as the competition for colonies gradually became fierce, stricter requirements were demanded for possession to be effective. Ineffective possession only created incomplete rights, which were later recognized as complete rights only when they were effective. Looking at past international precedents, the expression of state administrative power is considered the most important element of effective control. In the past, European powers regarded non-European areas as *terra nullius* and targeted them for occupation, but in the Western Sahara case, the ICJ ruled that the residences of politically and socially organized tribes could not be considered *terra nullius.*[20]

Through the historical theory of the occupation of *terra nullius*, Sakutaro Tachi simultaneously emphasizes the “legitimization of colonial invasion” as a means for European countries to acquire imperialist territories and “effective control” as the reality of occupation of *terra nullius.*

The seriousness of the problem lies in the fact that the historical theory of the occupation of *terra nullius* by Sakutaro Tachi not only combines the method of territorial acquisition by European imperialist countries with occupation of *terra nullius*, but also emphasizes effective control, which is the core of Japan’s claim to Dokdo.

In other words, by emphasizing the ‘legalization of invasion’ in the process of acquiring imperialistic colonies by European countries and ‘effective control’ as requirement of the occupation of *terra nullius*, it can be evaluated as nothing more than an attempt to establish the foundation for Japan’s typical distortion of the principles of international law that infringes upon Korea’s sovereignty over Dokdo.

3-2. A Review on the Notification Requirements Related to the Occupation by Sakutaro Tachi

3-2-1. Sakutaro Tachi's Claim Regarding the Requirements of Occupation of Terra Nullius

Sakutaro Tachi first argues as follows regarding the requirements for occupation: The intention of a state to acquire territory, which is one requirement for effective occupation, is expressed (1) by notifying a foreign country of the intention to preoccupy, (2) by publicly declaring such intention domestically, (3) by raising the national flag or erecting a sign indicating that it is the territory of the home country in the area where the occupation is to be carried out, or (4) by implicitly expressing an act that clearly falls under sovereignty by exclusively, that is, performing on the relevant land.

Sometimes, the intention to acquire territorial rights is expressed by notifying a foreign country, but it has not yet been established as a necessary condition under international law that notification to a foreign country must be made at the time of occupation. There are also cases where a declaration to the effect that the local country will recognize the land thereafter, or a declaration, or a ceremonial act such as raising the national flag, is called taking possession of the relevant land, but this is different from the so-called effective possession, or the so-called real possession that Vattel refers to.[21]

In cases where a sign erected locally expresses the intention to maintain territorial rights, the sign must also be recognized as a means of expressing the intention of the state, but it must be erected by a relevant organ of the state, or erected by a private individual with the authorization of the state, or at least ratified by the state after being erected by a private individual. Even if a private individual or private enterprise erects a sign declaring the territory of the state without contacting the state, such a sign does not express the state's intention to possess the territory, and therefore cannot be recognized as expressing the state's intention to acquire the territory, which is one of occupation requirements. In addition, even if there is a sign expressing the state's intention to possess territorial rights, its existence does not serve as absolute evidence proving the state's intention to retain territorial rights, and when the intention to renounce becomes clear due to other circumstances, the loss of territorial rights due to renunciation must be recognized regardless of the existence of the sign.

Sakutaro Tachi secondly argues as follows regarding the notification of occupation. In occupation, notification to a foreign country was one way of expressing the intention of a country to acquire territorial rights, but it is not a requirement under international law today. However, some scholars argue that notification to a foreign country is a necessary condition for occupation.

This is probably due to a misunderstanding that the general resolution of the African Conference in 1885, which specifically stated diplomatic notification as one of the requirements for occupation to be valid, naturally applies to occupation of general land, and that they do not recognize that the provisions of the African Conference resolution, the so-called Congo resolution, regarding the requirements for occupation are not recognized at all according to the 1919 Treaty of Saint-Germain, which is generally a treaty between a number of countries including major countries.

It is also often argued among international law scholars due to the misunderstanding of the opinion of the International Law Society in 1888 that diplomatic notification is one of the requirements for occupation, as declaring the provisions of actual international law, or because it is appropriate for international convenience to notify foreign countries, and because it is immediately recognized as current international law according to the natural legal point of view.

It should be said that current international law does not require expressing the intention to acquire territorial rights in a specific form such as notification to foreign countries for occupation of general land. It is not undesirable to notify foreign countries when preoccupying land because it is convenient to confirm whether other countries have claims regarding the land in question and to clarify the area covered by the occupation, but it cannot immediately decide the issue of actual international law depending on convenience.

In this way, it should be said that notification of occupation to foreign countries has not yet been established as a requirement that must be done as one of the requirements for occupation under actual international law. And at the same time, as long as the effective occupation has not been completed, it can be argued that even if a foreign country receives notification of occupation, it is not necessary to recognize the acquisition of territory.[22]

3-2-2. A Review of the Requirement of Occupation of Terra Nullius by Sakutaro Tachi

Sakutaro Tachi's arguments regarding the requirements for occupation can be analyzed as follows: Sakutaro Tachi's interpretation of the requirements for occupation can be evaluated as not being different from the general theory of the time. Sakutaro Tachi also presented *terra nullius* as an expression of intent to occupy, and effective control as requirements for occupation. In addition, he mentioned the Berlin Protocol of 1885 in relation to occupation, and introduced that the notification of occupation was stipulated as a requirement for occupation in this Protocol.

However, in his writings until 1913, Sakutaro Tachi did not specifically explain whether this requirement was a requirement under general international law regarding occupation or a special requirement that was applied only to the parties to the Berlin

Protocol. Sakutaro Tachi only stated the fact that after the Berlin Protocol, "in the case of occupation, notification was to be implemented".[23] This point is evaluated as being in sharp contrast to Masanosuke Akiyama's description.[24]

At this point, what should be noted is that just as Masanosuke Akiyama is denying the duty to notify in a different way,[25] Sakutaro Tachi is also changing his argument by saying that notification of occupation to a foreign country has not yet been established as a mandatory requirement for occupation under existing international law. At the same time, he argued that unless effective preemptive occupation is completed, a foreign country does not need to recognize the acquisition of territory even if it receives notification of occupation.[26]

Therefore, it can be evaluated that he distorted the principles of international law by emphasizing effective control and denying the obligation of notification thereby ultimately establishing the requirement of *terra nullius* to justify Japan's invasion of Dokdo.

3-3. A Review on the Commentary of the Clipperton Island case by Sakutaro Tachi

The *Clipperton Island* case concerned a dispute between France and Mexico over sovereignty over Clipperton Island.[27] The arbitrators ruled that in the case of uninhabited, inhospitable, and isolated islands, the usual strict requirement of effective control as a manifestation of sovereign power is relaxed, with no requirement that the sovereign effectively occupy, and the arbitrators further held that the first decisive act of sovereignty (such as notification to the Hawaiian government and publication in newspapers and magazines in the Clipperton Island dispute) was sufficient to create a valid title.

Regarding this ruling, Sakutaro Tachi argues that it is contrary to existing theories and practices to say that it is not necessary to meet the requirements for effective occupation of uninhabited islands. Sakutaro Tachi argues that if a state that claims to occupy land or an island does not have the requirements for effective possession, but another state expresses no interest in the island in question, it should not raise an issue related to the existence of the substantive requirements for occupation and should not dispute the validity of the occupation. He further argues that a State that feels an interest in the island claimed for occupation does not have to immediately recognize the sovereignty of the state claiming the occupation even after receiving notification of the occupation. After examining the conditions required for occupation of international law, especially whether the conditions for effective occupation are met, it is argued that trying to determine the attitude of recognizing the occupation for its effectiveness is not illegal, nor should it be said to be an unfriendly attitude.

This argument by Sakutaro Tachi can be ultimately evaluated as emphasizing effective control in the theory of occupation of *terra nullius*. This is something that subsequent insisters of occupation of *terra nullius* in the Japanese Society of International Law have presented as core arguments for the invasion of Dokdo by mobilizing the Clipperton Island case, the Eastern Greenland case,[28] the Minquiers and Ecrehos case,[29] but since they are all international precedents that correspond to the substantive truth of effective control over uninhabited islands, isolated locations and remote areas, they cannot be free from criticism that they are nothing more than arbitrary interpretations and citations based on Japanese colonialism, the foundation of the invasion of Dokdo.[30]

4. A Review on the Problems of Transmission of the Theory of Occupation of Terra Nullis by Sakutaro Tachi

4-1. A Review on the Theory of History of the Occupation of Terra Nullius by Kanae Daijudo

Sakutaro Tachi's theory of the history of territorial occupation is directly inherited to Daijudo Kanae's theory of the principle of occupation in international law. Daijudo Kanae describes it as follows.

The history of occupation in international law has been developed based on two issues: the conflict of interest in the competition for colonies among European countries and the justification of domination over non-European peoples. Occupation was a legal principle that arose during the colonial division struggles of European countries since the discovery of geography, with the goal of acquiring areas outside Europe. It was a legal theory provided by natural law scholars as a basis for England, France, and the Netherlands, which belatedly began acquiring colonies, compared to advanced colonial countries such as Spain and Portugal, which claimed rights based on the Pope's permission or discovery as a priority basis.[31]

And through a complex process, it eventually became established as a principle of international law in the late 18th century, in line with the latter's victory in the struggle to divide the colonies and the needs of the international community. Justifying the acquisition of non-European regions through occupation was not done in the time of Vittoria or Grotius, and only with Vatel was it possible to justify occupation based on labor, and the theory and practice were consistent.[32]

In this way, occupation was established as a legal principle governing the division of colonies, and with the partition of Africa in the 19th century, the legal content was developed, and the requirement of effective occupation, which means the establishment of local power, was newly imposed. This rule was established because the legal beliefs of the countries that it was necessary for the international community were consistent, and the motivation for its confirmation was also acknowledged as a conflict of interest between the colonial countries. In addition, the justification of domination over the colonial people was achieved by the idea of superior European civilization.[33]

In this way, the fact that occupation was established as a norm of international law while stagnating amid the struggles and frictions of many countries can be seen as a result of it meeting the needs of the international community in each era.[34]

Then, Kanae Daijudo's argument is evaluated as a deja vu of Sakutaro Tachi's theory of the history of the preoccupation of *terra nullius*, and it cannot be free from the same criticism given to Sakutaro Tachi. This is because by repeating the argument of 'effective control' as the substance of the occupation requirement and the legalization of colonial acquisition by mobilizing occupation as a method of imperialistic territorial acquisition by European countries, it is tolerating Japanese colonialism as the basis for the legalization of Japan's invasion of Dokdo.

4-2. Review on the Notification Requirements Related to the Occupation by Tetsuya Nagano

The denial of the notification obligation regarding the territorial sovereignty of Sakutaro Tachi is directly inherited to Nakano Tetsuya's theory of denial of the notification requirement, and the following section reviews the representative views of scholars from both Korea and Japan.[35]

First, in the view of Korean scholars, regarding the issue of sovereignty over Dokdo, Dokdo was historically Korean territory and not *terra nullius*, but Japan claimed that it completed the occupancy by incorporating Dokdo into its prefecture on February 22, 1905, through the so-called 'Shimane Prefecture Notice'. However, considering the following reasons that (1) there was no notification to the interested countries, (2) the announcement of the intent to preoccupy was merely a domestic local government notice, and (3) Japan effectively deprived Korea of its diplomatic rights by the Korea-Japan Treaty in 1905, it is not in a position to cite the fact that there was no formal protest from Korea regarding Japan's incorporation of Dokdo. Accordingly, Japan's claim is weakly based on these reasons.[36]

In the view of Japanese scholars, the cabinet decision is the will of the state, but it is a domestic matter, and unless there is an official announcement by a government agency, it is insufficient as a requirement for territorial acquisition. In addition, it is said that the requirements under international law were satisfied by the Shimane Prefecture notice, but it was made through a public announcement by a local government, and the decision of the local government is to inform the local residents, and can never be an expression of the state's external intent.

If, as Tetsuya Nakano argues, the local government's decision, the public notice, is considered an expression of the country's external will, then there is no need to mention international law and the theories of international law scholars. This is because it cannot be free from the criticism that it is sufficient to apply the local autonomy law, which is domestic law, to resolve other international issues.[37]

Furthermore, it can be argued that Japan violated the notification requirement by the fact that the Korea-Japan Treaty was forced on November 17, 1905, depriving Korea of its diplomatic rights without notifying Korea, a country with an interest in the incorporation of Dokdo, and then the following year, the Oki Island officials visited

Ulleungdo to notify it.

5. Conclusion

This year marks the 120th anniversary of Japan's invasion of Dokdo and its forced Japan-Korea Treaty of 1905. The Japanese Society of International Law, which was established in 1897 to lay the groundwork for Japan's policy of aggression before and after the invasion of Dokdo in 1905, and the Japanese Temporary Investigation Committee(1904.3-1906.2) of the Ministry of Foreign Affairs, which the Japanese government has concealed, are confidential organizations that consist of international law scholars to legally legalize the policy of aggression under Japanese colonialism.

This article discusses the acts of Sakutaro Tachi by examining the distortion of the principles of international law centered on the theory occupation of *terra nullius* of Dokdo by Sakutaro Tachi, who led the policy of invasion of Korea based on Japanese colonialism as an advisor to the Japanese Ministry of Foreign Affairs until his death in 1943.

It is noteworthy that Sakutaro Tachi's presentation of the historical theory of the occupation of *terra nullius* as a right of European imperialist states to acquire territory and the principles of international law of effective control has been inherited on to subsequent studies of the Japanese Society of International Law, which has laid the policy foundation for the Japanese government's claim to Dokdo, and has been embraced by Kanae Daijudo's historical theory of the occupation of *terra nullius* and Tetsuya Nakano's negation of the obligation of notification.

In relation to the Dokdo invasion, Sakutaro Tachi cannot be free from criticism in that he not only distorted the principles of international law regarding the title of Dokdo by linking the colonial acquisition method of European imperialism with the theory occupation of *terra nullius*, but he also emphasized effective control and - exclusion of the obligation of notification, and led Japanese-style legal positivism in the subsequent forced protection and annexation process of Korea, thereby laying the foundation for harsh colonization of Korea.[38]

Regarding the assessment of Sakutaro Tachi's recognition of international law, it should be noted that Tachi's perfect fulfillment of his role in response to a strict request from the Japanese government, with the excuse that it was obvious that someone else would take up the task even if he abandoned his role, cannot be criticized as anything other than the epitome of the Japanese colonialist distortion of international law jurisprudence, as he used international law as the basis for his policy of invading Dokdo.[39]

Therefore, Sakutaro Tachi's theory of *terra nullius* occupation based on Japanese colonialism ultimately abuses the theory of effective colonial rule by European imperialist countries, and was succeeded by Kanae Daijudo's historical theory of the occupation of *terra nullius* and Tetsuya Nakano's theory of the denial of the duty to notify *terra nullius* occupation, and it is rooted as the basis of the Japanese government's claim to Dokdo. We must recognize that the essential reality of the deep-rooted violence and greed declared in the Cairo Declaration was Japanese colonialism.

As a symbol of Korean territorial sovereignty and a cornerstone for building an East Asian peace community, Japan itself recognized Korea's sovereignty over Dokdo through the Edo shogunate's order of prohibition of passage on Crossing the Seas of 1696 and the Meiji government's Daijokan directive in 1877. However, regarding Japan's claim to Dokdo that has been mobilized by the distortion of the principle of international law by the Japanese Society of International Law since 1905, the author argues that Japan should fulfill its true historical and international legal responsibilities.

Notes

1 See-hwan Doh, "Korea's sovereignty over Dokdo and Japanese colonialism", Korea Times, February 28, 2025, p.18.
2 See-hwan Doh, "Japan's ongoing invasion of Dokdo and Korea's sovereignty over Dokdo", Dong-A Daily News, February 27, 2025, p.A28.
3 See-hwan Doh, "A Review of Sakutaro Tachi's distortion of international legal principles on Japan's invasion of Dokdo in 1905 and Japanese colonialism", The Journal of Dokdo, Vol.35, 2023, pp.69-105.
4 Rikiya Takahashi, "After Sakutaro Tachi: The Plan to Establish Legal Advisors in the Ministry of Foreign Affairs during the War", Journal of International Law and Diplomacy, 116(3), 2017, p.118.
5 Shinichi Tanaka, "The Global Position of Land Survey Projects in Korea: The Unique Japanese-Korean Character of Imperialist and Colonial Land Policies (1)", Social Science Research 29-3, Institute of Social Science Research, University of Tokyo. 1977, p.55.
6 See-hwan Doh, 2023, p.78.
7 Sakuye Takahashi, "Advancement of International Law Research in Japan", Tokyo Nichnich Shinbun, November 10, 1904.
8 Shinichi Tanaka, *op. cit.*, pp.60-61.
9 See-hwan Doh, 2023, pp.80-81.
10 Records of Ministry of Foreign Affairs, Chinda Sutemi: Advance and Retreat from Duties, Meiji 37.
11 Records of the Ministry of Foreign Affairs, Russian-Japanese War Service Award, <Ministry of Foreign Affairs Personnel Department> (No. 4, Employment, Entrustment, and Mercenary Department).
12 Sakutaro Tachi, "A Historical Study on occupation of land", Journal of International Law and Diplomacy, Volume 38, No.3., 1939, pp.183-184.
13 Sakutaro Tachi, 1939, p.186
14 Sakutaro Tachi, 1939, p.188.
15 Sakutaro Tachi, 1939, p.189.
16 Sakutaro Tachi, 1939, p.190.
17 Sakutaro Tachi, 1939, p.192.
18 Si-jin Oh, "Implications for Dokdo Sovereignty from the principles of the International Law of Colonialism and the title of Occupation", Dokdo's Territorial Sovereignty and International Legal titles Ⅲ, Northeast Asian History Foundation, 2022, p.93.
19 D. Greig, "Sovereignty, Territory and the International Lawyer's Dilemma", Osgoode Hall Law Journal, Vol.26, 1988, p.140.
20 In-seop Chung, New Lectures on International Law, Parkyoungsa, 2017, pp.515-516.
21 Emer de Vattel, Le droit de Gens ou Principles de la Loi Naturalle, Vol.1, Société typographique, 1775, §18, para.207.
22 Sakutaro Tachi, "Legal principles and precedent for the occupation of an island of terra nullius", Journal of International Law and Diplomacy, Volume 32, No.8., 1933, pp.9-12.
23 Sakutaro Tachi, International Public Law in Peacetime, Vol. 1, Lectures of the Tokyo Imperial University in 1913, mimeograph edition, 1913, pp. 186-187.
24 Pae-keun Park, "Theories of International Law concerning Occupation of Terra

Nullius around the Year 1905", Territory and Seas, Vol.6, 2013, p.53.
25 Masanosuke Akiyama, International Public Law, Japananese-French Law School, Shoshimyohodo, 1913, pp.219-221.
26 Sakutaro Tachi, 1933, pp.25-29.
27 Arbitral Award of His Majesty the King of Italy on the Subject of the Difference Relative to the Sovereignty over Clipperton Island(France v. Mexico), Jan. 28, 1931, American Journal of International Law, Vol.26, 1932, p.390.
28 Legal Status of Eastern Greenland, 1933, p.22, 52.
29 The Minquiers and Ecrehos Case, France/U.K., ICJ Reports 47, 1953.
30 See-hwan Doh, 2021, pp.236-237.
31 Kanae Daijudo, International Law of Territorial Attribution, Toshindo, 1998, p.75.
32 Kanae Daijudo, 1998, p.75.
33 Kanae Daijudo, 1998, pp.75-76.
34 Kanae Daijudo, 1998, p.76.
35 See-hwan Doh, "A review on Dokdo sovereignty and Japan's claim of original title from the Perspective of International Law", The Journal of Dokdo, 2021, pp.232-237.
36 Han-ki Lee, Lectures on International Law, New Edition, Parkyoungsa, 2007, p.310.
37 Hideyoshi Kawamoto, "The Historical·Legal Position of Dokdo", Aichi University Society of Korean Culture Research, 1960, p.30.
38 Nishi Taira, Toyoda Tetsuya, Kawazoe Rei, Kwon Namhee, Wakatsuki Tsuyoshi, "Controversy on protectorate: A case study on the practical meaning of European international law doctrines in East Asia", *Nomos*, Kansai University Institute of Law (ed.), 2022, pp.111.
39 Rei Kawazoe, "Sakutaro Tachi's Peace Plan, the Issue of Recognition of 'Manchukuo' and the Theory of Application of Sovereignty", *Journal of Peace Studies*, No.41, 2013, p.120.

The International Tribunal for the Law of the Sea's Advisory Opinion on Climate Change: A Rift Among Equals?

Lucas Carlos LIMA

Abstract

On May 21, 2024, the International Tribunal for the Law of the Sea (ITLOS) issued a landmark Advisory Opinion on climate change and international law, in response to a request by the Commission on Small Island States and Climate Change (COSIS). This was the first advisory opinion by an international tribunal focused on climate change, addressing States' obligations under UNCLOS to prevent and mitigate marine environmental harm caused by anthropogenic greenhouse gas emissions. While the Opinion affirmed key legal duties, its silences—particularly regarding the differentiation of obligations between developed and developing States—are equally telling. This article investigates whether the Tribunal explicitly acknowledged such differentiation, especially under the Principle of Common But Differentiated Responsibilities (CBDR). It analyzes ITLOS's legal reasoning, omissions, and the submissions of States, with particular focus on Brazil and the Republic of Korea. The study concludes that while the advisory process was framed generically, geopolitical divides significantly shaped both the proceedings and their legal implications.

Key Words

International Tribunal for the Law of the Sea, Advisory Opinions, Climate Change

1. Introduction

On May 21, 2024, the International Tribunal for the Law of the Sea ('ITLOS' or 'the Tribunal') issued its Advisory Opinion on Climate Change and International Law – the first of a triad of opinions requested from three international courts between 2022 and 2024 on the subject of the climate emergency. The Opinion was requested by the Commission on Small Island States and Climate Change ('COSIS' or 'the Commission'), an international organization created on October 3, 2021, through the Agreement for the Establishment of COSIS. The Opinion, eagerly awaited by the international community – the first time that an international court has expressed its views on climate change in an advisory capacity – was eloquent in setting out the standards and obligations that protect the marine environment from the effects of climate change. However, its silences are equally eloquent, and reveal dynamics prior to the Opinion that lie at the foundations of international climate law. More fundamentally, the Opinion highlights a clear distinction between developed and developing States, particularly in terms of the obligations assigned to each.

The request for an advisory opinion submitted by COSIS to ITLOS was accepted by the Tribunal after having satisfied itself of the requirements necessary for the exercise of its advisory jurisdiction under Art. 138(1) and (2) of UNCLOS.[1] The Tribunal concluded that the COSIS Agreement is an international agreement in relation to the purposes of the Convention, which expressly states that the Commission is authorized to request advisory opinions from the International Tribunal for the Law of the Sea. ITLOS further concluded that the questions raised by the Commission are of a legal nature and that, since an advisory opinion as such has no binding force and the consent of States which are not members of the requesting entity is not relevant, the Commission is entitled to request an advisory opinion from ITLOS. The request is made up of two separate but interrelated questions. Neither of them was rejected or modified by the exercise of the Tribunal's advisory function. The Commission asked the Court "what are the specific obligations of States Parties to the United Nations Convention on the Law of the Sea ('UNCLOS'), including under Part XII":

(a) to prevent, reduce and control pollution of the marine environment in relation to the deleterious effects that result or are likely to result from climate change, including through ocean warming and sea level rise, and ocean acidification, which are caused by anthropogenic greenhouse gas emissions into the atmosphere?

(b) to protect and preserve the marine environment in relation to climate change impacts, including ocean warming and sea level rise, and ocean acidification?"[2]

The questions submitted to the Tribunal have some features that reveal the strategy of the States with regard to the request. Firstly, they were formulated in a relatively open way. A reading of the headings of the questions could suggest either a restriction of the request to the obligations of the States parties to UNCLOS to those arising from the Convention itself or, on the other hand, an expansion beyond the obligations of the States parties to the Convention, including those arising from UNCLOS itself. In other words, the request seems to have left it to the Court to decide on the law applicable to answering the questions and, more specifically, on the use of rules foreign to the Convention's legal regime. Secondly, the questions deal exclusively with the environmental effects caused by climate change, ignoring other dimensions of the Law of the Sea potentially affected by climate change, for instance, maritime delimitation in the face of rising sea levels. Thirdly, and perhaps most importantly, the request makes no explicit mention of specific obligations imposed only on developed or developing states, nor does it point to any kind of differentiation between the recipients of the Advisory Opinion.

This latter characteristic of the request is the angle from which this article wishes to analyze the Advisory Opinion and, more broadly, the advisory procedure as a whole. At first glance, the request submitted to ITLOS seems generic in nature. However, a careful reading of the Advisory Opinion and, more importantly, of the participation of States in the course of the advisory proceedings, shows that the split between developed and developing states permeates the entire procedure, especially with regard to the effects of the Principle of Common But Differentiated Responsibilities (CBDR). In total, 34 States (including Brazil and the Republic of Korea) submitted written statements to the advisory procedure (31 within the established time limit and 3 out of time), and the majority of which explicitly addressed the Principle of CBDR or specific obligations of developed States towards developing States arising from cooperation duties under UNCLOS. In this sense, the aim here is to comprehend how States' interpretations of the CBDR Principle and other obligations specifically imposed on developed states have been integrated or disregarded by ITLOS.

Some scholars have tried to anticipate the content and consequences of the Advisory Opinion.[3] The objective of this article is to address the following question: Is it possible to conclude that the Advisory Opinion explicitly recognized the distinction between the obligations imposed by UNCLOS on developed and developing states in the field of protecting the marine environment from the effects of climate change? Section 2 will highlight the key developments and conclusions of the Advisory Opinion, emphasizing the salient points of its operative part and the legal reasoning behind each conclusion. Section 3 will examine certain "silences" in the Advisory Opinion, addressing the angles of the questions posed to the Court that were either explicitly or implicitly chosen not to be addressed. This section will also hypothesize on the reasons for these choices. Section 4 will address the issue of the divide between developed and developing States, highlighting how it was incorporated into the Advisory Opinion, particularly the treatment of the Principle of Common but Differentiated Responsibilities (4.1), as well as other pertinent obligations (4.2). In addition to the Court's position, the section will investigate the treatment of the same issue by the states participating in the advisory procedure, with a focus on the approaches between Brazil and the Republic of Korea (4.3). Finally, the conclusion will qualitatively delineate the existence of a split between developed and developing states with regard to their obligations under UNCLOS to combat environmental damage to the marine environment caused by climate change.

2. The Content of the Opinion

The Advisory Opinion serves a dual function. First, it clarifies the existing norms and obligations of States under UNCLOS in relation to climate change, affirming the applicability of the Convention to contemporary environmental challenges. Second, it contributes to the progressive development of international law—not by creating new rules, but by interpreting and framing the normative content and applicable standards of existing provisions. In doing so, the Tribunal enhances legal certainty and strengthens the coherence of the law of the sea with international environmental law.[4] It also sets important interpretative benchmarks that may influence the practice of States and the reasoning of other international courts and tribunals. This interpretative function is particularly relevant in areas where treaty provisions are open-ended or where legal obligations intersect with evolving scientific understanding.

A noteworthy aspect of the Advisory Opinion is its incorporation of binding instruments of international climate change law in its reasoning, effectively connecting the law of the sea with the climate change law.[5] Although framed in response to two questions under the Law of the Sea, the Opinion reaffirms the critical importance of addressing States' obligations under international climate change law. The core of this normative system is, according to the Opinion, the United Nations Framework Convention on Climate Change (UNFCCC),[6] whose central objective is to achieve "stabilization of greenhouse gas concentrations in the atmosphere at a level that avoids dangerous anthropogenic interference in the climate system".[7]

The main operational obligations and mechanisms imposed by the 1997 Kyoto Protocol and the 2015 Paris Agreement are also highlighted by the Opinion as developments built under the UNFCCC that envisage further perfectioning the climate change international legal regime.[8] The role of the Conferences of the Parties (COPs) in the development of mechanisms capable of enabling the measures imposed in the agreements—with emphasis on the Sharm el-Sheikh Implementation Plan—and mechanisms for monitoring the parties in relation to compliance with their obligations is specially recognized.[9] In addition to describing the obligations imposed on States under the UNFCCC and its subsequent agreements, the Opinion also highlights the role of the ozone layer protection regime, centered on the Vienna Convention for the Protection of the Ozone Layer and the Montreal Protocol on Substances that Deplete the Ozone Layer, as well as other regimes implemented under the International Maritime Organization (IMO) and the International Civil Aviation Organization (ICAO).

The mention of obligations imposed on States by other instruments is not incidental. The specificity of the issues presented to ITLOS by COSIS requires the Tribunal to be aware of the need to use rules external to UNCLOS when addressing them—if not through direct application, at least as a means of interpreting the Convention. The first possibility is provided for in Article 293(1) of UNCLOS, which states that "a court or tribunal having jurisdiction under this section shall apply this Convention and other rules of international law not incompatible with this Convention". In turn, the interpretative possibility is explicitly provided for in Article 31(3)(c) of the Vienna Convention on the Law of Treaties (VCLT), according to which the interpreter must take into account, in the interpretation of treaties, beyond the context of their conclusion, "any relevant rules of international law applicable in the relations between the parties".[10] Given the need to rely on rules external to UNCLOS to address the issue, the Tribunal stated that "coordination and harmonization between the Convention and external rules are important to clarify, and to inform the meaning of, the provisions of the Convention and to ensure that the Convention serves as a living instrument".[11] Furthermore, and more specifically, the Tribunal asserted that "the Convention and external rules should, to the extent possible, be interpreted consistently" so as to give rise to compatible obligations.[12] These statements highlight the Tribunal's understanding that the purpose of the Advisory Opinion is to guide States in fulfilling their obligations. More specifically, it aims to do so in a way that does not conflict with or hinder the fulfillment of other obligations imposed on them. In this sense, the Opinion demonstrates a strong effort to align the climate regime with the Law of the Sea obligations established under UNCLOS.

Having identified these two structural characteristics of the Advisory Opinion, we can now proceed directly to an analysis of its key findings and conclusions. The first question posed to the

Tribunal concerns the specific obligations of States Parties to the Convention to "prevent, reduce and control marine pollution in relation to the harmful effects that result or are likely to result from climate change and ocean acidification, which are caused by anthropogenic GHG emissions into the atmosphere".[13] To provide an answer, the first conclusion the Tribunal had to reach was whether anthropogenic GHG emissions fall within the definition of marine pollution under the Convention. Emphasizing that this correlation could not be assumed, the Tribunal noted that "the large majority of the participants in the proceedings recognized that anthropogenic GHG emissions meet the definition of 'pollution of the marine environment' under the Convention", though some participants expressed concern about this broad interpretation—fearing it would grant the Tribunal legislative powers.

The Tribunal stated that Article 1(1)(4) of UNCLOS sets out three criteria for what constitutes such pollution: (1) there must be a substance or energy; (2) this substance or energy must be introduced by humans into the marine environment; and (3) such introduction must result or be likely to result in deleterious effects.[14] In determining whether GHG emissions meet these criteria, ITLOS not only draws on scientific concepts to define terms such as "substance", "energy", or "gas", but also (1) refers to the text of UNCLOS itself, whose preamble asserts that "one of the main goals of the Convention is to establish a legal order for the seas and oceans that will promote the protection and preservation of the marine environment", (2) and also turns to other international treaties and agreements to define terms like "ecosystem"— for example, the 1992 Convention on Biological Diversity (CBD).[15] As a result of this interpretative exercise, the Tribunal concludes that "anthropogenic GHG emissions into the atmosphere constitute pollution of the marine environment within the meaning of Article 1(1)(4) of the Convention".

After overcoming this preliminary step, the Tribunal moves on to the analysis of the substantive obligations of States related to the protection and preservation of the marine environment from pollution caused by GHG emissions. The epicentre of these obligations lies in Article 192 of UNCLOS, which imposes on States the obligation to protect and preserve the marine environment. The rest of Part XII of the Convention elaborates on this central obligation in terms of the prevention, reduction, and control of marine pollution—establishing "specific obligations" in relation to the obligation outlined in Article 192. The Opinion acknowledges that the key provision in this regard is Article 194 of the Convention, which requires States to adopt measures to prevent, reduce, and control marine pollution from "any source".[16] This provision imposes three main duties on States:

> First, the obligation under paragraph 1 to take necessary measures to prevent, reduce and control marine pollution; second, the obligation under paragraph 2 to take necessary measures to ensure that certain situations relating to pollution do not occur; and third, the obligation under paragraph 5 to take necessary measures to protect and preserve rare or fragile ecosystems as well as the habitat of depleted, threatened or endangered species and other forms of marine life.[17]

Regarding the first of the obligations, the Opinion is clear in stating that the Convention does not establish a fixed concept of "necessary measures", although paragraph 3 of the same provision stipulates that such measures may include "those designed to minimize, to the fullest possible extent, the release of toxic, harmful or noxious substances, especially those which are persistent".[18] According to the Opinion, such measures must be determined objectively and in accordance with the scientific evidence provided by the work of the IPCC. Yet, some of the States involved in the proceedings argued that the best scientific evidence is only one of the factors to be considered when defining the obligations of States regarding the prevention, reduction, and control of marine pollution.[19] This position seems to have been adopted by the Tribunal, which, although recognizing that science "plays a crucial role, as it is key to understanding the causes, effects, and dynamics of such pollution", also stated that it cannot solely determine the content of such necessary measures.[20] Further sources of insight may be found in the relevant international rules and standards of the international climate regime. However, the Opinion was clear in separating the compliance requirements of the obligation imposed under Article 194 of UNCLOS from those imposed, for example, under the UNFCCC or the Paris Agreement, stating that:

> The Tribunal does not consider that the obligation under article 194, paragraph 1, of the Convention would be satisfied simply by complying with the obligations and commitments under the Paris Agreement. The Convention and the Paris Agreement are separate agreements, with separate sets of obligations. While the Paris Agreement complements the Convention in relation to the obligation to regulate marine pollution from anthropogenic GHG emissions, the former does not supersede the latter.[21]

The above excerpt demonstrates that, according to the Tribunal, international instruments related to climate change do not constitute *lex specialis* in relation to UNCLOS. There can be no mutual derogation or exclusion of obligations imposed by each of the treaties. Finally, regarding the nature of this obligation, the Tribunal concluded that the duty to prevent, reduce, and control marine pollution constitutes an obligation of conduct rather than an obligation of result. This imposes on States the duty "to deploy adequate means, to exercise best possible efforts, to do the utmost" to achieve the intended result, under a due diligence standard – which is "stringent, given the high risks of serious and irreversible harm to the marine environment from such emissions".[22] The stringent criterion is one of the great novelties of the opinion. For this reason, the obligation is also closely linked to the precautionary approach. The Tribunal asserts that the duty to exercise due diligence extends even to activities for which there is no scientific certainty.[23] Thus, the Opinion concludes that States are obligated to make their best efforts to prevent, reduce, and control marine pollution from anthropogenic GHG emissions under a due diligence standard.

As to the duty to take necessary measures to ensure that certain pollution-related situations do not occur, particularly situations of transboundary pollution, some novelties can also be identified. This provision draws on the well-established customary duty to prevent transboundary harm in international environmental law,[24] applicable whether the damage is caused by private entities or the State, provided that the activity in question falls within the State's jurisdiction or control.[25] In the specific case of GHG emissions, Article 194 of the Convention requires States to take all necessary measures to ensure that emissions under their jurisdiction or control do not cause harm to other States or their respective environments.[26] Yet, the Opinion acknowledges that "GHG emissions are not the type of activities to which Article 194(2), of the Convention is directed".[27]

The Tribunal determined that the obligation in question constitutes "an obligation of due diligence" for the same reason as the obligation set forth in paragraph 1.[28] The Tribunal then emphasized that the duty of due diligence "should not be understood as an obligation which depends largely on the discretion of a State or necessarily requires a lesser degree of effort to achieve the intended result", stressing that it must be fulfilled objectively. Regarding the specific obligation imposed by Article 194(2), the Tribunal highlighted that, due to the nature of transboundary pollution, the protective standard of the due diligence obligation under Article 194(2) may be even stricter than that established in paragraph 1.[29]

The Opinion then proceeds to examine the complex framework

of obligations imposed on UNCLOS member States concerning pollution from specific sources.[30] The Tribunal appeared to find it particularly challenging to trace the sources of pollution as defined by the Convention. However, it ultimately concluded by stating that "most anthropogenic GHG emissions into the atmosphere causing marine pollution originate from land-based sources. In addition, such emissions originate from vessels or aircraft. There are also some GHG emissions from other sources, including from certain seabed activities such as venting and flaring".[31]

The Opinion then proceeds to analyze other obligations relevant to the issue of climate change and its effects on the marine environment under UNCLOS, particularly those stemming from Part XII of the Convention. Firstly, the Tribunal analyzes the scope of specific obligations of cooperation under the Convention. The Opinion acknowledges that the participating States have recognized the need to cooperate in countering the effects of GHG emissions on the marine environment through various forms and fora, and recalls that the duty to cooperate is enshrined both in the Convention and in general international law, as well as in climate change conventions such as the UNFCCC and the Paris Agreement.[32] According to Article 197 of UNCLOS, cooperation may occur at the global or regional level, with the aim of formulating and developing rules, standards, practices, and procedures for the protection and preservation of the marine environment. The Tribunal stated that this obligation "does not oblige States to achieve a normative outcome but to participate meaningfully in the formulation and elaboration of rules", thus constituting a duty of conduct under due diligence.[33]

However, the Opinion emphasizes that the duty to cooperate is not limited to Article 197 but is further developed in other provisions. According to Article 200 of the Convention, States must cooperate to promote studies, scientific research programs, and the exchange of information, while Article 201 states that, based on the results obtained from fulfilling the obligations under Article 200, States parties must cooperate to establish appropriate scientific criteria and standards for regulations. The Opinion affirms that these obligations are applicable in the context of marine pollution from anthropogenic GHG emissions and are important to allow the development of a common regulatory framework.[34] In this regard, the Opinion stated that regulatory measures for the protection and preservation of the marine environment, on the one hand, and the results of scientific research and the criteria produced by them, on the other, have a "close relationship".[35]

Regarding the obligation of technical and scientific assistance, the Opinion recalls Article 202 of the Convention, which stipulates that States parties must promote scientific, educational, technical, and assistance programs to help developing States fulfill their obligations to protect and preserve the marine environment.[36] This obligation will be further discussed later, but it is important to note that the Tribunal determined that this obligation must be particularly fulfilled with respect to States "vulnerable to the adverse effects of climate change".[37]

In turn, the Opinion stated that the environmental monitoring and assessment obligations imposed on States Parties under Articles 204 and 205 of the Convention require them to cooperatively develop means to observe, measure, assess, and analyze the effects of marine pollution, as well as publish reports with the results. Furthermore, under Article 206, States parties are obligated to assess the potential harmful effects of activities carried out under their jurisdiction or control that could credibly cause substantial pollution or significant and detrimental changes to the marine environment. Interestingly, the Opinion stated that such obligations are "procedural in nature", and that compliance with them may serve as an important element in assessing the compatibility between States' actions and their general obligations under Articles 192 and 194 of UNCLOS.[38]

Regarding the monitoring obligation imposed by Article 204, the Opinion notes that it is continuous in nature, as surveillance must be ongoing in order to first collect the risks and effects of pollution on the marine environment through "scientifically recognized methods".[39] In the second phase, States parties must analyze the data collected.[40] Paragraph 2 of the same Article presents an obligation to adopt an even stricter threshold of surveillance over activities "that States have permitted, or in which they are engaged".[41] Under Article 205, in turn, States are obligated to submit reports demonstrating the results of their surveillance activities – a complementary duty to the obligations enshrined in Article 204.

Article 206 conveys another widely recognized and well-established obligation in international environmental law—namely, the duty to conduct an environmental impact assessment. According to the Advisory Opinion, the environmental impact assessment is "an essential part of a comprehensive environmental management system"[42] and "encompasses the duty of vigilance and prevention".[43] The Tribunal acknowledges that Article 206 does not specify the scope and content required for conducting the assessment. However, it asserts that the assessment must pertain to "planned activities" over which the State has "jurisdiction or control" and for which there are "reasonable grounds for believing" that they may cause substantial pollution or significant and harmful changes to the environment.[44] Such assessments must also take into account the cumulative effects of the activity in question with a view to mitigating and adapting its deleterious effects.

After extensively addressing the first question posed by the Request, the Tribunal then shifts its focus to the second question: What are the specific obligations of State Parties to UNCLOS, including under Part XII, to safeguard and preserve the marine environment in response to the impacts of climate change, including ocean warming, sea level rise, and ocean acidification?

According to the Tribunal, the interrelation between the two questions is emphasized, with the second question being broader in scope. It also recognized that the provisions of the Convention relevant to addressing Question (b) are found not only in Part XII but also throughout other sections of the Convention.[45]

The Tribunal begins its response to Question (b) by revisiting its analysis of Article 192, which was previously examined in addressing the first question. According to the Opinion, Article 192 "has a broad scope, encompassing any type of harm or threat to the marine environment" and comprises two key elements: the duty to prevent or mitigate environmental harm and the duty to preserve the marine environment.[46] According to the Opinion, Article 192 also imposes the obligation to "restore" damaged marine environments as part of their duty to preserve the marine environment, although it does not specify the particular harms and threats to which it applies, nor does it delineate the precise measures required to protect the marine environment against both present and future harms.[47]

The Tribunal holds the view that State Parties are under the obligation to adopt measures of adaptation and mitigation to alleviate the harmful effects of GHG emissions.[48] Interestingly, the Opinion immediately links this finding to Article 2 of the Paris Agreement, emphasizing that the Agreement "establishes the global goal of enhancing adaptive capacity, strengthening resilience, and reducing vulnerability to climate change".[49] This duty is, therefore, an obligation of due diligence — though one of an especially rigorous nature. The Opinion asserts that, in light of the risks posed to the marine environment, States, in fulfilling their obligations under Article 192 of the Convention, are required to adopt measures that are as comprehensive and effective as possible to prevent or mitigate the deleterious effects of climate change and ocean acidification on the marine environment.[50]

The Opinion ultimately turns to Article 194(5) of UNCLOS, a

provision that applies the general rule of marine environmental protection imposed by Article 192 to the context of "rare or fragile ecosystems, as well as the habitat of depleted, threatened or endangered species and other forms of marine life". It is interesting to note that the Court does not consider ecosystems and habitats to be "inherently" vulnerable, rare, or fragile. Rather, it holds that these conditions can change over time as a result of human activity.[51] Still, the Opinion draws on elements such as the definition of habitats from the Convention on Biological Diversity and the classification of species in the appendices to CITES as important sources of guidance for States in fulfilling their obligations.[52] Furthermore, the Opinion contends that the provision in question may necessitate the adoption of "context-specific" measures, governed by the relevant domestic legal framework, and permitting a degree of discretion. However, this discretion is circumscribed by scientific assessments and, crucially, by the obligation of good faith with respect to measures that could pose a threat to the collective interests of mankind.[53]

The Opinion continues by identifying additional obligations pertinent to addressing the second question. The Tribunal emphasizes that, pursuant to Article 61 of UNCLOS, State Parties bear the obligation to implement conservation and management measures, at their discretion, to ensure that the maintenance of living resources in the exclusive economic zone is not imperiled by overexploitation.[54] Specifically, these measures must be informed by a range of scientific data — including the movements of marine resource populations — with a view to ensure their populations are maintained or restored at levels above which their reproduction may become seriously threatened.[55] Article 119, in turn, stipulates the duty to conserve natural resources in the high seas, indicating that this obligation is fundamentally the same as that imposed on States within their exclusive economic zones.[56]

Regarding the general obligation of cooperation, the Opinion acknowledges its significance in addressing the second question of the Request. Following Article 63, the Court identifies that when the same stock or associated species are found within the exclusive economic zones of multiple coastal States, these States must cooperate, either directly or through regional arrangements, to coordinate measures for their conservation. Furthermore, if the same stock occurs both within the exclusive economic zone and in an adjacent area beyond the zone, the coastal State and States fishing in the adjacent area must agree on conservation measures for these stocks, either directly or through regional organizations.[57] By its turn, according to Article 118 of the Convention, States are obligated to cooperate in the conservation and management of living resources in the high seas. States whose nationals exploit identical or distinct living resources in the same area must engage in negotiations to implement the necessary measures for the conservation of those resources. As appropriate, they shall collaborate to establish subregional or regional fisheries organizations to this end.[58] In a similar vein, the Court highlights the obligations arising from the Fish Stocks Agreement.

Under Article 196 of the Convention, States shall take all necessary measures to prevent, reduce, and control pollution of the marine environment resulting from technologies under their jurisdiction or control, as well as the intentional or accidental introduction of alien or new species into a specific part of the marine environment, which may cause significant and harmful changes. The Opinion asserts that, with regard to the introduction of new species, the purpose of this provision is "to address the disturbance of the ecological balance of the marine environment as a result of human activities".[59] It also notes that the provision "implies the precautionary approach" through the usage of the word "may".[60]

Finally, regarding the so-called "marine protected areas" and "area-based management tools", the Court notes that these categories are not explicitly present in UNCLOS. However, it asserts that their implementation through regional treaties and collaborative arrangements is not prohibited by the Convention, and serves to provide a higher protective standard for certain marine environments.[61] However, it also notes that "such measures must be consistent with the Convention and other rules of international law"[62] – explicitly positing the Convention at the center of the global regime concerning the Law of the Sea and the protection of the maritime environment.

3. The Silences of the Opinion

Albeit comprehensive in scope, the Advisory Opinion rendered by ITLOS is not an all-encompassing piece. Rather, it is a product of legal reasoning shaped by both the methodological and political choices made by the Tribunal itself and the parties who authored the request.[63] While silences reflect zones of indecision, they function as evidentiary artifacts of the coalition of forces that shape the formulation of an advisory opinion in practice. In this section, only "explicit" silences will be discussed,i.e., silences acknowledged openly by the Court.

Examples of silences can be found in the section of the Advisory Opinion concerning the Scope of the Request (Section VI, A). The Tribunal notes that the two questions presented are self-limiting, as they ask ITLOS to identify the "specific obligations imposed on States Parties to the United Nations Convention on the Law of the Sea… including Part XII".[64] In this regard, the Tribunal must also limit itself to providing clarifications and guidance solely on the application of obligations arising from UNCLOS, while recognizing that it should "take into account external rules, as appropriate", in order to interpret those obligations.[65] The consequence is a definitive silence regarding the scope and content of obligations external to UNCLOS – such as those stemming from the UNFCCC or the Paris Agreement. This differs from the earlier assertion that the Advisory Opinion extensively employs the obligations of States arising from other climate instruments in an instrumental-interpretative manner, both to define the precise content of obligations under UNCLOS (i.e., treating them as other relevant norms of international law for interpretative purposes) and to promote a "harmonious interpretation" of the States' obligations from different sources.[66]

A second example of an "explicit" silence concerns the Tribunal's consideration of issues related to State responsibility and their relevance to the scope of the Request. While some States involved in the proceedings argued that addressing issues of responsibility would be relevant to answering the questions posed to the Tribunal, others asserted that such issues exceeded the scope of the Request, which is limited to addressing primary obligations under the Convention and does not consider the "legal consequences arising from the breach of obligations".[67] The Tribunal noted that the Request presented was notably different from previous instances in which it was called upon to address issues related to State responsibility—specifically in the Advisory Opinion Responsibilities and obligations of States with respect to activities in the Area, where the interpretation of the scope of secondary rules and their application was explicitly requested from the Tribunal.[68] In addressing the dilemma, the Tribunal took a stricter stance—yet still left room for flexibility: it limited itself to examining "primary obligations", but acknowledged that "to the extent necessary to clarify the scope and nature of primary obligations, the Tribunal may have to refer to responsibility and liability".[69]

A third explicit silence in the Opinion concerns the previously mentioned Law of the Sea issues of a non-environmental nature—specifically, issues related to sea level rise and its effects on maritime claims and entitlements. The Tribunal affirms that the

Request explicitly mentions sea level rise in its two questions and further pointed out that the Preamble of the COSIS Agreement recognizes that the maritime zones delineated "in accordance with the Convention, and the rights and entitlements that flow from them, shall continue to apply, without reduction, notwithstanding any physical changes connected to climate change-related sea-level rise".[70] However, the Tribunal acknowledges that the States involved did not request to address the issue of "base points, baselines, claims, rights, or entitlements" related to maritime zones, focusing instead solely on issues related to marine environmental protection. In the absence of an explicit request on this matter, the Tribunal adopted a restrictive interpretation of the Request and opted to exclude maritime boundary delimitation issues from the scope of the Opinion.

4. The Division Between Developed and Developing States

Of all the structural features of the Advisory Opinion, the most pervasive is the distinction between developed and developing States, and consequently, the differentiation of the specific obligations imposed on each. This cleavage is, in fact, a fundamental element of International Environmental Law, nearly ubiquitous across all environmental regimes within international law.[71] In the specific context of the climate regime, this cleavage underscores the historical disparity between developed States, which bear the largest responsibility for GHG emissions, and developing States, whose contribution to the causes of climate change was minimal in comparison. Consequently, the interests and interpretations put forward by developing countries have played a crucial role in the evolution of international environmental norms since the Stockholm Conference of 1972 and the Rio Conference of 1992.

The most prominent manifestation of the developed-developing division is the application of the CBDR Principle.[72] This principle acknowledges the unequal capacities and historical contributions of states to environmental degradation, particularly in relation to climate change. The logic of the principle implies that while all countries share the collective responsibility to address climate change, developed nations, as the primary historical emitters of greenhouse gases, are expected to bear a larger burden in terms of mitigation and financial support for developing nations. Conversely, developing countries are recognized as having the right to pursue economic growth and development, which may necessitate a more gradual approach to environmental obligations. As will be seen in the following, the CBDR Principle was largely applied by the Tribunal as both a substantive obligation and an interpretative mechanism.

However, the developed-developing distinction also extends and affects other obligations. Overall, the Tribunal supports the view that certain obligations arising from UNCLOS have different scopes of application, content, or protective standards depending on the State implementing them—whether developing or developed. This perspective is also widely shared by many of the States participating in the advisory proceedings. Nauru, for instance, asserts the pertinence of the developing-developed cleavage, highlighting that the Convention's Preamble expressly mentions "the special interests of developing countries" as one of its pivotal concerns. By its turn, Portugal highlights that, in accordance with the UNFCCC, "the responsibility for climate change is not evenly distributed, with developed and developing countries contributing differently to global GHG emissions".[73] In a solemn tone, Sierra Leone asserts that developing states encounter considerable obstacles in addressing climate change, with their ability to take action frequently constrained by limited resources and capacities.[74]

This brief introduction illustrates how the developed-developing divide is deeply embedded in the lexicon of international environmental law and how seamlessly it found its way into the judicial reasoning of ITLOS. Subsequently, its presence in the Advisory Opinion will be analyzed, first through the lens of the CBDR Principle, and then in relation to other obligations derived from the Convention.

4.1. Common But Differentiated Responsibilities

The CBDR Principle, although not always explicitly referenced by the Advisory Opinion when addressing the developing-developed divide, is nonetheless treated as a fundamental principle within the legal framework established by UNCLOS – or, at the very least, in the interpretation of it provided by the Tribunal. Its rationale is evident when the Opinion emphasizes that the Preamble of the Convention aligns its objectives with the promotion of a just and equitable international economic order, one that appropriately acknowledges the special interests and needs of developing States.[75]

The Advisory Opinion acknowledges that UNCLOS State Parties are also bound by the CBDR Principle through other relevant instruments. For example, Article 3 of the UNFCCC directly refers to "common but differentiated responsibilities and respective capabilities, specific needs, and special circumstances of developing country Parties" and establishes it as one of the Convention's guiding principles.[76] Article 4 of the same Convention establishes general obligations applicable to all Parties to the UNFCCC, as well as other obligations that apply only to States listed in Annex 1 – developed country Parties and country Parties undergoing the transition to a market economy. In a similar vein, the Opinion references the Paris Agreement, particularly Article 4(2), which mandates that State Parties "prepare, communicate, and maintain successive nationally determined contributions" that take into account "common but differentiated responsibilities and respective capabilities, in light of differing national circumstances".[77] In addition, Article 4(4) of the Paris Agreement posits that developed country Parties should continue taking the lead by undertaking economy-wide absolute emission reduction targets, while developing country Parties should continue enhancing their mitigation efforts, and are encouraged to move over time towards economy-wide emission reduction or limitation targets in the light of different national circumstances.[78]

In several instances throughout the Advisory Opinion, the Court asserts that certain obligations arising from the Convention, although not codifying the CBDR Principle, contain "underlying elements of the principle". This is the case, for example, with the obligation to provide assistance and support to developing States, as outlined in Article 202 of UNCLOS.[79] These cases will be analyzed in the next section, demonstrating that the CBDR Principle operates not merely as a standalone legal norm but as an underlying rationale that encapsulates the developed-developing divide and guides the interpretation and application of other norms, in other words, as a general principle of international law.[80]

The CBDR Principle was also prominently invoked by numerous participants in the advisory proceedings. Several States participating in the consultative proceedings acknowledged the significance of the CBDR Principle in addressing the issues raised in the Request. For instance, in its written submission, the Democratic Republic of the Congo (DRC) asserted that, given the historical and ongoing responsibility of industrialized nations for greenhouse gas emissions, as well as the heightened vulnerability of developing states to climate change, "industrialized countries must bear the greatest burden in this respect in accordance with the principle of common but differentiated responsibilities and respective capabilities".[81] In the same vein, the DRC affirmed that if an industrialized State fails to bear responsibility for its fair share of the burden in the fight against climate change, "it does not prevent it and thus transfers the damage or hazards of climate change to developing countries".

Other States prefer to highlight the applicability of the CBDR principle through instruments of the international climate change regime. New Zealand and Portugal underscored that the CBDR Principle is explicitly preserved within the framework of the Paris Agreement, as enshrined in Article 2(2),[82] while China maintains that "the international community should adhere to the principle of common but differentiated responsibilities" enshrined in the UNFCCC.[83] The Chinese contribution also posits that the CBDR principle is "the cornerstone of global governance on climate change, [and] must always serve as the guiding principle for addressing climate change".[84] By its turn, Australia's and Canada's contributions emphasizes that "common but differentiated responsibilities and respective capabilities" should guide each country's NDC, ensuring their highest possible ambitions are reflected,[85] a similar perspective to Singapore's, which highlights the "difficulties that some Parties face in switching to alternative energy options due to geographical constraints", emphasizing the relevance of national circumstances and the CBDR principle to the fairness and ambition of Parties' NDCs.[86] France asserts that both the UNFCCC and the Paris Agreement "reflect" the CBDR principle, "echoing the approach of UNCLOS".[87] Finally, Chile argues that States Parties to the Paris Agreement should "aim for a progressive reduction in GHG emissions" reflecting their highest possible ambitions, while ensuring these reductions account for the principle of common but differentiated responsibilities and respective capabilities, in light of different national circumstances.[88]

Other States explored more qualitative avenues when referring to the CBDR Principle. For example, Mozambique asserts that the CBDR principle is intimately connected with the obligation to reduce greenhouse gas emissions in such a way as "the majority of the burden falls on developed States".[89] Mozambique also acknowledges that the CBDR Principle—albeit sometimes subtly—permeates the entire Convention, ensuring that it considers the interests and needs of humanity as a whole, while placing particular emphasis on the special interests and needs of developing countries, whether coastal or landlocked.[90] Singapore states that the CBDR principle is the basis for providing all kinds of "differentiated obligations on developed and developing countries" in such a way as to take into account "the economic capacity of developing States and their need for economic development".[91] In the same vein, Sierra Leone affirms that the CBDR principle "ensures that the responsibilities of countries to address climate change are proportional to their historical contributions and capabilities".[92] This position aligns with that of Djibouti, whose written submission explicitly acknowledges the CBDR principle as outlined in Article 194 of UNCLOS.[93] Even more clearly, Rwanda affirms that the CBDR principle "is not in conflict with UNCLOS", but aligns with key provisions that recognize that some states may require assistance to comply with environmental obligations or impose the duty on developed States to assist in various forms developing States to fulfill their obligations.[94]

Some states evoked the interpretative function of the CBDR principle in relation to other pertinent norms of international law. For instance, the DRC affirmed that the obligation not to transfer damage or hazards or transform one type of pollution into another under Article 195 of the Convention "must be interpreted and applied in light of the principle of common but differentiated responsibilities and respective capabilities and thus applies to industrialized States in particular".[95] The DRC posits the same reasoning in relation to the obligation enshrined in Article 207 concerning measures to combat pollution of the marine environment from land-based sources.[96] By its turn, Mozambique interprets the phrase "in accordance with their capabilities" in Article 194(1) as evidence that the CBDR principle is reflected in the Convention, arguing that it implies developed States should bear the largest burden of adopting measures and assist developing countries in fulfilling their responsibilities.[97] Further,

Mozambique states that the CBDR principle must be understood as a relevant norm of international law in the sense of Article 31(3)(c) of the Vienna Convention on the Law of Treaties (VCLT), in such a way as it is "relevant in giving content to the measures to be adopted".[98] Mauritius is particularly eloquent in this respect:

> Article 2(2) of the Paris Agreement provides that it will be implemented to "reflect equity and the principle of common but differentiated responsibilities and respective capabilities, in the light of different national circumstances". Under an integrated approach to the climate-related duties arising under Part XII of the Convention, it will be necessary to consider the extent to which these principles relate to specific obligations, having regard to the support that Developed Country Parties are required to provide Developing State Parties, especially those particularly vulnerable to the adverse effects of climate change and having significant capacity constraints, such as the Least Developed Countries and Small Island Developing States.[99]

In a similar vein, Portugal asserts that international cooperation to address climate change must be based on a mechanism of differentiated responsibility, reflecting the varying capabilities and economic and social conditions of nations.[100] The Portuguese declaration affirms that the CBDR Principle serves as an interpretative link between the two legal regimes – the law of the sea and climate change. The CBDR principle guides cooperative action among States to (i) address the adverse impacts of climate change and (ii) preserve and protect the marine environment, with particular emphasis on the connection between the ocean and the climate system.[101] Also notably, Viet Nam regards the CBDR principle as "a relevant rule of international law" which is vital for "determining obligations related to the protection of the environment".[102]

4.2 Other Obligations

The Tribunal does not limit its engagement with this divide to explicit references to the CBDR Principle; rather, it weaves the distinction between developed and developing States into its broader legal reasoning. This is evident in its recognition of disparities in capacity and resource access, which in turn shape the specific obligations imposed on States under UNCLOS—ranging from the adoption of measures to due diligence and cooperation. This underscores the pervasive influence of the CBDR Principle's rationale, affirming its role as a guiding framework within the Convention's interpretative structure.

First, some participating States seem to directly link the developed-developing States distinction to the Tribunal's authority to exercise its advisory jurisdiction. For instance, New Zealand emphasized that "the importance of the questions posed to members of the Commission and other small island developing States, and the collective interest of State Parties to the Convention in the protection of the marine environment, are factors that weigh in favour of the Tribunal exercising its discretion to issue an advisory opinion".[103] This argument suggests that the Tribunal's advisory jurisdiction is not merely a matter of discretion or of cold application of statutory rules, but is also influenced by considerations of equity and global environmental governance. By framing the exercise of jurisdiction by ITLOS within the context of the developed-developing divide, States reinforce the notion that differentiated obligations are not only substantive but also relevant to procedural determinations within UNCLOS.

Second, the developed-developing divide is evident in the context of the specific obligation under Article 194(1) to adopt necessary measures for the prevention, reduction, and control of marine pollution—particularly that arising from anthropogenic GHG emissions. The Tribunal affirms explicitly that Article 194 does not encapsulate the CBDR principle, though "it contains some elements common to this principle".[104] The Opinion asserts that the application of this obligation must consider various factors, including the means and capacities available to the State in question.[105] This means that the measures adopted must vary based on each State's "scientific, technical, economic, and financial capabilities".[106] This "degree of flexibility", according to the Tribunal, "aims to accommodate the needs and interests of States with limited means and capabilities" and "'to lessen the excessive burden that the implementation of this obligation may entail for those States". Nevertheless, the Opinion warns that differences in technical or financial capacities cannot serve as a justification for avoiding or postponing the adoption of necessary measures under Article 194(1).[107] In this context, the provision primarily serves as a "call to leadership" for developed countries, rather than a concession to developing parties.[108] Judge Kulyk adopted an even more stringent stance, asserting in his declaration that "the absence of capabilities does not negate the necessity of action; rather, it demands the prioritization of essential measures and concerted efforts to enhance capabilities".[109] In the judge's view, the inconsistent treatment of the obligation to undertake all necessary measures undermines the uniform application of the highest standards for the protection and preservation of the marine environment.[110]

Still concerning the obligation to adopt necessary measures to prevent, reduce, and control marine pollution, Norway asserted that such measures must be implemented "taking into account the best practical means at their disposal" and "in accordance with their capabilities".[111] By its turn, France affirms that "while the Convention is stringent, it allows flexibility for States to use the best practicable means at their disposal and in accordance with their capabilities".[112] The French pronunciation also underscores that the criteria for implementing obligations under the Convention may be stricter for developed States compared to developing States, depending on scientific knowledge and technical and financial capabilities.[113]

Another compelling example of how the scope of obligations under UNCLOS varies between developed and developing States pertains to the standard of due diligence. The Advisory Opinion is unequivocal in asserting that the protective standard of due diligence must be "stringent". Still, it also acknowledges that its implementation "may vary according to States' capabilities and available resources", indicating that a State with "greater capabilities and sufficient resources" is expected to take more extensive action than a less resource-endowed State.[114] Yet, this does not suggest that a developing State is absolved from its obligation or may neglect to utilize all available means and capacities to uphold due diligence. It merely states that the capacities of developed and developing states must be taken into account on analyzing whether a given State was duly diligent when fulfilling its obligations. This very position is advanced by the European Union in its contribution to the advisory proceedings, according to which "the different financial and technical resources at the disposal of a State can contribute to determine the precise standard of due diligence required by a given State".[115] In the same vein, Singapore states that "the individual capacities, capabilities and constraints of a State would also be relevant in determining the content of the due diligence obligation".[116] Interestingly, Singapore's contribution highlights that the due diligence threshold depends on the "context and nature of the primary obligation relied upon", citing Article 194 of the Convention, which explicitly references "best practicable means at their disposal and in accordance with their capabilities" as a key factor in its application.[117]

The developed-developing divide is perhaps mostly visible in relation to the obligations of cooperation that permeate UNCLOS. The DRC, for instance, highlights that Article 207(4) of the Convention conveys the need "to take into account characteristic features of each region, the economic capacities of developing States and their need for development" when fulfilling the obligation.[118] New Zealand's submission states that, in accordance with the obligations stemming from Article 9 of the Paris Agreement, "developed country Parties should provide financial resources to assist developing country Parties with respect to both mitigation and adaptation".[119] In addition, it submits that "enhanced efforts are required to build the capacity of developing State Parties to respond to the impacts of climate change, including mitigation and adaptation actions".[120] Accordingly, China, while also recalling the States' obligations under the international climate regime, affirms that developing states must benefit from an enhancement of "cooperative action on technology development and transfer" assisting them in adaptation and capacity-building action[121]—while Mozambique understands that compliance and fulfillment of obligations under Article 207 of the Convention must "tak[e] into account characteristic regional features, the economic capacity of developing States and their need for economic development".[122] France, by its turn, delineates that the obligation to cooperate must necessarily comprehend "the allocation of appropriate funds and technical assistance to developing States", including through existing mechanisms such as the Global Environment Fund.[123] For the United Kingdom, cooperation under the Convention's Part XII can take many forms, but must necessarily include "the provision of technical assistance to developing States".[124] Finally, Sierra Leone reminds that Article 203 stresses preferential treatment for developing countries, ensuring they receive financial and technical support to mitigate environmental damage.[125]

More specifically, a minority of participating States have delineated a connection between the developed-developing divide and the obligations of adaptation stemming whether from the climate regime or the Convention. For instance, Canada affirms that adaptation is a key component of the global response to climate change, aimed at protecting people, livelihoods, and ecosystems, particularly addressing the urgent needs of developing country Parties that are especially vulnerable to climate change impacts.[126] Canada also reminds that the international climate change regime has long included efforts on adaptation, including bodies like the Global Goal on Adaptation, which seeks to enhance adaptive capacity, strengthen resilience, and reduce vulnerabilities, as well as the Least Developed Countries Expert Group (LEG), which accelerates support for national adaptation plans in least developed countries.

The Advisory Opinion also identifies specific obligations that, while not imposing more stringent standards of conduct on developed States in relation to a shared duty with developing States, do require assistance and support for the latter. This benefit seems to be not only a consequence of the unfavorable technical and economic situation of developing states, but also of the fact that "such States suffer more severely from their effects on the marine environment".[127] An example can be found in Article 202 of UNCLOS, which pertains to technical and scientific assistance to developing States. According to the Tribunal, such assistance "seeks to alleviate the difficulties of developing States in addressing this issue and to enhance their capacity to do so" and is "a means of addressing an inequitable situation".[128] Consequently, the assistance may equip developing States with the means to participate in "relevant international research and capacity-building programs", enabling them to develop autonomous capacities for research and technological advancement.[129] Similarly, Article 203 establishes preferential treatment for developing States—an obligation that must be fulfilled by the States, though not exclusively, "through the international organizations of which they are members".[130] The Tribunal asserts that the fulfillment of these obligations can take various forms, including utilizing the multiple assistance mechanisms that enable developing States to address the issue of marine pollution from GHG emissions, which coexist with those established under the UNFCCC and the Paris Agreement.[131] It is also noted that the means of assistance outlined in Articles 202 and 203 of the Convention are not exhaustive of the possibilities available for States to pursue[132] and its choice is left for their discretion.[133]

Participating States have also identified a connection between the developed-developing divide and the duty to provide technical and financial assistance. China, for instance, emphasized that the Opinion should "give special consideration to the unique challenges and critical concerns of developing countries, while enhancing support in financing, technology, and capacity building to facilitate their transition toward low greenhouse gas emissions and climate-resilient development".[134] The Chinese contribution goes as follows:

> Developed countries should effectively fulfill their obligations to substantially reduce emissions, honor their commitment to provide funding of US $100 billion annually to developing countries by 2020, develop a road-map for doubling adaptation finance, and provide financial resources to the Loss and Damage Fund in order to effectively assist developing countries, including small island developing States and least developed countries, and help them to enhance their climate resilience and address loss and damage associated with the adverse effects of climate change.[135]

Regarding the obligation to conduct an environmental impact assessment under Article 206 of UNCLOS, the Tribunal stated that the Convention does not prescribe a specific procedure or content for its implementation, emphasizing that "such content and procedure are to be determined by each State in its legislation".[136] The Opinion recalls the dictum of the International Court of Justice in Pulp Mills on the River Uruguay, which held that domestic legislation on the matter must "have regard to the nature and magnitude of the proposed development and its likely adverse impact on the environment, as well as to the need to exercise due diligence in conducting such an assessment".[137] The Tribunal advanced the interpretation that "the different capabilities of States, especially developing States", must be taken into account in the course of conducting environmental impact assessments, thereby ensuring them a certain degree of flexibility.[138]

4.3. Approximations between Brazil and Korea

Both Brazil and the Republic of Korea adhere to the division between developed and developing States as the basis for imposing differentiated obligations on each category, taking into account the economic conditions, technical factors, and respective capacities of each Party. Both countries emphasized that developing States should be given more leeway in fulfilling their obligations and affirmed that a fair and equitable distribution of responsibilities requires accounting for both the socio-economic realities and the environmental needs of each State.

The Republic of Korea is perhaps a bit more succinct in establishing the developed-developing divide in its contribution. To begin with, Korea does not mention the CBDR Principle. The Korean text establishes, in fact, particular concern for countries that are especially affected by sea-level rise and other serious impacts of climate change. Its participation in the proceedings underscores that Article 202 of the Convention establishes the obligation to provide scientific and technical assistance to developing States as a key measure to mitigate the "deleterious effects that result or are likely to result from climate change"—an affirmation that is also extended to the obligations under Section 4 of Part XII, which deals with monitoring and environmental assessment.[139] The Korean position also emphasizes that for the fulfilment of obligations under Articles 207, 212, 213, and 222 of the Convention—all related to adopting and enforcing laws and international regulations to prevent, reduce, and control marine pollution—it is essential to consider additional obligations imposed on States, including those concerning international cooperation and assistance to developing States, particularly Small Island States and low-lying States that are especially affected.[140]

The Brazilian contribution, by its turn, is centered on two aspects. First, the CDBR principle; second, the various forms of the obligation to cooperate under the Convention. Regarding the CBDR Principle, Brazil asserts that international law unequivocally recognizes it through its formulation in Principle 7 of the Rio Declaration (1992).[141] In addition, it recognizes that the principle is enshrined in several climate change instruments, domestic legislations and decisions of international bodies, as well as national courts of countries of very distinct development levels.[142] Interestingly, Brazil affirms that, in the context of climate change, the CBDR principle "reinforces" all cooperation obligations under the Convention, suggesting that it may also serve an interpretative function within UNCLOS.[143]

The Brazilian contribution acknowledges that the obligation to cooperate under UNCLOS manifests in various forms and serves as a cornerstone for fostering "fair and productive cooperation between developed and developing countries" in the collective effort to protect the marine environment. Brazil underscores that "the duty to cooperate is a fundamental principle in the prevention of marine pollution under Part XII of the Convention and general international law", highlighting the Convention's explicit obligation for developed States to "grant special treatment to developing States" by facilitating financial support, technical assistance from international organizations, and access to specialized services[144] as well as to promote "financing, capacity building, transfer of knowledge and technology to developing States".[145] In the same vein, Brazil reaffirms that Article 202 of the Convention delineates a suite of duties for developed

States, reinforcing their overarching obligation to foster scientific and technical cooperation with developing nations.[146] Again, Brazil understands that the obligations of cooperation of marine scientific research under Part XIII of UNCLOS imposes on developed States an obligation to "actively promote the flow of scientific data and information and the transfer of knowledge resulting from marine scientific research, especially to developing States" as well as "strengthening of the autonomous marine scientific research capabilities of developing States" and assuring the transfer of technology "on fair and reasonable terms and conditions".[147]

5. Conclusion: A Rift Among Equals

The Advisory Opinion delivered by the International Tribunal for the Law of the Sea in 2024 marks a significant normative shift at the intersection of the Law of the Sea and international climate law. The text is, at once, innovative and diplomatic, ambitious and restrained. What stands out most is how it makes visible—even in its silences—one of the most enduring fault lines in environmental international law: the divide between developed and developing States. And rather than ignoring this cleavage, the Tribunal opts to embed it within the interpretive logic of the United Nations Convention on the Law of the Sea.

From a strictly legal standpoint, the Opinion affirms that the obligations to protect and preserve the marine environment, particularly under Articles 192 and 194 of UNCLOS, apply fully to anthropogenic greenhouse gas emissions. The novelty lies less in the existence of the obligation than in the articulation of its scope: it is framed as a duty of conduct governed by a high standard of due diligence—one that is informed by the best available science, though not limited to it. The Opinion's methodological openness to incorporating principles and norms from the climate regime,such as the UNFCCC and the Paris Agreement, demonstrates a deliberate move toward systemic harmonization across legal frameworks that, while distinct, are functionally interrelated.

Yet the strength of the Opinion lies not only in what it affirms, but also in what it strategically emphasizes—or omits. The deliberate silence on State responsibility, the legal implications of sea level rise for maritime boundaries, and the broader content of climate obligations beyond UNCLOS reveal a careful political calibration. While this ensures broader institutional legitimacy and State buy-in, it also circumscribes the Opinion's transformative potential. In all of these areas, the Tribunal chooses a narrow reading of the questions posed, even while acknowledging their systemic significance.

It is in its treatment of the developed/developing divide, however, that the Opinion makes its most meaningful contribution to the evolving grammar of international environmental law. Although the CBDR Principle is not explicitly codified in UNCLOS, the Tribunal affirms its interpretive relevance—at times as a general principle of international law, at others as an implicit distributive logic underpinning the Convention itself. The integration of CBDR as a guiding parameter for obligations of due diligence, cooperation, and capacity-building lends the Opinion both ethical depth and political maturity. It also repositions developed States not merely as duty-bearers, but as actors with a particular responsibility to lead and support global responses.

The submissions of participating States—particularly Brazil, China, and small island developing States—demonstrate a collective effort to rebalance the normative discourse. The recognition, across most State contributions, that technical and financial capacity must inform the scope of obligations affirms the centrality of CBDR as a hermeneutic tool for both present and future developments in environmental law.

The Opinion thus emerges as a sophisticated legal construction under real and persistent tensions: between universality and differentiation; between precaution and pragmatism; between historical responsibility and the imperative of collective action. By affirming the legitimacy of asymmetric obligations, without compromising legal coherence, ITLOS articulates a more nuanced vision of environmental multilateralism—a vision in which equity and legality are not in contradiction, but rather co-constitutive of an international legal order that seeks, ultimately, to be just.

Notes

1 See, on the issue of jurisdiction, Yoshifumi Tanaka, 'The Role of an Advisory Opinion of ITLOS in Addressing Climate Change: Some Preliminary Considerations on Jurisdiction and Admissibility' (2023) 32(2) *Review of European, Comparative & International Environmental Law* 206.

2 International Tribunal for the Law of the Sea, Request for Advisory Opinion submitted by the Commission of Small Island States, ITLOS Reports (12 December 2022).

3 Monica Feria-Tinta, 'On the Request for an Advisory Opinion on Climate Change under UNCLOS before the International Tribunal for the Law of the Sea' (2023) 14(3) Journal of International Dispute Settlement 391; Rozemarijn J Roland Holst, 'Taking the Current When It Serves: Prospects and Challenges for an ITLOS Advisory Opinion on Oceans and Climate Change' (2023) 32(2) Review of European, Comparative & International Environmental Law 217 and Donald R Rothwell, 'Climate Change, Small Island States, and the Law of the Sea: The ITLOS Advisory Opinion Request' (2023) 27(5) ASIL Insights 1; Irini Papanicolopulu, 'The Climate Change Advisory Opinion Request at the ITLOS' (2023) (102) *QIL Questions of International Law* 7; Andrea Longo, 'Beyond Climate Change Obligations: Which Lessons from the ITLOS Advisory Opinion on Climate Change and Ocean Acidification for the Progressive Development of the Law of the Sea?' (2025) 27(1-2) *International Community Law Review* 112; Benoit Mayer, 'Request for an Advisory Opinion Submitted by the Commission of Small Island States on Climate Change and International Law' (2025) 119(1) *American Journal of International Law* 153; Daniel Bodansky, 'Advisory Opinions on Climate Change: Some Preliminary Questions' (2023) 32(2) *Review of European, Comparative & International Environmental Law* 185.

4 Jiangtao Qian, Kangjie Sun, and Yen-Chiang Chang, 'The Impact of the ITLOS Climate Change Advisory Opinion on the Development of International Law' (2024) 170 *Marine Policy* 106406 See also Pierre Clément Mingozzi, 'The Contribution of ITLOS to Fight Climate Change: Prospects and Challenges of the COSIS Request for an Advisory Opinion' (2023) 3(2) *The Italian Review of International and Comparative Law* 306.

5 Roberto Virzo, 'Fondamento ed esercizio della competenza consultiva del Tribunale internazionale del diritto del mare: considerazioni a margine del parere del 21 maggio 2024' (2024) 79(4) La Comunità Internazionale 603.

6 Arno Dal Ri Jr and L C Lima, 'O estabelecimento da Convenção-Quadro das Nações Unidas sobre mudança do clima como base do regime jurídico climático internacional (1985-1992)' in Jahyr Philippe Bichara and Arno Dal Ri (eds), Direito Internacional do Clima: Os limites do Acordo de Paris nos planos internacionais e internos (1st edn, Lumen Juris 2025) 13-39

7 International Tribunal for the Law of the Sea, Advisory Opinion on Climate Change and International Law, OC No 31, ITLOS Reports (21 May 2024) 68.

8 ITLOS, Advisory Opinion 70.

9 ITLOS, Advisory Opinion 72.

10 Vienna Convention on the Law of Treaties (opened for signature 23 May 1969,

entered into force 27 January 1980) 1155 UNTS 331, art 31.
11 ITLOS, Advisory Opinion (n 5)130. See Eduardo Jiménez Pineda, 'The UNCLOS as a Legal Living Instrument to Combat Climate Change and Its Deleterious Effects: The Specific Obligations of State Parties According to the Interpretation of ITLOS' (2024) 28 *Spanish Yearbook of International Law* 289-300.
12 ITLOS, Advisory Opinion 136.
13 ITLOS, Advisory Opinion 154.
14 ITLOS, Advisory Opinion 161.
15 ITLOS, Advisory Opinion 169.
16 ITLOS, Advisory Opinion 189.
17 ITLOS, Advisory Opinion 195.
18 ITLOS, Advisory Opinion 205.
19 ITLOS, Advisory Opinion 211.
20 ITLOS, Advisory Opinion 212. The Tribunal also reiterated that, in the absence of scientific certainty regarding the potential harm or adverse effects of a particular activity or substance, States must adopt a precautionary approach OC para 213. the precautionary approach has been incorporated into a growing number of international treaties and other instruments, many of which reflect the formulation of Principle 15 of the Rio Declaration. In the view of the Chamber, this has initiated a trend towards making this approach part of customary international law. (International Tribunal for the Law of the Sea, Responsibilities and Obligations of States with Respect to Activities in the Area, Advisory Opinion, 1 February 2011, ITLOS Reports 2011, 10, 47 [135]).
21 ITLOS, Advisory Opinion 212.
22 ITLOS, Advisory Opinion 234.
23 ITLOS, Advisory Opinion 242.
24 Rebecca M Bratspies and Russell A Miller (eds), *Transboundary Harm in International Law: Lessons from the Trail Smelter Arbitration* (CUP 2006); Hanqin Xue, *Transboundary Damage in International Law* (CUP 2003); Julio Barboza, *The Environment, Risk and Liability in International Law* (Brill 2010) and Robert Barnidge, 'The Due Diligence Principle under International Law' (2006) 8(1) *International Community Law Review* 81-121.
25 ITLOS, Advisory Opinion 247.
26 ITLOS, Advisory Opinion 250.
27 ITLOS, Advisory Opinion 251.
28 ITLOS, Advisory Opinion 254.
29 ITLOS, Advisory Opinion 258.
30 Including land-based sources, seabed activities under national jurisdiction, activities in the Area, pollution by dumping, pollution from vessels, and pollution from or through the atmosphere.
31 ITLOS, Advisory Opinion 263.
32 ITLOS, Advisory Opinion 296.
33 ITLOS, Advisory Opinion 307
34 ITLOS, Advisory Opinion 314-316.
35 ITLOS, Advisory Opinion 317. See also The Chamber held that measures adopted to prevent pollution of the marine environment may need to change over time to become stricter "in light ... of new scientific or technological knowledge" (ITLOS, Responsibilities and Obligations of States 117).
36 ITLOS, Advisory Opinion 323.
37 ITLOS, Advisory Opinion 339.
38 ITLOS, Advisory Opinion 345.
39 ITLOS, Advisory Opinion 348.
40 ITLOS, Advisory Opinion 348.

41 ITLOS, Advisory Opinion 349.
42 ITLOS, Advisory Opinion 354.
43 ITLOS, Advisory Opinion 356.
44 ITLOS, Advisory Opinion 359-361.
45 ITLOS, Advisory Opinion 379.
46 ITLOS, Advisory Opinion 385.
47 ITLOS, Advisory Opinion 386.
48 ITLOS, Advisory Opinion 392
49 ITLOS, Advisory Opinion 393
50 ITLOS, Advisory Opinion 399.
51 ITLOS, Advisory Opinion 402.
52 ITLOS, Advisory Opinion 404.
53 ITLOS, Advisory Opinion 405
54 ITLOS, Advisory Opinion 413-414.
55 ITLOS, Advisory Opinion 414.
56 ITLOS, Advisory Opinion 417.
57 ITLOS, Advisory Opinion 424-425
58 ITLOS, Advisory Opinion 424.
59 ITLOS, Advisory Opinion 432.
60 ITLOS, Advisory Opinion 434.
61 ITLOS, Advisory Opinion 439
62 ITLOS, Advisory Opinion 440.
63 See Roberto Virzo, 'Fondamento ed esercizio della competenza consultiva del Tribunale internazionale del diritto del mare: considerazioni a margine del parere del 21 maggio 2024' (2024) 79(4) La Comunità Internazionale 603.
64 ITLOS, Advisory Opinion 139
65 ITLOS, Advisory Opinion 141.
66 Bastiaan E Klerk, 'The ITLOS Advisory Opinion on Climate Change: Revisiting the Relationship Between the United Nations Convention on the Law of the Sea and the Paris Agreement' (2024) *Review of European, Comparative & International Environmental Law.*
67 ITLOS, Advisory Opinion 145.
68 ITLOS, Advisory Opinion 147.
69 ITLOS, Advisory Opinion 148.
70 ITLOS, Advisory Opinion 150.
71 Duncan French, 'Developing States and International Environmental Law: The Importance of Differentiated Responsibilities' (2000) 49(1) *International and Comparative Law Quarterly* 35-60; Philippe Cullet, *Differential Treatment in International Environmental Law* (Routledge 2017); Daniel Bodansky and Harro van Asselt, *The Art and Craft of International Environmental Law* (OUP 2024) & Anita Margrethe Halvorssen, *Equality Among Unequals in International Environmental Law: Differential Treatment for Developing Countries* (Routledge 2019).
72 Rio Declaration on Environment and Development (adopted 14 June 1992) UN Doc A/CONF.151/26 (Vol I). "States shall cooperate in a spirit of global partnership to conserve, protect and restore the health and integrity of the Earth's ecosystem. In view of the different contributions to global environmental degradation, States have common but differentiated responsibilities. The developed countries acknowledge the responsibility that they bear in the international pursuit of sustainable development in view of the pressures their societies place on the global environment and of the technologies and financial resources they command".
73 Written Statement of Portugal, Written Proceedings of States Parties (16 June

2023) 30.
74 Written Statement of Sierra Leone, Written Proceedings of States Parties (16 June 2023) 62.
75 ITLOS, Advisory Opinion 328.
76 ITLOS, Advisory Opinion 62.
77 ITLOS, Advisory Opinion 218.
78 ITLOS, Advisory Opinion 228.
79 ITLOS, Advisory Opinion 326.
80 International Law Commission, *General Principles of Law*, UN Doc A/78/10 (2023), ch V.
81 Written Statement of the Democratic Republic of the Congo, Written Proceedings of States Parties (13 June 2023) 170.
82 Written Statement of New Zealand, Written Proceedings of States Parties (15 June 2023) 6; Written Statement of Portugal, Written Proceedings of States Parties (16 June 2023) 39.
83 Written Statement of the People's Republic of China, Written Proceedings of States Parties (15 June 2023) 27.
84 Written Statement of the People's Republic of China, Written Proceedings of States Parties (15 June 2023) 27.
85 Written Statement of Australia, Written Proceedings of States Parties (16 June 2023) 36. Written Statement of Australia, Written Proceedings of States Parties (16 June 2023) preamble.
86 Written Statement of Singapore, Written Proceedings of States Parties (16 June 2023) 57.
87 Written Statement of France, Written Proceedings of States Parties (16 June 2023) 113.
88 Written Statement of Chile, Written Proceedings of States Parties (16 June 2023) 4.
89 Written Statement of Mozambique, Written Proceedings of States Parties (16 June 2023) 55.
90 Written Statement of Mozambique, Written Proceedings of States Parties (16 June 2023) 115.
91 Written Statement of Singapore, Written Proceedings of States Parties (16 June 2023) 58.
92 Written Statement of Sierra Leone, Written Proceedings of States Parties (16 June 2023) 81.
93 Written Statement of Djibouti, Written Proceedings of States Parties (16 June 2023) 78.
94 Written Statement of Rwanda, Written Proceedings of States Parties (17 June 2023) 301.
95 RDC, para 10.
96 RDC, para 12.
97 Mozambique, para 48.
98 Mozambique, para 66.
99 Mauritius, para 7.
100 Portugal, para 30
101 Portugal, para 94.
102 Viet Nam, para 87.
103 New Zealand, para. 29.
104 ITLOS, Advisory Opinion 202.
105 ITLOS, Advisory Opinion 207.
106 ITLOS, Advisory Opinion 225.
107 ITLOS, Advisory Opinion 226.
108 ITLOS, Advisory Opinion 229.

109 International Tribunal for the Law of the Sea, Declaration of Judge Kulyk in Advisory Opinion on Climate Change and International Law, OC No 31, ITLOS Reports (21 May 2024) IV.1.
110 Declaration of Judge Kulyk in ITLOS, Advisory Opinion on Climate Change (n 9), IV.1.
111 Norway.
112 France, para 113.
113 France, para 113
114 ITLOS, Advisory Opinion 241.
115 European Union, para 73.
116 Singapore, para 35.
117 Singapore, para 35.
118 RDC, para. 216.
119 New Zealand, para 72(c).
120 New Zealand, para 72(d).
121 People's Republic of China,para 30.
122 Mozambique, para 116.
123 France, para 114.
124 United Kingdom, para 84
125 Sierra Leone, para 62.
126 Canada, para 49.
127 ITLOS, Advisory Opinion 327.
128 ITLOS, Advisory Opinion 325 and 327.
129 ITLOS, Advisory Opinion 332.
130 ITLOS, Advisory Opinion 338. Mozambique also stresses this point in its commentary (116).
131 ITLOS, Advisory Opinion 329.
132 ITLOS, Advisory Opinion 333.
133 ITLOS, Advisory Opinion 334.
134 People's Republic of China, para 29.
135 People's Republic of China, para 29.
136 ITLOS, Advisory Opinion 363.
137 Pulp Mills on the River Uruguay (Argentina v Uruguay), Judgment, ICJ Reports 2010, 14, 83 [205].
138 ITLOS, Advisory Opinion 364.
139 Korea, para 18.
140 Korea, para 19.
141 States shall cooperate in a spirit of global partnership to conserve, protect and restore the health and integrity of the Earth's ecosystem. In view of the different contributions to global environmental degradation, States have common but differentiated responsibilities. The developed countries acknowledge the responsibility that they bear in the international pursuit of sustainable development in view of the pressures their societies place on the global environment and of the technologies and financial resources they command.
142 Brazil, para 19.
143 Brazil, para 17.
144 Brazil, para 15.
145 Brazil, para 16.
146 Brazil, para 16.
147 Brazil, para 16.

Artificial Intelligence and Human Rights: A Double-Edged Sword

Aziz Tuffi SALIBA[1]
Lutiana Valadares Fernandes BARBOSA[2]

Abstract

This paper aims to draw preliminary reflections on the implications of artificial intelligence (AI) to the obligations to protect, respect, and fulfill economic, social, and cultural rights (ESCR) by analyzing international human rights obligations, the United Nations' relevant instruments on AI, and soft law instruments. To do so, it draws reflections on the human rights to culture, health, and work, which are topics recognized and protected by international human rights treaties and are experiencing challenges in the context of the AI revolution. Next, it questions the specific issues AI poses to ESCR rights. The paper concludes that while AI poses significant challenges to protecting ESCR, it also offers opportunities for advancement in these rights when implemented ethically.

Key Words

Artificial Intelligence, AI, Human Rights, Health, Culture, Work

1. Introduction[3]

Artificial intelligence (AI) has been increasingly transforming daily human life and has even been called the Fourth Industrial Revolution.[4] A foundation for the paper's discussion requires a definition of AI, while acknowledging that "it is not a single monolithic concept".[5] AI is a range of computer programs designed to perform tasks that, until recently, only humans could do. This means those programs can solve problems by using inferential reasoning, classifications, and optimization to make decisions in a setting where information is incomplete or uncertain. AI programs differ in their levels of autonomy and problem-solving capabilities. Some rely on predefined rules to assess alternatives and draw conclusions, while others, based on machine-learning algorithms, learn from data without predefined rules.[6]

The impact of AI on human rights is profound, as it has the potential to both enhance and undermine those rights depending on how it is developed and deployed. Therefore, AI's transformative impact on human rights must be addressed through the lens of international obligations. Economic, social, and cultural rights ("ESCR") ensure access to fundamental services and resources, often requiring States to take proactive measures. These rights encompass immediate and progressively realized obligations,[7] [8] requiring a specific approach while considering AI risks and opportunities. When discussing AI with ESCR lenses, there is a challenge to avoid apocalyptic pessimism as much as excessive optimism. This paper aims to answer the question and open the debate on the challenges and opportunities AI presents to ESCR. The hypothesis is that those technologies are a double-edged sword that can be a propelling force for the protection of ESCR[9] and human rights violations due to risks of bias and inequality. Therefore, AI requires proactive governance and ethical and legal frameworks.

In this context, this paper examines the dual impact of AI technologies on human rights by analyzing the rights to culture, health, and work[10] — widely recognized and protected under both UN and regional human rights treaties.[11]

The analyses were conducted from a human rights-based approach.[12] Using the human rights framework means considering legally binding obligations towards protecting human beings and humanity, as well as ethical or aspirational considerations and good practices while considering the new scenarios presented by AI. The authors conducted bibliographical research regarding ESCR and AI to answer this paper's question. Its results were analyzed using the hypothetical-deductive method. A documentary survey was carried out in the United Nations Office of the High Commissioner for Human Rights publications regarding ESCR obligations applicable to AI.

1-1. AI and the Human Right to Culture

Regarding the human right to culture, the UNESCO Recommendation on the Ethics of AI is a soft law instrument and, therefore, not legally binding. However, its unanimous adoption by all 193 UNESCO member states in November 2021 reflects a collective commitment to the objectives and principles it sets forth. It encourages States to incorporate AI systems "in the preservation, enrichment, understanding, promotion, management, and accessibility of tangible, documentary and intangible cultural heritage, including endangered languages as well as Indigenous languages and knowledge",[13] while also highlighting the importance of a participatory approach.[14]

AI offers promising solutions for preserving endangered languages and cultural heritage, thereby reinforcing cultural rights. One example is a joint project by the Universidade Federal de Minas

Gerais ("UFMG"), Brazil, and the universities of Auckland, New Zealand, and Pretoria, South Africa. The initiative focuses on creating a dataset for the endangered Khelovedu language, integrating ethical and intellectual property considerations grounded in "Indigenous Knowledge Systems" (IKS).[15] Community involvement ensures that data collection respects cultural sensitivities and promotes co-ownership by native speakers. Thus, the project aims to preserve linguistic heritage and provide a replicable model for developing datasets for other under-documented languages. Another example of AI technologies aiming at enhancing the right to culture is in Korea, where the National Strategy for a Great Transformation foresees the construction of one hundred and sixty smart museums and galleries based on ICT.[16]

On the other hand, while cultural rights encompass the protection of diverse identities, languages, and traditions, AI systems might reinforce dominant cultural norms, sidelining or even silencing minority languages and traditions. For example, AI translation tools widely used often do not offer indigenous languages, which contributes to undermining cultural diversity. Moreover, AI-driven globalization tends to favor dominant cultural narratives, eroding minority identities and traditions. Algorithmic content moderation can also disproportionately suppress cultural expressions from underrepresented communities, contributing to their invisibility. For instance, moderation algorithms may overlook cultural, language, or gender-based contexts and sensitivities or public interest in certain content. As a result, they have, for example, led to the removal of historically significant photographs with cultural meaning.[17] Many States and scholars, particularly in China and the European Union, are concerned about protecting culture in the development of AI, especially large language models (LLMs) like ChatGPT.[18] From an international human rights perspective, States' international obligations might be breached if they do not comply with the human right to culture and non-discrimination, for instance.[19]

The Committee on the Rights of the Child's General Comment No. 25 on children's rights in the digital environment provides valuable insights. While it highlights that the "digital environment promotes children's right to culture, leisure, and play, which is essential for their well-being and development",[20] it states the importance of benefiting children and promoting their "differing identities, in particular their cultural identities, languages, and heritage. They [digital technologies] can facilitate children's social skills, learning, expression, creative activities, such as music and art, and a sense of belonging and a shared culture".[21] It also mentions the importance of balancing the digital environment with "attractive alternatives in the physical locations where children live"[22] and that face-to-face communication, and physical recreation are key to the development of their social and emotional skills is essential.[23]

Regarding the right to culture, this paper argues that, in alignment with the obligations outlined in international human rights treaties such as the International Covenant on Economic, Social and Cultural Rights ("ICESCR")[24] and providing a solid ground for further development of the legal standards, the UNESCO Recommendation on the Ethics of AI offers important recommendations to States. It encourages States to assess and address the cultural implications of AI systems, particularly those regarding natural language processing ("NLP"), such as voice assistance or automated translations. These evaluations should offer insights for strategies that enhance the benefits of these systems by bridging cultural divides and fostering greater human understanding. At the same time, they should mitigate adverse effects, such as reduced use of endangered languages, local dialects, and tonal or cultural nuances, which could contribute to their disappearance.

Furthermore, the UNESCO Recommendation also advises Member States to promote AI education and training for creative professionals and artists, enabling them to evaluate the relevance of

AI technologies for their work and to participate in the development and implementation of technologies "as AI technologies are being used to create, produce, distribute, broadcast and consume a variety of cultural goods and services, bearing in mind the importance of preserving cultural heritage, diversity, and artistic freedom". States shall also prevent the risk of concentration in the cultural market by raising awareness and promoting assessment of AI applications within local cultural industries and small and medium-sized enterprises operating in the cultural sector. Finally, Member States should collaborate with technology companies and other stakeholders to ensure a diverse supply and broad access to cultural expressions. Special attention should be given to algorithmic recommendations, ensuring they improve the visibility and discoverability of local content.[25]

Whereas AI presents both risks and opportunities for the human right to culture, it should be noted that the risks may be protracted over time, potentially delaying the progressive realization of this right. A preliminary analysis indicates that possible negative impacts might affect populations, especially experiencing situations of social vulnerability, whose cultural voices have been traditionally silenced, such as indigenous peoples and children.

Among the cultural practices AI might impact are traditional healing practices, such as those of indigenous shamans. As AI-driven systems become more widespread, these culturally rooted methods risk being marginalized, threatening the preservation of indigenous knowledge. The following section explores how AI impacts the human right to health, examining its potential to transform healthcare systems while raising critical challenges, particularly for vulnerable populations.

2. AI and the Human Right to Health

AI is transforming the healthcare sector by replicating human reasoning and processing large volumes of information quickly and efficiently.[26] In practice, AI is being developed and researched to perform tasks that traditionally require significant time or are prone to human error, such as analyzing medical images like X-rays or MRIs to identify signs of disease. For instance, AI systems can detect subtle patterns that might go unnoticed by the human eye, aiding in the early detection of conditions such as cancer or heart disease.[27] These tools save time and enhance diagnostic accuracy, allowing doctors to focus on more complex aspects of patient care.

AI may also play an important role in personalized medicine, where treatments are tailored to patients' individual needs. Using advanced algorithms, AI analyzes large datasets, such as electronic medical records, to predict health outcomes and recommend specific treatments based on each patient's unique characteristics, including their genetic profile, lifestyle, and medical history.[28] This approach helps physicians deliver more effective treatments while reducing the risk of adverse reactions.

Beyond diagnostics and treatments, AI-based tools like chatbots and virtual assistants enhance patient engagement. These systems can assist with answering basic medical inquiries, scheduling appointments, and sending medication reminders, thereby streamlining healthcare processes. By improving efficiency and accessibility, AI technologies play a crucial role in bridging gaps in healthcare delivery, particularly for individuals in remote or underserved areas, ensuring they receive timely and accurate medical support.[29]

An example of AI technologies regarding the right to health can be found in the Korean National Strategy for a Great Transformation, which foresees[30] "[d]igital health care services, such as Internet of Things ("IoT") sensors that measure the heart rate, blood sugar levels and activities, and AI speakers that engage in conversations to enhance cognitive functions, will be provided to 120,000 elderlies and others vulnerable to health implications. Wearable devices will be provided to 200,000 people with chronic conditions, such as high blood pressure or diabetes, to help them manage their conditions".[31]

AI is also accelerating progress in genetics by analyzing DNA to identify connections between genetic traits and diseases. This supports the development of new drugs and therapies that target diseases at their root. Simultaneously, AI is revolutionizing prosthetics, enabling devices that adapt to users' movements and needs, significantly improving the quality of life for individuals with physical disabilities.[32]

In this context, the UNESCO Recommendation on the Ethics of AI underscores that States should work towards leveraging efficient AI systems to enhance the protection of the right to life and health, which includes the mitigation of disease outbreaks, "while building and maintaining international solidarity to tackle global health risks and uncertainties, and ensure that their deployment of AI systems in health care be consistent with international law and their human rights law obligations".[33]

Despite these advances, integrating AI into healthcare raises significant ethical, legal, and social challenges. Issues such as data privacy, algorithmic bias, marginalization of traditional healing practices, transparency, and equitable access must be addressed to ensure that the benefits of this technology are distributed fairly and responsibly.[34]

AI's ability to process large volumes of information, including sensitive health data like medical histories and test results, raises concerns about patient privacy and the ethical use of such information. Respecting confidentiality is essential, and robust measures must be implemented to prevent unauthorized access or data breaches. Ensuring the security of these systems is critical to maintaining patient trust and avoiding misuse.

Another challenge is combating algorithmic bias. Many AI systems are trained on datasets that may reflect implicit biases, leading to decisions that disproportionately impact vulnerable and historically marginalized groups. For instance, the outcomes may perpetuate inequalities if training data lacks representative samples of various ethnicities, genders, or socioeconomic conditions. Furthermore, they might erode traditional health practices such as those of indigenous peoples. Identifying and correcting these biases is essential to ensure fairness in access to AI benefits and the results it delivers.

Additionally, the transparency and explainability of AI tools are critical concerns. AI often operates as a 'black box', making its decisions difficult for healthcare professionals and patients to understand. This opacity can lead to distrust in the reliability or motivations behind algorithm-generated recommendations. Therefore, AI systems must be explainable and transparent, enabling doctors and patients to comprehend and trust the decisions made.

Equity in access to AI technologies also requires attention. Countries and communities with fewer resources face significant barriers to adopting these tools, potentially deepening healthcare disparities. Furthermore, populations in rural or low-income areas are often at a disadvantage. Ensuring that innovations are globally accessible is indispensable for sharing AI's benefits widely.

The World Health Organization ("WHO") has also acknowledged that AI can be transformative in health, presenting both opportunities and risks of biases and data health being unethically collected and used. According to WHO, "[t]here are also potential serious negative consequences if ethical principles and human rights obligations are not prioritized by those who fund, design, regulate or use AI technologies for health".[35]

Regarding the right to health of persons with disabilities and AI, the Report of the United Nations Special Rapporteur on the rights of persons with disabilities has highlighted AI opportunities such as "contribut[ing] to better outcomes for persons with disabilities if used to diagnose illnesses and recommend treatments, uses that are helpful to everyone and could usefully be extended to applications in rehabilitation contexts as well". On the risks, the report has stated that AI assessments based on certain disability types can result in an increase in health insurance premiums or even in private health insurance being denied, and the AI reasoning for such a decision might be unknown or even unknowable.[36]

Furthermore, the report has also acknowledged that AI "is transforming the relationship of the State with persons with disabilities; for example, research has revealed that, in certain instances, artificial intelligence and emerging technologies have become gatekeepers for social protection benefits". In this regard, AI systems can restrict access to benefits, such as unemployment assistance, by relying on biased datasets and discriminatory algorithms. Given the high level of poverty among persons with disabilities globally, including many living in extreme poverty, it is essential to ensure that AI systems do not unjustly deny their eligibility for services and support. Lack of transparency in the logic behind machine learning and automated decision-making creates significant challenges for the general population and can disproportionately affect persons with disabilities, who already face marginalization in health and life insurance markets.[37]

According to the Special Rapporteur on the Rights of Persons with Disabilities, the benefits of AI devices, such as the ability to personalize patient treatment recommendations and improve access to specialist medical and rehabilitation advice, must be distributed equitably to individuals with disabilities. AI presents risks of discrimination in healthcare, particularly when outcomes like cost-cutting are programmed, potentially compromising patient well-being and disproportionately affecting persons with disabilities.

Article 25 of the United Nations Convention on the Rights of Persons with Disabilities ("CRPD") addresses such discrimination by prohibiting the denial of healthcare or health services based on disability. Additionally, the article's prohibition of discrimination in providing health and life insurance based on disability extends to the use of AI in determining access to insurance coverage.[38]

Regarding children and the right to health, General Comment No. 25 on children's rights in relation to the digital environment acknowledges the potential benefits, such as facilitating access to healthcare and information and improving diagnostics and treatment of children and adolescents of all ages. Digital technologies also present valuable opportunities to support children in disadvantaged or vulnerable circumstances and those in remote communities. These technologies may be the sole means of accessing health services and information during public emergencies or health and humanitarian crises. According to the general recommendation, applications involving children's data should restrict their processing to what is strictly necessary for delivering the service. These services should be delivered by professionals or individuals with appropriate training under-regulated oversight mechanisms. States parties must guarantee that digital health products and services do not generate or exacerbate inequities in children's access to in-person healthcare. Furthermore, State parties should establish or revise regulations requiring health technologies and services providers to incorporate children's rights into their design, functionality, content, and distribution. Regulations should address known harms and proactively consider emerging research and evidence in public health to prevent the dissemination of misinformation and materials or services that could harm children's mental or physical health.[39]

Concerning AI and the human right to health, this paper argues that the UNESCO recommendation on the ethics of AI, while a soft law instrument, provides guidance to States to fulfill their international human rights obligations, as it is aligned with the ICESCR and other international human rights obligations[40] and provide a solid ground for further development of international human rights standards regarding the right to health in the AI context. It recommends that Member States should prioritize the regulation of AI applications in healthcare, particularly those used for prediction, detection, and treatment, by: (a) implementing oversight mechanisms to minimize and address bias; (b) involving professionals, patients, caregivers, or service users as "domain experts" at all relevant stages of the AI toll development; (c) safeguarding privacy, especially given the potential need for medical monitoring, and ensuring compliance with all applicable national and international data protection standards; (d) establishing effective measures to ensure individuals whose personal data is analyzed are informed and provide consent for its use, without restricting access to healthcare services; (e) maintaining human oversight in the care process, ensuring that diagnoses and treatment decisions are always made by humans while recognizing the assisting role AI systems can play; and (f) requiring, where appropriate, the review of AI systems by an ethics committee before their clinical application.[41]

While AI has immense potential to transform the healthcare sector positively, its risks must be carefully managed to preserve trust and efficacy in its applications. Ethical and human rights legal commitments are essential to overcoming these challenges, ensuring that the technology contributes to building more inclusive, efficient, and humane healthcare systems. Populations facing social vulnerability are particularly susceptible to the risks posed by AI in healthcare, with potential short- and long-term impacts, including challenges in accessing health insurance and the perpetuation of bias and discrimination within the healthcare system.

AI can enhance healthcare access and improve workplace safety and productivity, significantly benefiting both sectors. On the other hand, the widespread adoption of AI raises concerns about job displacement, inequality in healthcare access, and the potential for biased decision-making. The following section offers reflections on AI and the human right to work.

3. AI and the Human Right to Work

AI will significantly impact the future of work, affecting social rights. The most profound changes should occur with the automation of repetitive tasks, the expansion of human capabilities, and the creation of new roles, such as data analysts and AI ethics specialists.[42] For example, automation in the manufacturing sector has increased efficiency, while AI systems in the logistics sector optimize supply chains.[43] However, these advancements raise concerns about job displacement, particularly in roles that require lower educational levels, such as routine administrative work or industrial tasks. AI-enabled management tools can also perpetuate inequalities in the workplace through biases in hiring algorithms or salary allocation, disproportionately affecting marginalized groups.[44] In this context, the press release to the Korean New Deal states that the "transition towards a digital and green economy creates new industries and jobs, diversifying the forms of work and enabling platform labor and remote working. At the same time, it could also lead to a mismatch between jobs and skills and a lower demand for low-skilled labor".[45] Still, according to the Korean New Deal, the increasing challenges of unemployment and rising polarization highlight the need for a more robust and comprehensive employment safety net that offers advanced job training and safeguards emerging forms of employment.[46]

In addition to altering work structures, AI may influence meaningful work experience. While it can amplify complex human skills, such as critical thinking and creativity, it can also reduce autonomy and lead to alienation in roles where workers become mere "machine operators". Furthermore, the unequal adoption of AI creates disparities in its impact, favoring developed economies and regions with higher educational levels while leaving others vulnerable to economic polarization.[47]

Integrating AI in hiring processes presents significant risks, including inconsistencies in key aspects of personality assessments,[48] as well as inherent bias and discrimination. Studies have shown that AI-based personality prediction tools often exhibit substantial instability, leading to unreliable hiring outcomes. AI systems operate on a much larger scale, potentially affecting hundreds of thousands of applicants if biases are present, thus raising critical civil rights concerns regarding fairness and equity in employment, such as "[a] human hiring manager can only discriminate against a limited number of people. If an AI system that turns out to be biased is used on all job candidates in a large corporation, hundreds of thousands of people could potentially be affected".[49]

Furthermore, the United Nations High Commissioner for Human Rights observed that the foundation of many AI systems used in people management relies on quantitative social science, which is often flawed and susceptible to biases. For instance, an AI hiring algorithm trained on historical datasets that prioritize male, white, and middle-aged candidates will inherently disadvantage women, people of color, and individuals outside this age group, even if they are equally qualified for the role. It further recommended implementing decisive measures to promote diversity within the teams responsible for developing AI systems.[50]

The Special Rapporteur on the rights of persons with disabilities highlighted that "AI program only looks for people with education and jobs that people with disability have been excluded from before. The past unfair decisions about education and work can lead to more unfair decisions if this is not thought about properly".[51] The report stated that the United Nations Convention on the Rights of Persons with Disabilities safeguards against discrimination based on disability in the workplace, covering aspects such as recruitment, hiring, job retention, career progression, and the provision of safe and healthy working conditions, which includes the obligation to offer reasonable accommodations. In this context, reasonable accommodation might involve offering alternative testing and screening methods to support applicants with disabilities, ensuring they can fully utilize their skills without being restricted. Reasonable accommodations during testing should be treated with equal importance, and establishing a parallel, non-algorithmic hiring process for a percentage of all candidates could help eliminate bias and stigma.[52]

Public policies and organizational initiatives must proactively address these challenges through reskilling initiatives, equitable policies, and ethical frameworks to ensure that AI benefits all workers while mitigating health, safety, and social equity risks.[53] Reskilling initiatives are essential as AI transforms work, automating routine tasks and creating demand for roles requiring technical expertise, creativity, and emotional intelligence. Governments can establish national programs, such as the European Union's Digital Skills and Jobs Coalition, to reduce digital skills gaps.[54] Some tech companies have already launched internal programs to upskill their employees in areas like data analysis and AI model training, while NGOs and community organizations offer accessible or free training for underrepresented populations. Emphasis on continuous learning and partnerships between academia and industry is crucial to prepare workers for the ever-evolving demands of an AI-driven economy.

Moreover, equitable policies are crucial to ensure that the benefits of AI are distributed fairly across society. Governments can implement targeted strategies, such as subsidies for training programs aimed at low-income individuals and tax incentives for companies investing in developing an AI-oriented workforce. Expanding digital infrastructure, particularly in rural and disadvantaged areas, is essential to provide equal access to AI-driven opportunities. Income support measures, such as universal basic income or tailored unemployment benefits, can help workers navigate transition periods. Marginalized groups, including women, older workers, and low-income communities, should receive special attention to mitigate the risks of exclusion in AI-transformed labor markets.

In this sense, while not a legally binding instrument, UNESCO's Recommendation on the Ethics of AI provides an important path to further development of standards regarding existing international obligations concerning the human right to work. The recommendation stresses that States should "assess and address the impact of AI systems on labor markets and its implications for education requirements, in all countries and with special emphasis on countries where the economy is labor-intensive". According to UNESCO, this involves integrating a broader range of core and interdisciplinary skills into education at all levels to help current and future workers adapt to a rapidly evolving job market while understanding the ethical implications of AI. Skills like "learning how to learn", communication, critical thinking, teamwork, empathy, and cross-domain knowledge transfer should complement technical and low-skill training. Transparency about in-demand skills and regularly updating curricula are essential.[55] The recommendation also advises States to "work with private sector companies, civil society organizations, and other stakeholders, including workers and unions, to ensure a fair transition for at-risk employees".[56] This should involve implementing upskilling and reskilling programs, creating effective mechanisms to retain employees during transition periods, and exploring "safety net" initiatives for those who cannot be retrained.

Furthermore, States should create and execute programs to address the identified challenges, which may include strategies such as upskilling, reskilling, enhanced social protection, proactive industry policies, tax incentives, and new forms of taxation. Additionally, Member States should ensure adequate public funding to support these initiatives. Relevant regulations, such as tax policies, should be carefully reviewed and modified if necessary to mitigate the impact of unemployment caused by AI-driven automation.[57]

Ethical and legal frameworks must be developed to ensure AI adoption aligns with principles of justice, transparency, and accountability. These frameworks address critical concerns, such as algorithmic biases, data privacy, and transparency of AI systems in hiring or performance evaluation processes. Companies should regularly audit and monitor AI systems to identify and correct biases, ensuring that decision-making processes are transparent and justifiable to those affected. Protecting worker autonomy is another fundamental principle, requiring that human oversight remains central in AI-influenced decisions. Regulatory frameworks should require transparency reporting and create accountability mechanisms to ensure compliance with ethical standards.

By integrating reskilling initiatives, equitable policies, and ethical frameworks, stakeholders can address the risks associated with AI while unlocking its potential to enhance productivity, creativity, and inclusion in the workplace. These measures are essential to ensure that the transition to an AI-driven economy creates opportunities for all workers, especially those traditionally marginalized, reducing inequalities and securing a future where humans and machines collaborate effectively.

Building on the reflections on the human rights to culture, health, and work, the following section presents a broader analysis of ESCR.

4. Reflections on Economic, Social, and Cultural Rights and AI

As demonstrated by the case studies in the previous sections on culture, health, and labor, AI holds immense potential for positive impact, ranging from opening new avenues of scientific research and optimizing energy grids to enhancing public health, agriculture, and advancing progress on the Sustainable Development Goals ("SDGs").[58] However, if left unregulated, AI may present significant problems that could undermine these benefits.

Human rights organizations and scholars have increasingly emphasized the critical need to prioritize human rights in designing, deploying, and regulating AI to mitigate the risks associated with this technology. They argue that human rights standards shift the conversation from ethical considerations to legally binding obligations.[59] In this context, this section highlights the interdependence of civil, political, economic, social, cultural, and environmental rights, recognizing that the fulfillment of one often facilitates the realization of others. For instance, the right to education—an ESCR—empowers individuals to actively participate in political life, while the right to free expression—a civil and political right ("CPR")—enables advocacy for improved healthcare access, an ESCR. With this foundation, the paper aims to initiate a discussion on the unique characteristics of ESCR and their implications within the transformative paradigm shift introduced by AI.

Economic, social and cultural rights are often meant to reduce inequality and poverty, focusing on social justice and redistribution of resources. Those rights are also frequently positive in nature, which means they often require active State action to be fulfilled, such as providing access to education, healthcare, or housing. On the other hand, civil and political rights are often negative, meaning they protect individuals and collectivities from State interference, such as the right to free speech or a fair trial. Furthermore, in the context of ESCR, States have two kinds of obligations: immediate enforceability and progressive realization,[60] meaning this might involve mid- and long-term strategies and resource allocation.[61] Implementing those rights will likely require significant state investment and the improvement or creation of public systems. On the other hand, regarding CPR, States have an immediate duty to respect, protect, and fulfill,[62] and its implementation often requires the guarantee of legal frameworks to ensure individual freedoms and mechanisms for individuals to seek redress.

Considering the specific features of ESCR, while recognizing that AI can be beneficial for ESCR, it is necessary to reflect on the main risks that the literature points in relation to AI, and that were also presented in the previous sections regarding the human rights to culture, health, and work, among which are bias and discrimination, and exacerbation of inequality.[63] In the same sense, the Council of Europe Framework Convention on Artificial Intelligence and Human Rights, Democracy and the Rule of Law, in its preamble, expresses concern about the risk of discrimination in the context of AI, as well as that it may potentially create or worsen inequalities, particularly for women and vulnerable individuals, in terms of enjoying their human rights and fully, equally, and effectively participating in economic, social, cultural, and political activities.[64]

Regarding bias and discrimination, AI systems are often based and trained on existing data, which might reflect societal prejudice and bias. Therefore, AI systems might reinforce or even amplify social inequality and injustices. AI enables the processing of vast amounts of data at a speed and scale not achievable by humans, potentially serving public safety, health, and national security. However, those systems "rely on datasets that, in their design or implementation, may allow for bias and thus produce discriminatory effects".[65] Excessive dependence on and trust in automated decisions and a failure to acknowledge this fundamental issue can undermine the scrutiny of AI outcomes and prevent individuals from accessing remedies for harmful AI-driven decisions. Automation may hinder the transparency and accountability of a process, making it difficult for even well-intentioned authorities to explain the results.[66] Bias emerging from AI is potentially more dangerous and pernicious than human bias as "AI tools can be used broadly, systematizing bias and also cloaking it in the guise of a neutral technology. Bias harbored by specific individuals—even many individuals—can still be overcome".[67]

For instance, women, migrants, indigenous peoples, and people of African descent may face disproportionate negative impacts from biased AI-driven decisions.[68] What happens is that human biases are encoded and thus perpetuated by the algorithms as they "rely on data capturing the past, thus automating the status quo unless preventative measures are taken".[69] As the Committee on the Elimination of Racial Discrimination observed, "the increasing use of new technological tools, including artificial intelligence, in areas such as security, border control and access to social services, has the potential to deepen racism, racial discrimination, xenophobia and other forms of exclusion".[70] According to the Committee, there are numerous entry points through which bias can be incorporated into algorithmic profiling systems, decisions regarding the origin and scope of the datasets used for training, societal and cultural biases incorporated by developers into those datasets, the AI models themselves, and how the outputs of the AI models are applied in practice. Specifically, the following data-related factors can contribute to adverse outcomes: (a) the inclusion of information about protected characteristics in the data; (b) the use of so-called proxy information, such as postal codes linked to segregated urban areas, which can indirectly reveal race or ethnic origin; (c) the data being biased against a particular group; and (d) the use of poor-quality data, including data that is poorly selected, incomplete, inaccurate, or outdated.[71]

A report by the United Nations High Commissioner for Human Rights highlighted how the COVID-19 pandemic has underscored

AI's rapid and widespread influence across various sectors. AI-driven contact-tracing systems, leveraging data such as geolocation, health records, and personal networks, were deployed to monitor the virus's spread. Furthermore, AI systems have identified individuals as potentially infected, leading to isolation or quarantine measures, while predictive grading algorithms have resulted in discriminatory outcomes, disproportionately affecting students from disadvantaged backgrounds.[72]

These examples illustrate AI's profound influence on daily life, particularly in relation to privacy and its intersection with fundamental rights such as health, education, freedom of movement, and freedom of expression. AI bias affects CPR and ESCR, influencing areas such as housing, incarceration rates, access to credit, and employment. However, based on the analysis in previous sections, AI-related biases in the context of ESCR, given their characteristic of progressive realization, pose a risk of long-term and socially enduring impacts—especially for historically marginalized populations. In contrast, biases affecting CPR often result in more immediate and individualized consequences.

Another significant risk posed by AI technologies concerning human rights is the exacerbation of inequality, as the benefits of AI are more likely to accrue to financially privileged individuals while traditionally marginalized populations risk being left behind. As noted, "widening digital divides could limit the benefits of AI to a handful of States, companies, and individuals".[73] In other words, those who develop AI or possess access and technical expertise are more likely to accumulate greater economic resources, whereas those excluded from technological advancements face further marginalization.[74]

AI technologies often rely on infrastructure such as internet connectivity and digital literacy—resources that remain unequally distributed across societies. This digital divide can further entrench disparities in accessing services essential for realizing ESCR. In the realm of ESCR, as governments increasingly adopt AI-driven e-governance platforms to manage social services and benefits—including healthcare and pensions—there is potential for improved speed and efficiency. However, these advancements also risk widening the gap in access for the most vulnerable populations, such as those who are illiterate or lack access to digital devices and the internet.

Moreover, "the cost of flawed AI is not borne equally by all. The use of predictive AI disproportionately harms groups that have been systematically excluded and disadvantaged in the past".[75] These biases threaten to reinforce existing inequalities and impede efforts to achieve inclusive social and economic development.

Many ESCR have collective dimensions, requiring policies and systems that benefit entire communities rather than just individuals. However, AI-driven solutions are predominantly market-driven, often prioritizing individual and corporate interests over broader community welfare. Additionally, ESCR are designed to protect marginalized individuals and groups experiencing social vulnerability or exclusion, such as children, women, Indigenous peoples, and persons with disabilities. Nevertheless, AI systems frequently overlook the unique needs of these groups, leading to further exclusion or even harm. For example, AI applications in social security systems may wrongfully deny benefits to vulnerable individuals due to biased or incomplete data, exacerbating existing inequalities.

ESCR are particularly susceptible to the challenges posed by the digital divide, as communities lacking access to technology and digital literacy are systematically excluded from AI-driven advancements in essential sectors such as education, healthcare, and agriculture. Adopting a human rights-based approach to AI development—emphasizing transparency, accountability, and inclusivity—can help mitigate these risks while maximizing the potential benefits of AI technologies for all.[76]

5. Final Considerations

This paper examines the impacts of AI on economic, social, and cultural rights (ESCR)—a set of rights that have traditionally received less attention in discussions on emerging technologies, despite their fundamental role in ensuring human well-being and social equity. These rights encompass both immediate obligations and obligations of progressive realization, making them particularly vulnerable to long-term AI-related risks, such as bias, discrimination, and the exacerbation of inequality, which disproportionately affect historically marginalized populations. Furthermore, the paper underscores the need for a balanced approach to AI governance. As explored, these technologies hold immense potential to positively transform critical areas such as health, work, and culture; however, their associated risks must be carefully assessed and mitigated. Further research is needed to deepen the debate on AI's intersection with ESCR.

While internationally binding human rights instruments exist to protect ESCR, they do not specifically address AI—a rapidly evolving field that remains largely unregulated and governed primarily by soft law instruments, which depend on the voluntary compliance of States. Though not legally binding, the UNESCO Recommendation on the Ethics of AI provides a valuable basis for aligning AI standards with international human rights obligations. Moving the discussion toward a human rights-based framework and establishing standards rooted in States' legal commitments can shift AI regulation from a discretionary matter to a binding obligation, potentially holding States internationally accountable for failing to meet their responsibilities.

Effectively addressing the challenges posed by AI requires a collective commitment from all sectors of society to ensure its development and deployment align with human rights principles—

ensuring AI is ethical, inclusive, transparent, and accountable. Any application of AI must be rigorously evaluated through the lens of States' international human rights obligations, a necessity that is particularly crucial in the context of ESCR. Ultimately, the goal must be to harness AI's transformative potential to enhance human capabilities and uphold fundamental values—fostering equity, dignity, and the universal protection of human rights in all their dimensions.

References

Arvind Narayanan and Sayash Kapoor, *AI Snake Oil: What Artificial Intelligence Can Do, What It Can't, and How to Tell the Difference*, (Princeton: Princeton University Press, 2024), p. 53.

Committee on the Rights of the Child, *General Comment No. 25 on children's rights in relation to the digital environment*, CRC/C/GC/25, (2021).

Council of Europe, *Framework Convention on Artificial Intelligence and Human Rights, Democracy and the Rule of Law*, Council of Europe Treaty Series - No. 225, (2024).

Didem Özkiziltan and Anke Hassel, *Artificial Intelligence at Work: An Overview of the Literature*, (2021), https://ssrn.com/abstract=3796746 or http://dx.doi.org/10.2139/ssrn.3796746 [Accessed on June 22, 2025].

European Commission, *Digital skills and jobs coalition*, https://digital-strategy.ec.europa.eu/en/policies/digital-skills-coalition, [Accessed on June 22, 2025].

Filippo Raso, Hannah Hilligoss, Vivek Krishnamurthy, Christopher Bavitz, and Levin Yerin Kim, *Artificial Intelligence & Human Rights: Opportunities & Risks*, Berkman Klein Center Research Publication No. 2018-6, (2018), http://dx.doi.org/10.2139/ssrn.3259344 [Accessed on June 22, 2025].

Fukuda-Parr, S., Lawson-Remer, T., & Randolph, S., *Measuring the progressive realization of human rights obligations: an index of economic and social rights fulfillment*, (2008).

Howard J., *Artificial intelligence: Implications for the future of work*, Am J Ind Med. 2019 Nov; 62(11): 917-926, (2019).

Inter-American Court of Human Rights, *Case Vera Rojas y Otros Vs. Chile*, Sentence of Oct 1, 2021, par. 96.

Iván Suazo Galdames, *Artificial Intelligence in Human Medicine*, 10 Int'l J. Med. & Surgical Sci. 1, (2023), https://revistas.uautonoma.cl/index.php/ijmss/article/view/2150.2023, [Accessed on June 18, 2025].

Judith Clifton, Amy Glasmeier, and Mia Gray, *When Machines Think for Us: The Consequences for Work and Place*, 13 Cambridge J. & Soc'yeon. & Soc'y 3, (2020).

Julia Carrie Wong, *Mark Zuckerberg accused of abusing power after Facebook deletes 'napalm girl' post*, The Guardian, (2016), https://www.theguardian.com/technology/2016/sep/08/facebook-mark-zuckerberg-napalm-girlphoto-vietnam-war.

Korean Ministry of Economy and Finance, *Korean New Deal: National Strategy for a Great Transformation*, Press Releases, (2020), https://english.moef.go.kr/pc/

selectTbPressCenterDtl.do?boardCd=N0001&seq=4948 [Accessed on June 18, 2025].

Leonardo Parentoni, *What should we reasonably expect from artificial intelligence?*, anno (XII) Fascicolo 2. Il Diritto Degli Affari, (2022).

Lilya Grace, *AI-powered Virtual Health Assistants: Enhancing Patient Engagement and Self-management*, 11 J. of Healthcare Data Science and AI 11, (2024), https://journalpublication.wrcouncil.org/index.php/JHDSA/article/view/37, [Accessed on June 18, 2025].

Mathias Risse, *Human Rights and Artificial Intelligence: An Urgently Needed Agenda*. Human Rights Quarterly, vol. 41 no. 1, (2019), p. 1-16.

Ministry of Foreign Affairs The People's Republic of China, *Position Paper of the People's Republic of China on Strengthening Ethical Governance of Artificial Intelligence (AI)*, (2022) [Accessed on June 18, 2025].

Mohd Faishal et al., *The Future of Work: AI, Automation, and the Changing Dynamics of Developed Economies*, 18 World J. Adv. Res. & Rev. 620, (2023).

Rhea A, Markey K, D'Arinzo L, Schellmann H, Sloane M, Squires P, et al., *LinkedIn URLs and Other Unexpected Influences on AI Personality Prediction in Hiring: Results of an Audit*, In: Proceedings of the 2022 AAAI/ACM Conference on AI, Ethics, and Society, (Oxford: ACM, 2022), p. 572–87.

Ryan Abbott, *The Reasonable Robot: Artificial Intelligence and the Law*, (Cambridge: Cambridge University Press, 2020).

Tebogo George Mahashe, Adriana Pagano et al., *Building a Low-Resourced-Language-Model Dataset: Considering Ethics and IP from an IKS Context* (unpublished manuscript, forthcoming publication on the Worldwide Universities Network), available soon at https://wun.ac.uk/.

UNESCO, *Recommendation on the Ethics of AI*, (2021), pars. 94–95, 95–98, 116, 118, 121, 123.

United Nations Committee on the Elimination of Racial Discrimination, *General Recommendation No. 36, 2020, on preventing and combating racial profiling by law enforcement officials*, CERD/C/GC/36, (2020).

United Nations General Assembly, *Artificial intelligence and the rights of persons with disabilities - Report of the Special Rapporteur on the rights of persons with disabilities*, OHCHR, A/HRC/49/52, (2021), pars. 32–34.

United Nations General Assembly, *Promotion and protection of the right to freedom of opinion and expression*, A/73/348, (2018).

United Nations General Assembly, *Report of the Special Rapporteur on the promotion and protection of the right to freedom of opinion and expression*, A/HRC/38/35, (2018), para. 2.

United Nations General Assembly, *The right to privacy in the digital age - Report of the United Nations High Commissioner for Human Rights*, A/HRC/48/31, (2021).

United Nations High Commissioner for Human Rights Volker Türk, *Human Rights: A Path for Solutions*, Vision Statement offered by the United Nations High Commissioner for Human Rights, United Nations Human Rights office of the High Commissioner, (2024), p. 29.

United Nations Human Rights Office of the High Commissioner, *Human Rights in the Digital Age: The International Legal Framework*, United Nations, (2018), p. 91.

United Nations Sustainable Development Group, *Universal Values, principle One: Human Rights-Based Approach*, UN, (2020).

United Nations, *Governing AI for Humanity, Final Report*, (2024).

United Nations, *International Covenant on Economic, Social and Cultural Rights* (ICESCR), (1966).

Yang Qiang, *The Fourth Revolution*, Unesco Courier n. 3, (2018).

Yavar Bathaee, *The Artificial Intelligence Black Box and the Failure of Intent and Causation*, 31 Harvard Journal of Law & Technology, (2018), p. 898.

Zaki Khoury and Yulia Lesnichaya, *Harnessing trustworthy artificial intelligence: A lesson from Korea*, World Bank Blog, (2022), [Accessed on June 20, 2025].

Notes

1 Professor of International Law at the Federal University of Minas Gerais (UFMG). Dean for International Affairs (UFMG). PhD in International Law (UFMG). Master of Laws (University of Arizona).

2 Postdoctoral researcher at Federal University of Minas Gerais (UFMG) and visiting researcher at the Center for Latin American Studies at Georgetown University. PhD in International Law (UFMG). Master of Laws (Columbia University).

3 The author expresses gratitude to Prof. Antonio Luiz Pinho Ribeiro (UFMG), Ana Luisa Vaz (UFMG), Fernanda Alves (UFMG), Isabela Mattos (UFMG), Maria Amaral Scheid (UFMG) and Samir Tuffi Saliba Júnior (UFMG), for their valuable insights and support. However, any errors or omissions are the sole responsibility of the authors.The opinions and analyses expressed in this work are solely those of the authors and do not necessarily reflect the views of any institution with which they are affiliated.

4 Yang Qiang, *The Fourth Revolution*, Unesco Courier n. 3, (2018). "After the internet and mobile internet triggered the Third Industrial Revolution, artificial intelligence (AI) technologies, driven by big data, are fuelling a Fourth Industrial Revolution". We recall that first industrial revolution was based on textile manufacturing and the innovation of the steam engine and the second industrial revolution on steel, electricity and automobile; Ryan Abbott, *The Reasonable Robot: Artificial Intelligence and the Law*, (Cambridge: Cambridge University Press, (2020). "Already impressive-sounding era titles such as the Fourth Industrial Revolutioin, the Second Machine Age, and the Automation Revolution are being used to describe the coming disruption".

5 Leonardo Parentoni. *What should we reasonably expect from artificial intelligence?*. anno (XII) Fascicolo 2. Il Diritto Degli Affari, (2022).

6 Yavar Bathaee, *The Artificial Intelligence Black Box and the Failure of Intent and Causation*, 31 Harvard Journal of Law & Technology, (2018), p. 898.

7 United Nations General Assembly, *Promotion and protection of the right to freedom of opinion and expression*, A/73/348, (2018). United Nations General Assembly, *Report of the Special Rapporteur on the promotion and protection of the right to freedom of opinion and expression,* A/HRC/38/35, (2018), para. 2. See also Julia Carrie Wong, *Mark Zuckerberg accused of abusing power after Facebook deletes 'napalm girl' post"*, The Guardian, (2016), https://www.theguardian.com/technology/2016/sep/08/facebook-mark-zuckerberg-napalm-girlphoto-vietnam-war.

8 Inter-American Court of Huma Rights, *Case Vera Rojas y Otros Vs. Chile*, Sentence of Oct 1, 2021, par. 96. Fukuda-Parr, S., Lawson-Remer, T., & Randolph, S., *Measuring the progressive realization of human rights obligations: an index of economic and social rights fulfillment, (2008).*

9 United Nations High Commissioner for Human Rights Volker Türk, *Human Rights: A Path for Solutions Vision Statement offered by the United Nations High Commissioner for Human Rights, Volker Türk,* United Nations Human Rights office of the High Commissioner, (2024), p. 29 "Unprecedented advances in digital technology, including generative Artificial Intelligence, offer us previously unimaginable

opportunities to move forward on the enjoyment of human rights and contribute to rescuing the 2030 Agenda. At the same time, the negative societal impacts are already with us and proliferating, and human rights harms are almost inevitably going to grow given the largely unregulated nature of some of these technologies".

10 In the context of the right to culture, health and work, an intersectional analysis regarding children or/and persons with disabilities will be also presented, considering UN reports on the topic.

11 For example: Universal Declaration of Human Rights, (1948), articles 22, 23, 25, and 27). International Covenant on Economic, Social and Cultural Rights, (1966), articles 6, 7, 12, and 15. Convention on the Elimination of All Forms of Discrimination Against Women, (1979), articles 11, 12, and 13. Convention on the Rights of the Child, (1989), articles 24 and 31. Convention on the Rights of Persons with Disabilities, (2006), articles 24, 25, and 27. Environmental rights are recognized in the Stockholm Declaration, (1972), principle 1. Rio Declaration, (1992), principle 10. Paris Agreement, (2015), preamble. Minamata Convention on Mercury, (2013), preamble and article 1. Regionally, these rights are protected under the Protocol of San Salvador, (1988), articles 6, 10, and 14. European Social Charter, (1961, revised 1996), articles 11, 15, and 22. Aarhus Convention, (1998), articles 1 and 3; the African Charter on Human and Peoples' Rights, (1981), articles 16, 22, and 24 and its Maputo Protocol, (2003), articles 13 and 14; the Arab Charter on Human Rights, (2004), articles 38, 40, and 42; and the ASEAN Human Rights Declaration, (2012), articles 28, 31, and 32.

12 United Nations Sustainable Development Group, *Universal Values*, principle One: Human Rights-Based Approach, UN, (2020). "The human rights-based approach (HRBA) is a conceptual framework for the process of human development that is normatively based on international human rights standards and operationally directed to promoting and protecting human rights. It seeks to analyses inequalities which lie at the heart of development problems and redress discriminatory practices and unjust distributions of power that impede development progress and often result in groups of people being left behind".

13 UNESCO, *Recommendation on the Ethics of AI*, (2021), parr 94.

14 UNESCO, *Recommendation on the Ethics of AI*, (2021), parr 94.

15 Tebogo George Mahashe, Adriana Pagano et al., *Building a Low-Resourced-Language-Model Dataset: Considering Ethics and IP from an IKS Context* (unpublished manuscript, forthcoming publication on the Worldwide Universities Network), available soon at https://wun.ac.uk/.

16 Korean Ministry of Economy and Finance, *Korean New Deal: National Strategy for a Great Transformation,* Press Releases, (2020), https://english.moef.go.kr/pc/selectTbPressCenterDtl.do?boardCd= N0001&seq=4948 [Accessed on June 18, 2025]. World Bank Blog, *Harnessing trustworthy artificial intelligence: A lesson from Korea Zaki KhouryYulia Lesnichaya,* (2022), Harnessing trustworthy artificial intelligence: A lesson from Korea [Accessed on June 18, 2025] "The Republic of Korea is emerging as a global leader in successfully harnessing trustworthy AI. Thanks to the government's longstanding support of the ICT sector, Korea boasts of strong digital infrastructure, sound industrial capabilities, and rapid 5G adoption and

commercialization — and now aspires to be a world leader in AI".

17 United Nations General Assembly, *Promotion and protection of the right to freedom of opinion and expression*, A/73/348, (2018). Julia Carrie Wong, *Mark Zuckerberg accused of abusing power after Facebook deletes 'napalm girl' post"*, The Guardian, (2016), https://www.theguardian.com/technology/2016/sep/08/facebook-mark-zuckerberg-napalm-girlphoto-vietnam-war [Accessed on June 18, 2025]. see also United Nations General Assembly, *Promotion and protection of the right to freedom of opinion and expression*, A/73/348, (2018). United Nations General Assembly, *Report of the Special Rapporteur on the promotion and protection of the right to freedom of opinion and expression,* A/HRC/38/35, (2018), par. 2.

18 Ministry of Foreign Affairs The People's Republic of China, *Position Paper of the People's Republic of China on Strengthening Ethical Governance of Artificial Intelligence (AI)*, (2022) Position Paper of the People's Republic of China on Strengthening Ethical Governance of Artificial Intelligence (AI)_Ministry of Foreign Affairs of the People's Republic of China [Accessed on June 18, 2025]. World economic Forum, *Fourth Industrial Revolution Can China and Europe find common ground on AI ethics?* (2021), Can China and Europe find common ground on AI ethics? | World Economic Forum [Accessed on June 18, 2025].

19 United Nations General Assembly, *Promotion and protection of human rights: human rights questions, including alternative approaches for improving the effective enjoyment of human rights and fundamental freedoms Promotion and protection of the right to freedom of opinion and expression*, A/73/348, (2018). See also Julia Carrie Wong, *Mark Zuckerberg accused of abusing power after Facebook deletes 'napalm girl' post"*, The Guardian, (2016). https://www.theguardian.com/technology/2016/sep/08/facebook-mark-zuckerberg-napalm-girlphoto-vietnam-war [Accessed on June 18, 2025]. United Nations General Assembly, *Report of the Special Rapporteur on the promotion and protection of the right to freedom of opinion and expression,* A/HRC/38/35, (2018), par. 2.

20 Committee on the Rights of the Child, *General Comment No. 25 on children's rights in relation to the digital environment*, CRC/C/GC/25, (2021).

21 Committee on the Rights of the Child, *General Comment No. 25 on children's rights in relation to the digital environment*, CRC/C/GC/25, (2021).

22 Committee on the Rights of the Child, *General Comment No. 25 on children's rights in relation to the digital environment*, CRC/C/GC/25, (2021).

23 Committee on the Rights of the Child, *General Comment No. 25 on children's rights in relation to the digital environment*, CRC/C/GC/25, (2021).

24 Article 15

1. The States Parties to the present Covenant recognize the right of everyone:
   (a) To take part in cultural life;
   (b) To enjoy the benefits of scientific progress and its applications;
   (c) To benefit from the protection of the moral and material interests resulting from any scientific, literary or artistic production of which he is the author.
2. The steps to be taken by the States Parties to the present Covenant to achieve the full realization of this right shall include those necessary for the conservation, the development and the diffusion of science and culture.
3. The States Parties to the present Covenant undertake to respect the freedom indispensable for scientific research and creative activity.

4. The States Parties to the present Covenant recognize the benefits to be derived from the encouragement and development of international contacts and co-operation in the scientific and cultural fields.

25 UNESCO, Recommendation on the Ethics of AI, (2021), pars. 95-98.

26 Iván Suazo Galdames, Artificial Intelligence in Human Medicine, 10 Int'l J. Med. & Surgical Sci. 1, (2023), https://revistas.uautonoma.cl/index.php/ijmss/article/view/2150.2023, [Accessed on June 18, 2025].

27 Iván Suazo Galdames, Artificial Intelligence in Human Medicine, 10 Int'l J. Med. & Surgical Sci. 1, (2023), https://revistas.uautonoma.cl/index.php/ijmss/article/view/2150.2023, [Accessed on June 18, 2025].

28 Feng Jiang et al., Artificial Intelligence in Healthcare: Past, Present and Future, 2 Stroke & Vascular Neurology 230, 2017, available at https://svn.bmj.com/content/2/4/230.

29 Lilya Grace, AI-powered Virtual Health Assistants: Enhancing Patient Engagement and Self-management, 11 J. of Healthcare Data Science and AI 11, (2024), https://journalpublication.wrcouncil.org/index.php/JHDSA/article/view/37, [Accessed on June 18, 2025].

30 Korean Ministry of Economy and Finance, Korean New Deal: National Strategy for a Great Transformation, (2020), Press Releases, [Accessed on June 18, 2025]. According Zaki KhouryYulia Lesnichaya, Harnessing trustworthy artificial intelligence: A lesson from Korea, World Bank Blog, (2022), Harnessing trustworthy artificial intelligence: A lesson from Korea, [Accessed on June 20, 2025] "The Republic of Korea is emerging as a global leader in successfully harnessing trustworthy AI. Thanks to the government's longstanding support of the ICT sector, Korea boasts of strong digital infrastructure, sound industrial capabilities, and rapid 5G adoption and commercialization — and now aspires to be a world leader in AI".

31 Korean Ministry of Economy and Finance, Korean New Deal: National Strategy for a Great Transformation, (2020), Press Releases, [Accessed on June 20, 2025].

According to Zaki KhouryYulia Lesnichaya, Harnessing trustworthy artificial intelligence: A lesson from Korea, World Bank Blog, (2022), Harnessing trustworthy artificial intelligence: A lesson from Korea, [Accessed on June 20, 2025] "The Republic of Korea is emerging as a global leader in successfully harnessing trustworthy AI. Thanks to the government's longstanding support of the ICT sector, Korea boasts of strong digital infrastructure, sound industrial capabilities, and rapid 5G adoption and commercialization — and now aspires to be a world leader in AI".

32 Iván Suazo Galdames, Artificial Intelligence in Human Medicine, 10 Int'l J. Med. & Surgical Sci. 1, (2023), https://revistas.uautonoma.cl/index.php/ijmss/article/view/2150, [Accessed on June 20, 2025].

33 UNESCO, Recommendation on the Ethics of AI, (2021), pars. 95-98.par. 121.

34 Iván Suazo Galdames, Artificial Intelligence in Human Medicine, 10 Int'l J. Med. & Surgical Sci. 1, (2023), https://revistas.uautonoma.cl/index.php/ijmss/article/view/2150.2023, [Accessed on June 18, 2025].

35 World Health Organization, Ethics and governance of artificial intelligence for health: WHO guidance, World Health Organization (2021).

36 United Nations General Assembly, *Artificial intelligence and the rights of persons with*

disabilities - Report of the Special Rapporteur on the rights of persons with disabilities, OHCHR, A/HRC/49/52, (2021), par. 32.

37 United Nations General Assembly, *Artificial intelligence and the rights of persons with disabilities - Report of the Special Rapporteur on the rights of persons with disabilities*, OHCHR, A/HRC/49/52, (2021), par. 33-34.

38 United Nations General Assembly, *Artificial intelligence and the rights of persons with disabilities - Report of the Special Rapporteur on the rights of persons with disabilities*, OHCHR, A/HRC/49/52, (2021)

39 Committee on the Rights of the Child, *General Comment No. 25 on children's rights in relation to the digital environment*, CRC/C/GC/25, (2021),parr. 44-45.

40 Article 12

1. The States Parties to the present Covenant recognize the right of everyone to the enjoyment of the highest attainable standard of physical and mental health.
2. The steps to be taken by the States Parties to the present Covenant to achieve the full realization of this right shall include those necessary for:
   (a) The provision for the reduction of the stillbirth-rate and of infant mortality and for the healthy development of the child;
   (b) The improvement of all aspects of environmental and industrial hygiene;
   (c) The prevention, treatment and control of epidemic, endemic, occupational and other diseases;
   (d) The creation of conditions which would assure to all medical service and medical attention in the event of sickness.

41 UNESCO, *Recommendation on the Ethics of AI*, (2021), par. 123.

42 Howard J., *Artificial intelligence: Implications for the future of work*, Am J Ind Med. 2019 Nov; 62(11): 917-926, (2019). Didem Özkiziltan, and Anke Hassel, Artificial Intelligence at Work: An Overview of the Literature, (2021), https://ssrn.com/abstract=3796746 or http://dx.doi.org/10.2139/ssrn.3796746 [Accessed on June 22, 2025].

43 Judith Clifton, Amy Glasmeier, and Mia Gray, *When Machines Think for Us: The Consequences for Work and Place*, 13 Cambridge J. & Soc'ycon. & Soc'y 3, (2020).

44 Didem Özkiziltan, and Anke Hassel, *Artificial Intelligence at Work: An Overview of the Literature,* (2021), https://ssrn.com/abstract=3796746 or http://dx.doi.org/10.2139/ssrn.3796746 [Accessed on June 22, 2025].

45 Korean Ministry of Economy and Finance, *Korean New Deal: National Strategy for a Great Transformation,* (2020), Press Releases, [Accessed on June 20, 2025].

46 Korean Ministry of Economy and Finance, *Korean New Deal: National Strategy for a Great Transformation,* (2020), Press Releases, [Accessed on June 20, 2025].

47 Judith Clifton, Amy Glasmeier, and Mia Gray, *When Machines Think for Us: The Consequences for Work and Place,* 13 Cambridge J. & Soc'ycon. & Soc'y 3, (2020).

48 Rhea A, Markey K, D'Arinzo L, Schellmann H, Sloane M, Squires P, et al. *LinkedIn URLs and Other Unexpected Influences on AI Personality Prediction in Hiring: Results of an Audit,* In: Proceedings of the 2022 AAAI/ACM Conference on AI, Ethics, and Society, (Oxford: ACM, 2022), p. 572-87.

49 Hilke Schellmann, *The Algorithm: How AI Can Hijack Your Career and Steal Your Future,* (London: C. Hurst & Co. Publishers, 2024), p. 21.

50 United Nations General Assembly, *The right to privacy in the digital age - Report of the United Nations High Commissioner for Human Rights,* A/HRC/48/31, (2021).

51 United Nations General Assembly, *Artificial intelligence and the rights of persons with disabilities - Report of the Special Rapporteur on the rights of persons with disabilities*, OHCHR, A/HRC/49/52, (2021).
52 United Nations General Assembly, *Artificial intelligence and the rights of persons with disabilities - Report of the Special Rapporteur on the rights of persons with disabilities,* OHCHR, A/HRC/49/52, (2021).
53 Howard J., *Artificial intelligence: Implications for the future of work,* Am J Ind Med. 2019 Nov;62(11):917-926, (2019). Mohd Faishal et al., The Future of Work: AI, Automation, and the Changing Dynamics of Developed Economies, 18 World J. Adv. Res. & Rev. 620, (2023).
54 European Commission, Digital skills and jobs coalition, https://digital-strategy.ec.europa.eu/en/policies/digital-skills-coalition, [Accessed on June 22, 2025].
55 UNESCO, *Recommendation on the Ethics of AI,* (2021), par.116.
56 UNESCO, *Recommendation on the Ethics of AI,* (2021), par. 118.
57 UNESCO, *Recommendation on the Ethics of AI,* (2021), par. 118.
58 United Nations, *Governing AI for Humanity*, Final Report, (2024).
59 United Nations High Commissioner for Human Rights Volker Türk, *Human Rights: A Path for Solutions Vision Statement offered by the United Nations High Commissioner for Human Rights, Volker Türk,* United Nations Human Rights office of the High Commissioner, (2024), p. 29.
60 Inter-American Court of Huma Rights, *Case Vera Rojas y Otros Vs. Chile,* Sentence of Oct 1, 2021, par. 96. Fukuda-Parr, S., Lawson-Remer, T., & Randolph, S., Measuring the progressive realization of human rights obligations: an index of economic and social rights fulfillment, (2008).
61 United Nations, *International Covenant on Economic, Social and Cultural Rights* (ICESCR), (1966).
62 United Nations, *International Covenant on Economic, Social and Cultural Rights* (ICESCR), (1966).
63 Filippo Raso, Hannah Hilligoss, Vivek Krishnamurthy, Christopher Bavitz, and Bavitz, Levin Yerin Kim, *Artificial Intelligence & Human Rights: Opportunities & Risks,* Berkman Klein Center Research Publication No. 2018-6, (2018), http://dx.doi.org/10.2139/ssrn.3259344 [Accessed on June 22, 2025]. Mathias Risse, *Human Rights and Artificial Intelligence: An Urgently Needed Agenda.* Human Rights Quarterly, vol. 41 no. 1, (2019), p. 1-16.
64 Council of Europe, Framework Convention on Artificial Intelligence and Human Rights, Democracy and the Rule of Law, Council of Europe Treaty Series - No. 225, (2024).
65 United Nations General Assembly, *Promotion and protection of the right to freedom of opinion and expression,* A/73/348, (2018).
66 United Nations General Assembly, *Promotion and protection of the right to freedom of opinion and expression,* A/73/348, (2018).
67 United Nations Human Rights Office of the High Commissioner, *Human Rights in the Digital Age: The International Legal Framework,* United Nations, (2018), p. 91.
68 Frederik J. Zuiderveen Borgesius, *Strengthening legal protection against discrimination by algorithms and artificial intelligence,* The International Journal of Human Rights, 24:10, 1572-1593, (2020).
69 Mathias Risse, *Human Rights and Artificial Intelligence: An Urgently Needed Agenda.* Human Rights Quarterly, vol. 41 no. 1, (2019), p. 1-16.
70 United Nations Committee on the Elimination of Racial Discrimination, *General*

Recommendation No. 36, 2020, on preventing and combating racial profiling by law enforcement officials, CERD/C/GC/36, (2020).

71 United Nations Committee on the Elimination of Racial Discrimination, *General Recommendation No. 36, 2020, on preventing and combating racial profiling by law enforcement officials,* CERD/C/GC/36, (2020).

72 United Nations General Assembly, *The right to privacy in the digital age - Report of the United Nations High Commissioner for Human Rights,* A/HRC/48/31, (2021).

73 United Nations, *Governing AI for Humanity Final Report,* (2024).

74 Mathias Risse, *Human Rights and Artificial Intelligence: An Urgently Needed Agenda.* Human Rights Quarterly, vol. 41 no. 1, (2019), p. 1-16.

75 Arvind Narayanan and Sayash Kapoor, AI Snake Oil: *What Artificial Intelligence Can Do, What It Can't, and How to Tell the Difference,* (Princeton: Princeton University Press, 2024), p. 53.

76 On recommendations to address the challenges see for instance United Nations Committee on the Elimination of Racial Discrimination, *General Recommendation No. 36, 2020, on preventing and combating racial profiling by law enforcement officials,* CERD/C/GC/36, (2020). "62. States should adopt measures to ensure that independent oversight bodies have a mandate to monitor the use of artificial intelligence tools by the public sector, and to assess them against criteria developed in conformity with the Convention to ensure they are not entrenching inequalities or producing discriminatory results. States should also ensure that the functioning of such systems is regularly monitored and evaluated in order to assess deficiencies and to take the necessary corrective measures. When the results of an assessment of a technology indicate a high risk of discrimination or other human rights violations, States should take measures to avoid the use of such a technology. (…)States should also ensure the adoption and periodic revision of guidelines and codes of conduct that companies must observe in the programming, use and commercialization of algorithms that may lead to racial discrimination or, in general, any other form of discrimination likely to be in violation of the Convention". "68. States should document cases of racial discrimination associated with artificial intelligence, as well as prevention measures, sanctions and remedies, and include such information in their reports to the Committee. 69. Human rights bodies, States, national human rights institutions and civil society organizations should carry out, and disseminate the results of, studies, identify good practices on effective measures addressing racial biases derived from artificial intelligence, including those related to human rights compliance and ethical aspects of machine learning, and identify relevant criteria in terms of interpretation or transparency in the processes of the programming and training of algorithms, and should do so through the lens of the International Convention on the Elimination of All Forms of Racial Discrimination".

Three Blades of Leverage: A Critical Perspective on the Korea-China Investment Treaty Framework

Changwan HAN
Attorney-at-Law; Ph.D. in International Law
Bae, Kim & Lee LLC, Seoul, Korea

Abstract

Korea and China have three coexisting international investment agreements (the BIT, TIT, and FTA), allowing investors to choose the most favorable treaty in investment arbitration. While these agreements share similarities, their differences in wording and substantive provisions create a complex legal framework, leading to varied interpretations and arbitration outcomes. Chronologically, the BIT (2007) offers the strongest protections to investors, the TIT (2012) strikes a middle ground, and the FTA (2015) provides the most regulatory flexibility to host states. This reflects a global trend toward granting host states greater policy discretion. The current treaty framework between Korea and China remains fragmented, allowing investors to choose among three different agreements based on their individual strategic interests. This flexibility may benefit investors, but it also creates legal uncertainty, and raises concerns about treaty shopping, and diminishes the effectiveness of the FTA. Unless Korea and China address the inconsistencies, the BIT will likely remain the dominant instrument in investment arbitration cases between Korea and China, effectively undermining the TIT and the investment provisions of the FTA. This creates an unresolved tension between the legal framework that investors rely on and the policy objectives that the two states may have intended to pursue.

Key Words

Investment Treaty, Korea, China, Treaty Shopping, Investment Arbitration

1. Introduction

Korea and China have adopted three International Investment Agreements ("IIAs"), forming the backbone of their bilateral investment protection framework. These agreements include: the Agreement between the Government of the Republic of Korea and the Government of the People's Republic of China on the Promotion and Protection of Investments, signed on September 8, 2007 (the BIT); the Agreement among the Government of the Republic of Korea, the Government of the People's Republic of China, and the Government of Japan for the Promotion, Facilitation, and Protection of Investment, signed on May 13, 2012 (the TIT); and the Free Trade Agreement between the Government of the Republic of Korea and the Government of the People's Republic of China, signed on June 1, 2015 (the FTA).

Despite the coexistence of these three instruments, none of them explicitly addresses their hierarchical relationship or provides guidance on how they should interact in cases of overlap. As a result, all three agreements remain concurrently valid and applicable between Korea and China, with no single instrument holding supremacy over the others.

A key commonality among these agreements is their inclusion of investor-state dispute settlement ("ISDS") mechanisms: Article 9 of the BIT, Article 15 of the TIT, and Article 12.12 of the FTA. This means that a Korean or Chinese investor seeking to initiate an investment claim against the other state may, in principle, select any of the three treaties as the legal basis for their claim. Naturally, potential claimants must weigh the advantages and disadvantages of each treaty, considering factors such as the scope of protection, procedural rules, and substantive standards.

The existence of multiple investment treaties raises critical legal and practical questions regarding their application, potential conflicts, and strategic treaty selection by investors. While such a framework provides flexibility, it may also lead to legal uncertainty, treaty shopping, and complex jurisdictional challenges in arbitration proceedings.

This article aims to explore the key similarities and differences among these three investment treaties, analyzing their legal implications for treaty parties and investors in dispute. In doing so, this article will also examine relevant arbitral awards to assess how different treaty provisions have been interpreted and applied in past investment disputes. By shedding light on these issues, this study seeks to contribute to a deeper understanding of the evolving investment treaty relationship between Korea and China.

2. Protected Investments and Investors

2.1 Protected Investments

BIT Article 1.1	TIT Article 1(1)	FTA Article 12.1
The term "investments" means every kind of assets, used as investment by investors of one Contracting Party within the territory of the other Contracting Party, in accordance with the applicable laws and regulations of that other Contracting Party at the	(1) the term "investments" means every kind of asset that an investor owns or controls, directly or indirectly, which has the characteristics of an investment, such as the commitment of capital or other resources, the expectation of gain or	**covered investment** means, with respect to a Party, an investment in its territory of an investor of the other Party that is in existence as of the date of entry into force of this Agreement or established, acquired, or expanded thereafter;

time of investment and shall include, in particular, though not exclusively: (a) movable and immovable property as well as any other property rights in rem such as mortgages, liens, pledges, usufruct and similar rights; (b) shares, stocks, bonds and debentures or any other forms of participation in a company, business enterprise or joint venture; (c) claims to money or to any performance having an economic value associated with an investment; (d) intellectual property rights, including copyrights, trade marks, patents, industrial designs, technical processes, know-how, trade secrets and trade names, and goodwill; (e) any right conferred by law or under contract and any licences and permits pursuant to law, including the right to search for, extract, cultivate or exploit natural resources	profit, or the assumption of risk. Forms that investments may take include: (a) an enterprise and a branch of an enterprise; (b) shares, stocks or other forms of equity participation in an enterprise, including rights derived therefrom; (c) bonds, debentures, loans and other forms of debt, including rights derived therefrom; (d) rights under contracts, including turnkey, construction, management, production or revenue-sharing contracts; (e) claims to money and claims to any performance under contract having a financial value associated with investment; (f) intellectual property rights, including copyrights and related rights, patent rights and rights relating to utility models, trademarks, industrial designs, layout-designs of integrated circuits, new varieties of plants, trade names, indications of source or geographical indications and undisclosed information; (g) rights conferred pursuant to laws and regulations or contracts such as concessions, licenses, authorizations and permits; and	investments means every kind of asset that an investor owns or controls, directly or indirectly, which has the characteristics of an **investment**, such as the commitment of capital or other resources, the expectation of gain or profit, or the assumption of risk. Forms that investments may take include: (i) an enterprise and a branch of an enterprise; (ii) shares, stocks or other forms of equity participation in an enterprise, including rights derived therefrom; (iii) bonds, debentures, loans and other forms of debt, including rights derived therefrom; (iv) rights under contracts, including turnkey, construction, management, production or revenue-sharing contracts; (v) claims to money and claims to any performance under contract having a financial value associated with investment; (vi) intellectual property rights, including copyrights and related rights, patent rights and rights relating to utility models, trademarks, industrial designs, layout-designs of integrated circuits, new varieties of plants, trade

	(h) any other tangible and intangible, movable and immovable property, and any related property rights, such as leases, mortgages, liens and pledges; Note: Investments also include the amounts yielded by investments, in particular, profit, interest, capital gains, dividends, royalties and fees. A change in the form in which assets are invested does not affect their character as investments	names, indications of source or geographical indications and undisclosed information; (vii) rights conferred pursuant to laws and regulations or contracts such as concessions, licenses, authorizations and permits; and (viii) any other tangible and intangible, movable and immovable property, and any related property rights, such as leases, mortgages, liens and pledges;

For IIAs to apply and for investment treaty arbitration to proceed, the existence of a protected investment is essential, along with a protected investor, which will be addressed later. Whether an investment qualifies for treaty protection depends on the definition of a protected investment under the applicable treaty.[1] Without a protected investment, the arbitral tribunal would lack jurisdiction over a claim against the respondent State.[2] Over time, investment treaties have adopted divergent approaches regarding what constitutes a protected investment. The investment protection framework between Korea and China has also evolved, with the three instruments taking different definitional approaches to protected investment.

2-1-1. Characteristics of Investment

All three instruments provide a broad asset-based definition of protected investments, referring to "every kind of asset(s)", followed by a list of investment forms. This illustrative list is non-exhaustive, meaning there may be other types of assets that can qualify as investments under the relevant treaty.[3]

However, unlike the BIT, the TIT and the FTA require that an investment must possess certain characteristics to qualify as an investment. Therefore, if either the TIT or the FTA is applicable, the claimant's investment must exhibit characteristics such as a commitment of capital or other resources, an expectation of gain or profit, or an assumption of risk. This may raise additional questions: What are the relevant characteristics of an investment? What is the relationship between these characteristics? And how many characteristics must be fulfilled to qualify as an investment? Despite these thorny questions, it is clear that at least some characteristics of an investment must exist in order to be get protection granted by the TIT or the FTA.[4]

By contrast, it is unclear whether an investment under a BIT must also meet these criteria. According to the so-called *Salini* test, if an investment dispute is brought before the ICSID and the ICSID Convention applies, the claimant's alleged rights must qualify as an investment under Article 25 of the ICSID Convention (objective meaning)[5] as well as the investment treaty (subjective meaning).[6] Consequently, the investment must possess the characteristics of an investment for the ICSID Convention to apply.

The *Salini* tribunal ruled that an investment entails (i) contributions, (ii) a certain duration of performance of the contract, (iii) participation in the risks of the transaction, and (iv) contribution to the economic development of the host state. The tribunal also emphasized that these elements should be assessed as a whole.[7] Several tribunals have agreed with this approach to varying degrees. For instance, some tribunals have held that, while jurisdiction over a claim requires meeting the investment requirements under both the investment treaty and the ICSID Convention, contribution to the economic development of the host state should not be considered a necessary characteristic of an investment.[8] Other tribunals have considered a contribution to the host state's economic development as a factor in determining whether it qualifies as an investment.[9] On the other hand, some hold the view that, since the ICSID Convention does not define what an investment is, the scope of protected investments must be determined based on the relevant investment treaty concluded by the contracting parties. These tribunals have ruled that the jurisdiction of an ICSID tribunal should be assessed in accordance with the parties' consent and that Article 25 of the ICSID Convention may not impose limits on this consent.[10]

Moreover, in non-ICSID cases where the ICSID Convention does not apply and other rules of arbitration, such as the UNCITRAL rules, are used, there are differing views on whether the term 'investment' has an objective meaning. For example, the *Romak* tribunal ruled that the term 'investment' under an investment treaty has an inherent meaning, irrespective of whether the investor resorts to ICSID or UNCITRAL arbitral proceedings. The tribunal further held that the term 'investment' entails a contribution, duration, and risk.[11]

To sum up, even under the BIT, which does not specify the characteristics of an investment, the claimant's claims might need to satisfy the objective meaning of an investment. If the investor initiates proceedings under the ICSID framework, it is somewhat more likely that the objective criteria must be met to qualify as an investment under the ICSID Convention. However, if the investor opts for other proceedings, such as UNCITRAL, it still remains possible that the tribunal may also require such criteria to determine the existence of a protected investment under the applicable investment treaty. In any case, unlike the other two instruments, the inadequate description of the characteristics of an investment in the BIT is likely to give rise to intense debate between the disputing parties in the event that the BIT is chosen as the basis for initiating the investment dispute proceedings.

2-1-2. Control of Asset

Both the TIT and the FTA state that control of an asset can qualify as an investment, whereas the BIT does not include such language. Therefore, under the TIT and FTA, an investor who does not fully own an asset but exercises control over it may still have an investment as defined by these treaties. Then, what does control mean? One tribunal held that an entity may be said to control another entity if it possesses the legal capacity to do so.[12] However, this abstract explanation is, on its own, insufficient. The determination of control should involve a complex analysis requiring the consideration of several factors, including equity participation, voting rights, and management rights.[13] This analysis should be conducted on a case-by-case basis, requiring flexibility and careful consideration of contextual facts and legal findings. Even if a claimant is a minority shareholder in a local company established in the host state, they may exert effective influence over operational control through their management role and, as a result, control the local company.[14] Holding a majority share may lead to a presumption of control, but this presumption can be rebutted by considering additional circumstances.[15]

As noted earlier, the BIT does not explicitly include control in its definition of an investment. This raises the question of whether an investor must have (at least partial) ownership of the asset to invoke the BIT, even if they exercise control over it. In contrast, both the TIT and the FTA refer to every kind of asset that an investor owns 'or' controls, making it clear that a claimant who owns or controls an asset may seek protection under these treaties. However, it is not immediately clear whether the definition of an investment under the BIT aligns with that of the TIT or the FTA. Most of the time, this is unlikely to pose a significant problem, as a claimant who controls an asset typically possesses certain rights to do so, which can themselves be considered an asset. The BIT explicitly refers to 'any other forms of participation in a company, business enterprise, or joint venture' as examples of assets. However, at least in theory, the respondent state may argue that a claimant who has the capacity to control the management of a local company established in the host state cannot invoke the BIT if they lack ownership of the asset.

2-1-3. Indirect Investment

The TIT and the FTA explicitly include indirect investments as protected investments by referring to 'every kind of asset that an investor owns or controls, directly or indirectly'. In contrast, the BIT makes no mention of indirect investments, which raises the question of whether such investments can be considered protected under the BIT.

An indirect investment refers to an investment held by an investor through one or more intermediaries. For example, the investor may hold shares in a company that, in turn, owns or controls the investment. This arrangement involves a chain of ownership and/or control that includes multiple entities.[16] The issue of indirect investment becomes evident in cases where an investor incorporates another entity to invest in the territory of the host state. In such scenarios, questions may arise as to whether the investor can look through the corporate structure to claim losses incurred by a separate juridical entity.[17] Under the TIT and FTA, it is clear that investors may pursue such a claim against a host state even if they do not directly own or control the investment.

However, the BIT does not explicitly reference indirect investments. Consequently, respondent States may argue that investors who hold only indirect investments in their territory are not entitled to assert investment claims against the host state. In practice, some respondent States have contended that, since the investment treaty does not explicitly permit investors with only indirect interests to pursue claims, such investors lack standing. It appears that most tribunals have rejected this argument, finding they have jurisdiction over claims brought by investors with indirect investments, as the term 'investment' under the applicable treaty is very broad and can include both direct and indirect investments.[18] However, at least one tribunal has ruled that indirect investments may not be protected under an investment treaty unless the treaty explicitly refers to the protection of indirect investments. This is particularly the case if the claimant fails to "demonstrate that the investment was made at the claimant's direction, that the claimant funded the investment, or that the claimant controlled the investment in an active and direct manner".[19] Therefore, it is possible that an investor relying on the BIT could face an argument from the respondent state challenging their claim if they hold only an indirect interest in the disputed asset.

2-1-4. Legality Requirement

The BIT defines the term 'investment' as every kind of asset used as investment "in accordance with the applicable law and regulations" of the host state. The requirement may allow the respondent State to potentially raise a jurisdictional defence if an investment was not made in accordance with the host state's applicable laws and regulations.[20] This legality requirement concerns the host state's laws governing the admission of investments.[21] Thus, including the above wording, the investment treaty aims to ensure that the treaty does not protect investments made in violation of the host state's laws,[22] though some tribunals have ruled that minor and trivial breaches of the host state's laws would not constitute a violation of the legality requirement under the relevant treaty.[23]

However, the TIT and the FTA lack such a definition, raising the question of whether the respondent state can invoke a jurisdictional defence if an investment was not made in compliance with its laws and regulations. In the *Achmea* case, the tribunal noted that the definition of "investment" in the Netherlands-Slovakia BIT did not include a requirement that investment be made in accordance with the host state's laws and regulations.[24] The tribunal found it unreasonable to assume that the treaty parties intended to protect investments violating a prohibition on foreign investment in a specified sector. At the same time, it held that the treaty could reasonably be interpreted without imposing a blanket requirement for compliance with the host state's laws at the time of the investment's making, as long as the investment fell within the scope of treaty protection.[25] In this case, there was no indication that investing in the sector in question was inherently unlawful. The respondent argued that certain aspects of how the investment was made constituted violations of Slovak law. However, the tribunal determined that these alleged violations were not serious enough to warrant the cancellation or termination of the investment. It concluded that such violations did not equate to breaching a prohibition on foreign investment in a specific sector. Consequently, the tribunal rejected the respondent state's argument that it lacked jurisdiction due to the investment being made in violation of Slovak law.[26]

Moreover, some tribunals have ruled that they had jurisdiction over claims even if the investment was not made in accordance with the host state's laws, but have denied substantive protection under the investment treaty to the investor, even though the treaty did not explicitly provide for such an outcome.[27] Other tribunals have held that compliance with national laws in the establishment of an investment is implicit, even if not explicitly stated in the relevant treaty,[28] or that this principle exists as a general norm independent of specific treaty language.[29]

Therefore, respondent States may raise jurisdictional or substantive defenses when the investment in question was not made in accordance with their domestic laws and regulations. However, it remains unclear what effect, if any, such an illegal investment would have on the investor's claims against the host states. Alternatively, treaty parties may specifically and explicitly condition investors' access to an investment dispute settlement mechanism on compliance with the host state's domestic legislation. In this regard, it is clear that under the BIT, a tribunal does not have jurisdiction over an investor's claims if the alleged investment was not made in compliance with the host state's laws. Conversely, under the TIT and the FTA, it is less certain whether a tribunal has jurisdiction, substantive protection can be granted, or the host state has any defense when the investment was made in violation of its laws.

2-2. Protected Investors

BIT Article 1.2	TIT Article 1(2)-1(4)	FTA Article 12.1
The term "investor" means any natural person or legal entity of one Contracting Party who invests in the territory of the other Contracting Party; (a) the term "natural person" means a natural person having the nationality of one Contracting Party in accordance with its laws; and (b) the term "legal entity" means any entity incorporated or constituted in accordance with the laws and regulations of one Contracting Party, including a company, public institution,	(2) the term "investor of a Contracting Party" means a natural person or an enterprise of a Contracting Party that makes investments in the territory of another Contracting Party; (3) the term "natural person of a Contracting Party" means a natural person that has the nationality of that Contracting Party in accordance with its applicable laws and regulations; (4) the term "enterprise of a Contracting Party" means any legal person or any other entity constituted or organized under the applicable laws	**investor of a Party** means a natural person or an enterprise of a Party that makes investments in the territory of the other Party; **natural person of a Party** means a natural person that has the nationality of that Party in accordance with its applicable laws and regulations; **enterprise of a Party** means any legal person or any other entity constituted or organized under the applicable laws and regulations of that Party, whether or not for profit, and whether private or government-owned or

foundation, partnership, firm, organisation, corporation or association	and regulations of that Contracting Party, whether or not for profit, and whether private-or government-owned or controlled, and includes a company, corporation, trust, partnership, sole proprietorship, joint venture, association or organization;	controlled, and includes a company, corporation, trust, partnership, sole proprietorship, joint venture, association or organization;

Like a protected investment, a protected investor is one of the most important criteria in light of the investment protection in accordance with the relevant investment agreement. Whether a claimant constitutes a protected investor under the applicable treaty affects the jurisdiction of the arbitral tribunal of an investment dispute.[30] Although the three treaties above use slightly different wording, they all essentially define an 'investor' in the same way, categorizing an investor as either a natural person or an enterprise (a legal entity).

2-2-1. State-Owned Enterprises

State-owned enterprises ("SOEs"), including sovereign wealth funds, have their own separate legal personality from states[31] and primarily engage in commercial or economic activities. However, they are wholly or partially owned or controlled by governments. During the last several decades, they have taken a significant role in the global market, with some of them making substantial investments abroad.[32] Consequently, several investment arbitration cases have been initiated by SOEs. The nature of SOEs and their close ties to their home states raise questions about whether they can qualify as an investor eligible to bring claims against host states.

Many investment treaties have included SOEs in their definition of "investor". The TIT and the FTA also stipulate that investors explicitly include any legal person or any other entity, "whether private or government-owned or controlled". Consequently, under the TIT and the FTA, it is evident that SOEs investing in the other treaty party may file an investment claim against the host state. However, the BIT does not include any reference to "government-owned or controlled" or any similar language, which may raise questions about whether SOEs from one treaty party can qualify as investors and bring claims against the other party.

Most SOEs engage in commercial or economic activities, even though they are wholly or partially owned or controlled by their home state governments. They are distinct legal entities, separate from the state itself, and can fall under the concept of "company" if "they are incorporated or constituted in accordance with the laws and regulations of one Contracting Party", thereby qualifying as investors capable of bringing claims against host states unless excluded by applicable treaty clauses.[33] Moreover, the BIT defines an "investor" to include public institutions. While it is unclear whether SOEs fall under the concept of a public institution in the BIT, the fact that public institutions can qualify as investors suggests there is no need to exclude SOEs from qualifying as investors. The question of whether SOEs acting in a governmental capacity qualify as investors remains contentious,[34] but SOEs acting in a commercial capacity appear to qualify as investors under all three instruments.

2-2-2. Denial of Benefits

Even if a claimant qualifies as an investor under the relevant investment treaty, the host state may deny the benefits of the treaty to certain categories of investors if it contains a denial of benefits clause. The most common example involves mailbox companies or shell corporations that are owned or controlled by entities from a third state and lack substantial economic activities in their home state.

The TIT and the FTA both contain provisions regarding the denial of benefits. Article 22 of the TIT and Article 12(15) of the FTA stipulate that treaty benefits may be denied in two scenarios: (1) when an enterprise of the other party is owned or controlled by an investor of a non-party, and the denying party either does not maintain normal relations with the non-party or adopts/maintains measures that prohibit transactions with the enterprise or would be violated or circumvented if treaty benefits were granted to the enterprise or its investments; (2) when an enterprise of the other party is owned or controlled by an investor of a non-party or of the denying party, and the enterprise lacks substantial business activities in the other party. Even though there is disagreement about whether invoking the clause has prospective[35] or retroactive[36] effects, it is clear that the clause provides the respondent state with an opportunity to preemptively avoid investment dispute claims.

However, the BIT does not contain a denial of benefits clause. Therefore, when a claimant qualifies as an investor, the host state cannot deny the benefits of treaty protection, even if the investor is owned or controlled by entities from a third country and has no substantial business activities in its home state.

3. Substantive Provisions

3-1. Fair and Equitable Treatment

BIT Article 2.2	TIT Article 5(1)	FTA Article 12.5
2. Each Contracting Party shall accord to investments in its territory of investors of the other Contracting Party fair and equitable treatment and full and constant protection and security	1. Each Contracting Party shall accord to investments of investors of another Contracting Party fair and equitable treatment and full protection and security. The concepts of "fair and equitable treatment" and "full protection and security" do not require treatment in addition to or beyond any reasonable and appropriate standard of treatment accorded in accordance with generally accepted rules of international law.	1. Each Party shall accord to covered investments treatment in accordance with customary international law, including fair and equitable treatment and full protection and security. 2. For greater certainty, paragraph 1 prescribes the customary international law minimum standard of treatment of aliens as the minimum standard of treatment to be afforded to covered investments. The concepts of "fair and equitable treatment" and "full protection and security" do not require treatment in addition to or beyond that which is required by that standard, and do not create additional substantive rights. ......

Three investment treaties between Korea and China use differing wordings regarding fair and equitable treatment, which could result in varying levels of investment protection. A key issue is whether fair and equitable treatment in each treaty aligns with the minimum standard of treatment to be afforded to foreign investors or investments. While the BIT does not mention whether fair and equitable treatment corresponds with the minimum standard, the FTA explicitly states that fair and equitable treatment is accorded in accordance with customary international law minimum standard of treatment for aliens.

The TIT stipulates that fair and equitable treatment does not extend beyond "any reasonable and appropriate standard of treatment accorded in accordance with generally accepted rules of international law". However, it does not define what "generally accepted rules of international law" entail or clarify whether they align with the minimum standard of treatment. It appears that the reference to "generally accepted rules of international law" in the TIT should be understood as referring to the international standard of treatment, which constitutes the minimum standard under customary international law.[37] Therefore, under the TIT, an investor will be accorded the minimum standard of treatment for aliens, as established under customary international law, aligning with Article 12(5) of the FTA.

This matter clearly relates to the discussion of differing concepts of the fair and equitable treatment standard: on one hand, fair and equitable treatment as the international minimum standard, and on the other, fair and equitable treatment as an autonomous standard independent of the minimum standard of treatment.[38]

When relevant investment treaties, such as the TIT and the FTA, refer to the "minimum standard of treatment" or "international standard", it can be reasonably concluded that the fair and equitable treatment standard in these treaties derives from the jurisprudence and decisions of international courts and tribunals. This interpretation traces back to the *Neer* decision made by the Mexico-US Claims Commission in 1926, the meaning of which has since evolved. The *Neer* Commission held that the minimum standard is breached by conduct amounting to "an outrage, to bad faith, to wilful neglect of duty, or to an insufficiency of government action so far short of international standards that every reasonable and impartial man would readily recognize its insufficiency".[39] The *Neer* standard sets a high threshold for breach under the minimum standard of treatment, requiring conduct amounting to an outrage or bad faith.

An earlier investment arbitration tribunal in the *Genin* case, where the relevant investment treaty (Estonia-US BIT) stipulates that "[i]nvestment shall at all times be accorded fair and equitable treatment .... and shall in no case be accorded treatment less than required by international law", held that the treaty requires adherence to the international minimum standard. It further stated that an act amounting to "a wilful neglect of duty, an insufficiency of action falling far below international standards, or even subjective bad faith" would violate the minimum standard.[40] This ruling appears consistent with the *Neer* standard. However, over time, international jurisprudence has evolved to interpret fair and equitable treatment under the minimum standard more broadly, incorporating concepts like transparency, legitimate expectations, and procedural fairness.[41] Unlike the *Genin* tribunal, other tribunals do not consider bad faith or malicious intent by the respondent State as a necessary element for a violation of fair and equitable treatment.[42]

On the other hand, when investment treaties, such as the BIT, do not include wording like 'minimum standard of treatment' or 'international standard', they establish an autonomous standard rather than aligning with the minimum standard under customary international law. In such cases, the meaning of fair and equitable treatment must be interpreted according to the interpretive principles of international law, as outlined in Articles 31 and 32 of the Vienna Convention on the Law of Treaties.[43] Many scholars and investment arbitration tribunals have opined that fair and equitable treatment, as an autonomous standard, is not confined by the minimum standard under customary international law and offers a higher level of protection to investors than the international minimum standard.[44]

On its face, the BIT does not refer to the international minimum standard, whereas the FTA and the TIT explicitly do. This suggests that the BIT treats fair and equitable treatment as an autonomous standard, while the FTA and the TIT regard it as part of the minimum standard. As its name suggests, the minimum standard may function as a baseline, potentially offering a lower level of protection compared to the autonomous standard. An autonomous standard might go beyond this baseline, offering more comprehensive or higher levels of protection. This could lead investors to perceive the BIT as providing a higher level of protection for fair and equitable treatment than the FTA and the TIT. In practice, claimants often argue that, since the fair and equitable treatment standard in applicable treaties is an autonomous standard without qualification or condition, it should be interpreted broadly.[45]

Having said that, there are also doubts whether these differences can make a real impact in actual cases.[46] The terms 'fair' and 'equitable' themselves are vague, and referencing the minimum standard provides little practical guidance when applying the standard to the specific facts of a case. Moreover, the minimum standard itself has evolved to demand a higher level of protection, which significantly overlaps with the autonomous standard, if at all. Ultimately, what matters is whether respondent States act in an unfair or inequitable manner toward investors or investments, regardless of the applicable standard.[47] In this context, it is unlikely that the differing formulations of fair and equitable treatment in the three investment treaties between Korea and China would lead to different outcomes in a specific case.

3-2. National Treatment

BIT Article 3.1	TIT Article 3.1	FTA Article 12.3(1)
1. Each Contracting Party shall in its territory accord to investors of the other Contracting Party and to their investments no less favourable than	1. Each Contracting Party shall in its territory accord to investors of another Contracting Party and to their investments treatment no less	1. Each Party shall in its territory accord to investors of the other Party and to covered investment treatment no less favorable than that it

the treatment it accords in like circumstances to its own investors and their investments (hereinafter referred to as "national treatment") with respect to the expansion, operation, management, maintenance, use, enjoyment, and sale or other disposal of investments (hereinafter referred to as "investment and business activities").	favorable than that it accords in like circumstances to its own investors and their investments with respect to investment activities	accords in like circumstances to its own investors and their investments with respect to investment activities.

National treatment under all three instruments requires a host state to treat foreign investors and their investments no less favorably than it treats its own domestic investors and investments in like circumstances. It is clear under these treaties that national treatment applies after the investment has been established, since a protected investor is defined as an entity that makes investments in a host state.[48]

One thing to note is that the BIT's national treatment clause also refers to the "expansion", which is not mentioned in the TIT and FTA. The TIT and FTA refer to "investment activities", which are defined as "management, conduct, operation, maintenance, use, enjoyment and sale or other disposition of investment".[49] This may raise the question of whether the national treatment provisions of the TIT and FTA do not apply to the expansion of an investment made previously.

The author of this article has not been able to find any case that attempts to define the "expansion" of an investment. According to dictionaries, "expansion" is defined as "the action of getting larger" (Cambridge Dictionary), "the act of becoming bigger or of making something bigger; the act of expanding" (Merriam-Webster

Dictionary), or "the action of becoming larger or more extensive" (Oxford Dictionary).

In the author's view, since an investor inherently seeks to grow their business or enhance their economic activities, and since the strategic or operational management of a business may involve its expansion, the terms "management, conduct, operation, maintenance, use" of an investment could encompass the act of becoming bigger. In this regard, the "expansion" of an investment does not significantly differ from "management, conduct, operation, maintenance, use" of an investment, unless there are special circumstances in which, for example, the investor attempts to enter an entirely different sector or field.

That being said, as mentioned earlier, the author has not found a single case that defines "expansion" in the context of investment or directly supports this interpretation. Additionally, there might be special circumstances where the term "expansion" could provide grounds for an investor to argue that national treatment should be granted when seeking to grow their business or enter another economic field or sector. If this is the case, the BIT's national treatment clause may be more favorable to investors compared to the TIT and FTA.

3-3. Most-Favoured-Nation Treatment

BIT Article 3.3	TIT Article 3.1	FTA Article 12.4
3. Each Contracting Party shall in its territory accord to investors of the other Contracting Party and to their investments and activities associated with such investments by the investors of the other Contracting Party treatment no less	1. Each Contracting Party shall in its territory accord to investors of another Contracting Party and to their investments treatment no less favorable than that it accords in like circumstances to investors of the third	1. Each Party shall in its territory accord to investors of the other Party and to covered investments treatment no less favorable than that it accords in like circumstances to investors of any non-Party and to their

favourable than that accorded in like circumstances to the investors and investments and associated activities by the investors of any third State (hereinafter referred to as "most-favoured-nation treatment") with respect to investments and business activities, including the admission of investment	Contracting Party or of a non-Contracting Party and to their investments with respect to investment activities and the matters relating to the admission of investment in accordance with paragraph 2 of Article 2. 3. It is understood that the treatment accorded to investors of the third Contracting Party or any non-Contracting Party and to their investments as referred to in paragraph 1 does not include treatment accorded to investors of the third Contracting Party or any non-Contracting Party and to their investments by provisions concerning the settlement of investment disputes between a Contracting Party and investors of the third Contracting Party or between a Contracting Party and investors of any non-Contracting Party that are provided for in other international agreements.	investments with respect to investment activities and the matters relating to the admission of investment in accordance with paragraph 2 of Article 12.2. 3. It is understood that the treatment accorded to investors of any non-Party and to their investments as referred to in paragraph 1 does not include treatment accorded to investors of any non-Party and to their investments by provisions concerning the settlement of investment disputes between a Party and investors of any non-Party that are provided for in other international agreements

Under all three instruments, a host state must grant investors from another treaty party the same level of treatment it provides to investors from any other country. This most-favoured-nation treatment aims to prevent discrimination between foreign investors based on nationality and promote equal competitive conditions.

As seen earlier, national treatment under these treaties will not be accorded concerning the admission of investment, i.e., the pre-establishment phase. However, when it comes to the most-favoured-nation treatment, some protection, albeit limited, will still be available even in the context of investment admission. The final part of Article 3(3) of the BIT, Article 3(1) of the TIT, and Article 12(4)(1) of the FTA state that the most-favoured-nation treatment will apply in the context of the admission of investment. Therefore, this treatment may apply to market access (the pre-establishment phase), meaning that if a host state allows a foreign investor from another country to invest in accordance with its domestic laws, an investor from another treaty party must also be allowed to invest in the host state. To clarify, these three treaties do not grant investors a right of admission. Rather, a host state is only required to admit foreign investments in accordance with its domestic legislation, which it can revise as necessary.[50] However, according to the most-favoured-nation treatment under the treaties, those rules governing the admission of investment must be applied no less favorably to foreign investors from another treaty party.

One major difference concerns the applicability of most-favoured-nation treatment to dispute settlement mechanisms. Investors may want to invoke the treatment to claim better procedural rights from other treaties, including access to investment arbitration. The TIT and the FTA explicitly exclude from their scope the treatment accorded to investors of non-party and to their investment under provisions concerning the investment dispute settlement. This exclusion may prevent investors from bypassing agreed arbitration mechanisms under the relevant treaty, meaning that an investor may not invoke the most-favoured-nation treatment clause in these two treaties to claim access to dispute settlement mechanisms from other treaties.

On the other hand, the BIT does not explicitly exclude most-favoured-nation treatment from dispute settlement provisions. This may raise the question of whether an investor can invoke most-favoured-nation treatment to access dispute settlement mechanisms available in other treaties the host state has with other countries. The key issue is whether, and if so, to what extent, the scope of the BIT's dispute settlement provisions may be modified if they provide less favorable treatment than that granted under another investment treaty between the host state and a third country. Investment arbitration tribunals have remained divided on this issue when the underlying treaties do not explicitly stipulate whether most-favoured-nation treatment extends to dispute settlement arrangements. In such cases, various tribunals have concluded that most-favoured-nation treatment may allow claimants to invoke more favorable dispute resolution clauses from other treaties.[51] Several other tribunals, however, have rejected this approach, thereby preventing claimants from relying on dispute settlement provisions in other investment treaties.[52] Thus, under the BIT, it might be possible that a claimant may be able to rely on the most-favoured-nation treatment clause to invoke more favorable dispute settlement arrangements in other treaties the host state has concluded with a third country.

3-4. Umbrella Clauses

Article 10(2) of the BIT states: "[e]ach Contracting Party shall observe any commitments it may have entered into with the investors of the other Contracting Party as regards to their investments". Similarly, Article 5(2) of the TIT stipulates: "[e]ach Contracting Party shall observe any written commitments in the form of an agreement or contract it may have entered into with regard to investments of investors of another Contracting Party". These clauses are often referred to as umbrella clauses. They essentially ensure that any obligations a host state has undertaken with respect to a foreign investor from the other treaty party, including commitments in investment contracts, licenses, or even domestic law, are enforceable under the treaty's dispute resolution mechanism. This is significant because the clause may enhance investor protection by (1) preventing host states from evading contractual or other obligations with foreign investors and (2) allowing investors to bring treaty-based claims for breaches of contractual or other commitments.[53] This means that even private contractual disputes between the investor and the host state can be elevated to an investment treaty dispute, allowing recourse to investment arbitration.[54]

The extent of protection provided by the umbrella clause depends on the specific wording of treaties and tribunal interpretation. The BIT, as seen above, requires a host state to observe "any commitments it may have entered into" with a foreign investor, while the TIT stipulates that "any written commitments in the form of an agreement or contract it may have entered into with regard to investments". There are two major differences between the two.

First, the TIT mentions 'any written commitments', whereas the BIT simply mentions 'any commitments' without specifying that they must be in writing. In theory, this means the BIT can provide protection even when a host state makes oral commitments without any documentation. However, the TIT does not extend protection to such oral commitments.

Second, under the TIT, protection under the umbrella clause is provided only when commitments are made in the form of "an agreement or contract". In contrast, the BIT does not require that commitments be made through an agreement or contract with a foreign investor. This means that, under the BIT, an investor may invoke the umbrella clause even without concluding an agreement or contract with the host state. The investor may also argue that the host state's commitments under its domestic law fall within the protection of the umbrella clause.[55] However, under the TIT, an investor can rely on the umbrella clause only if it has concluded an agreement or contract with the host state. The investor cannot claim that the host state's breach of its domestic law or other regulatory commitments falls within the protection of the umbrella clause.

Unlike the BIT and the TIT, the FTA does not contain an umbrella clause and defines an investment dispute as a dispute that arises from an alleged breach of any obligation of the host state under the treaty (Article 12(1)(1) of the FTA). Therefore, an investor cannot claim that the host state's breach of a contractual or other regulatory commitment is subject to investment arbitration under the FTA unless the alleged breach also constitutes a violation of treaty obligations.[56]

4. Exception Clause

One of the key mechanisms with international investment treaties is the exception clause, which allows states to deviate from their treaty obligations under specific circumstances. Exception clauses may serve as a safeguard, balancing investor rights with the regulatory autonomy of host states. The three investment treaties between Korea and China contain different types of exception clauses, resulting in varying degrees of balance between the interests of investors and host states.

4-1. Security Exception

The BIT does not contain a security exception clause. However, both the TIT and the FTA include a similarly worded security exception clause. Article 18 of the TIT provides the following, while Article 12(1) of the FTA contains a comparable provision:

> 1. Notwithstanding any other provisions in this Agreement other

than the provisions of Article 12, each Contracting Party may take any measure:

(a) which it considers necessary for the protection of its essential security interests:

(i) taken in time of war, or armed conflict, or other emergency in that Contracting Party or in international relations: or

(ii) relating to the implementation of national policies or international agreements respecting the non-proliferation of weapons;

2. In cases where a Contracting Party takes any measure, pursuant to paragraph 1, that does not conform with the obligations of the provisions of this Agreement other than the provisions of Article 12, that Contracting Party shall not use such measure as a means of avoiding its obligations.

The key feature of this exception is that a host state may take measures it deems necessary to protect its essential security interests not only during times of war or armed conflict but also in other emergencies, whether domestic or international. The concept of "essential security interests" is not defined, which may create uncertainty and ambiguity in its application to specific cases. Determining what qualifies as "essential" or what should be considered "security interests" or "other emergencies" is itself a challenging problem. Moreover, the exception clause contains seemingly self-judging language, such as "[the host state] considers necessary", which may raise questions about whether the host state's defence based on security exceptions is subject to review or entirely self-judging. Investment tribunals have taken somewhat different approaches to these issues.[57] Despite these uncertainties, it is clear that a host state may invoke essential security interests as a defence to justify actions that would otherwise be prohibited under the TIT or the FTA, although the state state shall not use such measure as a means to evade its obligations under the treaties (Article 18(2) of the TIT and Article 12(15)(2) of the FTA).[58]

4-2. Prudential Measures

Prudential measure clauses in investment treaties grant host states the authority to implement financial and economic measures aimed at safeguarding financial stability, maintaining monetary policy, or upholding regulatory frameworks. While the BIT does not include such a clause, both the TIT and the FTA contain a prudential measures clause, as follows.

TIT Article 20	FTA Article 9.5
1. Notwithstanding any other provisions of this Agreement, a Contracting Party shall not be prevented from taking measures relating to financial services for prudential reasons, including measures for the protection of investors, depositors, policy holders or persons to whom a fiduciary duty is owed by an enterprise supplying financial services or to ensure the integrity and stability of the financial system. 2. Where the measures referred to in paragraph 1 do not conform with the provisions of this Agreement, they shall not be used as a means of avoiding the Contracting Party's obligations under this Agreement.	1. Notwithstanding any other provisions of this Chapter or Chapter 12 (Investment), a Party shall not be prevented from adopting or maintaining measures for prudential reasons, including for the protection of investors, depositors, policy holders, or persons to whom a fiduciary duty is owed by a financial service supplier, or to ensure the integrity and stability of the financial system. 2. Where such measures do not conform to the provisions of this Agreement referred to in paragraph 1, they shall not be used as a means of avoiding the Party's commitments or obligations under such provisions.

On the other hand, due to the absence of such a clause in the BIT, it remains unclear whether a host state may adopt a prudential or comparable measure in response to financial difficulties under the BIT. This issue can be analyzed from two perspectives. First, under general public international law, a defence of necessity may be invoked when a host state takes a measure that is the only way to safeguard its essential interests against a grave and imminent peril.[59] However, this is a highly exceptional plea that requires extremely rigorous conditions.[60] In investment arbitration cases, tribunals have acknowledged that a host state may invoke the defence of necessity as stipulated in Article 25 of the ILC Articles. This requires elements such as "essential interest", "grave and imminent peril", "the only way", "impairment of other states or the international community as a whole", among others.[61] But most tribunals have ultimately rejected the respondent States' defense of necessity in one way or another,[62] with rare exceptions.[63] Despite the possibility of invoking the defense of necessity under general international law, this cannot be compared to the explicit recognition of prudential measures in the TIT and FTA.

Second, investment tribunals have increasingly recognized the host state's right to regulate under its police powers. This recognition allows host states to adopt measures aimed at achieving public policy objectives, such as public health, environmental protection, national security, and financial stability. However, these regulatory powers should be exercised in a non-discriminatory manner and in pursuit of the general welfare.[64] Therefore, even in the absence of an explicit prudential measures clause, a host state may rely on the police powers doctrine or the right to regulate in response to financial difficulties. However, such measures must be exercised in a non-discriminatory and good-faith manner, serve a legitimate public purpose, and be proportionate. That being said, this still cannot be equated with the explicit recognition of prudential measures in the TIT and FTA.

4-3. Taxation Measures

Both Article 21 of the TIT and Article 21(3)(2) of the FTA stipulate that the treaty does not apply to taxation measures, except as expressly provided, such as in cases of expropriation. However, the BIT does not contain such an exception.[65] By excluding the application of the TIT or the FTA, in whole or in part, to tax measures, the host state can retain greater flexibility in its tax policy decisions. For instance, the host state may grant more favorable tax benefits to domestic investors than to foreign investors (as an exception to the national treatment obligation) to promote the domestic industry. Alternatively, it may grant more favorable tax benefits to investors from a particular country (as an exception to the most-favoured-nation treatment obligation) to foster a more amicable relationship with that country.

However, in the author's view, the application of a tax exemption clause is unlikely to make a significant difference in most cases. In the *Hulley* and *Yukos* cases, the tribunals examined Article 21(1) of the Energy Charter Treaty (ECT), which contains the taxation carve-out provision. Both tribunals held that the carve-out applies only to *bona fide* taxation measures, namely, actions genuinely intended to raise general revenue for the State. According to the tribunals, measures taken under the guise of taxation but actually serving an entirely unrelated purpose do not qualify for exemption from the ECT's protection standards under Article 21(1).[66] The *EnCana* tribunal took a similar view.[67] Therefore, according to these views, treaty protections remain applicable even if a taxation exemption clause exists, as long as the host state's measures do not constitute *bona fide* taxation.

Moreover, if a host state exercises its taxation authority in accordance with established tax rules and without predominantly improper purposes—whether political or otherwise—it is highly unlikely that such measures would violate the state's obligations under the investment treaty. As the *RosInvestCo* tribunal explained, "the normal application of domestic tax law in the host state cannot be seen as an expropriatory act".[68] Furthermore, as the *EnCana* tribunal rightly pointed out, foreign investments are subject to taxation and other charges, and in the absence of a specific commitment from the host state, a foreign investor has neither the right nor any legitimate expectation that the tax regime will remain unchanged.[69]

Therefore, even if the BIT does not contain a tax exemption clause, *bona fide* taxation measures taken in accordance with a host state's legitimate sovereign authority are unlikely to result in a violation of the treaty on the merits. Conversely, even if both the TIT and the FTA include such a clause, the exemption will likely apply only to *bona fide* taxation measures, while improper taxation measures may still lead to a finding that the host state has violated its treaty obligations on the merits. In sum, when a host state implements *bona fide* taxation measures, it is highly unlikely to be found in breach of its treaty obligations, regardless of the presence of a taxation exemption clause. In this regard, these three treaties do not lead to significantly different outcomes concerning a host state's taxation measures.

4-4. Denial of Benefits

While the BIT does not include a denial of benefits clause, both Article 22 of the TIT and Article 12(15) of the FTA contain such a clause, as follows.

TIT Article 22	FTA Article 12.5
1. A Contracting Party may deny the benefits of this Agreement to an investor of another Contracting Party that is an enterprise of the latter Contracting Party and to its investments if the enterprise is owned or controlled by an investor of a non-Contracting Party and the denying Contracting Party: (a) does not maintain normal economic relations with the non-Contracting Party; or	1. A Party may deny the benefits of this Chapter to an investor of the other Party that is an enterprise of the latter Party and to its investments if the enterprise is owned or controlled by an investor of a non-Party and the denying Party: (a) does not maintain normal economic relations with the non-Party; or (b) adopts or maintains measures with respect to the non-Party that prohibit transactions with the enterprise or that

(b) adopts or maintains measures with respect to the non-Contracting Party that prohibit transactions with the enterprise or that would be violated or circumvented if the benefits of this Agreement were accorded to the enterprise or to its investments. 2. A Contracting Party may deny the benefits of this Agreement to an investor of another Contracting Party that is an enterprise of the latter Contracting Party and to its investments if the enterprise is owned or controlled by an investor of a non-Contracting Party or of the denying Contracting Party, and the enterprise has no substantial business activities in the territory of the latter Contracting Party	would be violated or circumvented if the benefits of this Chapter were accorded to the enterprise or to its investments. 2. A Party may deny the benefits of this Chapter to an investor of the other Party that is an enterprise of the latter Party and to its investments if the enterprise is owned or controlled by an investor of a non-Party or of the denying Party, and the enterprise has no substantial business activities in the territory of the latter Party

For example, pursuant to both the TIT and the FTA, if an investor does not have substantial business activities in its home state, the host state may deny the benefits of the treaty if the investor is owned or controlled by an investor from a non-party or the host state. Investment tribunals have been divided on whether invoking the denial of benefits clause would have only prospective effects. Investment tribunals have taken divergent views. The *Plama* tribunal required that the invocation of the clause occur even before an investor makes an investment.[70] Some tribunals have found that the invocation does not have a retroactive effect, meaning that the respondent State can only deny the benefits to an investor before a dispute arises.[71] On the other hand, other tribunals have taken the view that a host state may invoke such a clause even after a dispute or arbitration has begun, meaning that such invocation would have a retroactive effect and the tribunal would lack jurisdiction over the matter.[72] One tribunal held that such an invocation would also have retrospective effects, but the right to deny benefits must be exercised in good faith and in due course. The tribunal then denied the respondent state's right to invoke the denial of benefits because the state exercised it too late.[73]

Despite the tribunal's divergent views on the denial of benefits clause, an investor may, in any case, be unable to rely on the TIT or the FTA if they are owned or controlled by an investor from a non-party or the host state and lack substantial business activities in their home state. Such an investor would certainly prefer the BIT over the TIT or the FTA.

4-5. Environmental Measures

The BIT does not have an exception clause related to the host state's environmental measures. Similarly, the TIT and the FTA also lack such an exception for environmental protection, but they contain provisions on environmental measures.

The TIT's preamble recognizes that investment promotion and protection can be achieved without relaxing health, safety, and environmental measures of general application. Moreover, it emphasizes the importance of investors complying with the host state's laws and regulations to contribute to environmental progress. Article 23 of the TIT also provides that encouraging investment through the relaxation of environmental measures is inappropriate and such measures must not be waived or otherwise derogated from to incentivize the establishment, acquisition, or expansion of investments within its territory.

Article 12(16) of the FTA contains the same provisions as Article 23 of the TIT, as shown above. Additionally, Article 16(3) of the FTA reaffirms each party's sovereign right to establish its own levels of environmental protection and development priorities, as well as to adopt or modify its environmental laws and policies. It also requires each party to strive to improve its level of environmental protection. Moreover, Article 16(5) stipulates that neither party shall waive nor otherwise derogate from its environmental laws, regulations, policies, or practices in a way that weakens or reduces the protections afforded by those laws, regulations, policies, and practices.

These provisions do not constitute exception clauses for environmental measures per se. However, they may play a significant role in the interpretation of other treaty provisions and the assessment of host state measures, as they can form part of the context and/or the object and purpose of the treaties. Under customary international law on treaty interpretation, as codified in Articles 31 and 32 of the Vienna Convention on the Law of Treaties ("VCLT"), the ordinary meaning of treaty terms must be interpreted in their context and in light of the treaty's object and purpose. Investment tribunals have consistently adhered to these interpretive principles, frequently considering both the context of treaty terms and the overarching object and purpose of an investment treaty when construing specific provisions.[74]

In this regard, the above-mentioned provisions on environmental measures in the TIT and the FTA may reaffirm the host state's regulatory authority over environmental protection and guide the investment tribunal's interpretation of other treaty provisions, though concrete outcomes may vary depending on the specific circumstances and terms of the relevant treaty.

5. Concluding Remarks

As examined, Korea and China have three coexisting investment treaties—the BIT (2007), TIT (2012), and FTA (2015)—which share many similar provisions. These include a three-year statute of limitations (Article 9(7) of the BIT, Article 15(11) of the TIT, and Article 12(12)(10) of the FTA), a fork-in-the-road clause (Article 9(4) of the BIT, Article 15(5) of the TIT, and Article 12(12)(5) of the FTA), transparency obligations (Article 11 of the BIT, Article 10 of the TIT, and Article 12(8) of the FTA), and rules governing the transfer of funds (Article 6 of the BIT, Article 13 of the TIT, and Article 12(10) of the FTA).

However, these treaties are not identical; they contain differences in wording and substantive provisions, creating a complex and layered investment treaty regime between Korea and China. As a result, an investor filing an investment arbitration claim against a host state can choose which of the three treaties to invoke. Given these differences, the selection of the applicable treaty may lead to different legal interpretations and potentially different arbitration outcomes. This raises an important question: Which treaty should apply when an investor from one state brings a claim against the other?

According to Article 30(3) of the VCLT, when all parties to an earlier treaty are also parties to a later treaty, but the earlier treaty has not been explicitly terminated or suspended, the earlier treaty applies only to the extent that its provisions are compatible with the later treaty. Applying this principle, one could argue that the BIT remains in force only where its provisions do not contradict those of the later TIT and FTA. However, investment arbitration tribunals prioritize party autonomy, meaning that the investor can freely choose which treaty to base their claim on. If an investor decides to proceed under the BIT, then the arbitration agreement between the disputing parties, namely, the claimant and the respondent state, exists solely under the BIT. In such a case, the tribunal would derive its jurisdiction from the BIT alone, making it unclear whether the VCLT's compatibility rule would apply. This ambiguity further complicates the interpretation and application of the three treaties in actual disputes.

Interestingly, the TIT directly addresses the issue of treaty coexistence. Article 25 explicitly preserves the validity of any pre-existing bilateral investment treaties between the contracting parties, ensuring that investors can continue to rely on them. While the FTA does not contain a similar provision, it also does not expressly repeal or replace the earlier BIT or TIT. This reinforces the conclusion that all three treaties remain concurrently applicable, granting investors the flexibility to choose the treaty most advantageous to their case.

This "treaty shopping" phenomenon allows investors to leverage the most investor-friendly provisions across the three agreements.[75] For example, the BIT provides the broadest investor protections, including an autonomous fair and equitable treatment ("FET") standard and an unrestricted umbrella clause, while both the TIT and FTA contain exceptions that grant host states greater regulatory space. Additionally, while both the BIT and TIT contain umbrella clauses, the TIT narrows its scope by restricting it to written commitments in contracts or agreements, whereas the BIT's umbrella clause applies more broadly. Notably, the FTA does not include an umbrella clause at all, offering the least protective framework among the three agreements.

A clear pattern emerges when comparing these treaties chronologically: the BIT (2007) offers the strongest protections to investors, the TIT (2012) strikes a middle ground, and the FTA (2015) provides the most regulatory flexibility to host states.[76] This progression aligns with the global trend of states revising their investment treaty frameworks to incorporate greater policy discretion while reducing the rigid investor protections of earlier agreements. However, a puzzling question remains: *Why did Korea and China not terminate or replace their older treaties despite their evolving views on investment protection?* One possible explanation is strategic flexibility—both states may have wanted to retain a range of options for their investors, ensuring stronger protections when necessary. Article 25 of the TIT supports this interpretation, as it explicitly permits reliance on pre-existing bilateral treaties. However, the lack of official documentation or explanations leaves this issue open to debate.

From a practical perspective, the continued existence of the BIT alongside the FTA raises concerns about policy coherence. The BIT and FTA are bilateral agreements between the same two states—Korea and China—yet they provide significantly different levels of investment protection. If Korea and China truly intended to redefine their investment relationship through the investment chapter of the FTA, they would have likely replaced or suspended the BIT at the time of the FTA's conclusion in 2015.

A possible justification for maintaining the TIT is that it is a trilateral agreement involving Japan, whereas the BIT and FTA are strictly bilateral. However, no clear rationale exists for preserving the BIT in parallel with the FTA, as both apply exclusively to Korea and China. As a result, the FTA's investment chapter is largely ineffective in practice.[77] Investors have little incentive to choose the FTA when the BIT offers broader and more favorable protections. This situation contradicts the presumed intentions of Korea and China in concluding the FTA, as the BIT effectively overrides the FTA's investment provisions in terms of investor preference.

The current treaty framework between Korea and China remains fragmented, allowing investors to choose among three different agreements based on their individual strategic interests. This flexibility may benefit investors, but it also creates legal uncertainty, raises concerns about treaty shopping, and diminishes the effectiveness of the FTA. If Korea and China truly intended to align their investment policies with the evolving global trend—prioritizing greater policy space for host states over rigid investor protections—they should have taken steps to phase out the BIT or clarify the hierarchy among the three treaties. The absence of such action suggests either a deliberate choice to maintain broad investor protections or a lack of consensus between the two states on how to transition to a more modern investment regime.

Ultimately, unless Korea and China formally address the inconsistencies in their treaty framework, the BIT will likely remain the dominant instrument in investment arbitration cases between Korea and China, effectively undermining the investment provisions of the FTA. This creates an unresolved tension between the legal framework that investors rely on and the policy objectives that the two states may have intended to pursue.

Notes

1 Zachary Douglas, *The International Law of Investment Claims* (Cambridge: Cambridge University Press, 2009), paras. 121, 122, 345; C.L. Lim, Jean Ho and Martins Paparinskis, *International Investment Law and Arbitration*, Second Edition (Cambridge: Cambridge University Press, 2021), 276-277; Jeswald W. Salacuse, *The Law of Investment Treaties*, Second Edition (Oxford: Oxford University Press, 2015), 174-175; Campbell McLachlan, Laurence Shore and Matthew Weiniger, *International Investment Arbitration*, Second Edition (Oxford: Oxford University Press, 2017), 217-218; Rudolf Dolzer, Ursular Kriebaum and Christoph Schreuer, *Principles of International Investment Law*, Third Edition (Oxford: Oxford University Press, 2022), 83.

2 *Salini Costruttori S.p.A. and Italstrade S.p.A. v. Kingdom of Morocco [I]*, ICSID Case No. ARB/00/4, Decision on Jurisdiction, 31 July 2001, para. 44; *Joy Mining Machinery Limited v. Arab Republic of Egypt*, ICSID Case No. ARB/03/11, Award on Jurisdiction, 6 August 2004, para. 63; *Jin Hae Seo v. Republic of Korea*, HKIAC Case No. HKIAC/18117, Final Award, 27 September 2019, paras. 168-169.

3 *Siemens A.G. v. The Argentine Republic*, ICSID Case No. ARB/02/8, Decision on Jurisdiction, 3 August 2004, para. 137. "The specific categories of investment included in the definition are included as examples rather than with the purpose of excluding those not listed".

4 According to *Jin Hae Seo* tribunal, the listed characteristics must be assessed globally and holistically. It is not always necessary for all of these listed characterises to be present to qualify as an investment. *Jin Hae Seo v. Republic of Korea*, HKIAC Case No. HKIAC/18117, Final Award, 27 September 2019, para. 96.

5 Article 25 of the ICSID Convention stipulates that "[t]he jurisdiction of the Centre shall extend to any legal dispute arising directly out of relation to *an investment*, between a Contracting State (or any constituent subdivision or agency of a Contracting State designated to the Centre by that State) and a national of another Contracting State, which the Parties to the dispute consent in writing to submit to the Centre". (emphasis added)

6 The definition of investment under the investment treaty is often referred to as a subjective approach because it is determined by the treaty parties. On the other hand, the definition of investment under the ICSID Convention is often regarded as an objective approach, as it must be assessed independently of the intentions of the treaty parties.

7 *Salini Costruttori S.p.A. and Italstrade S.p.A. v. Kingdom of Morocco [I]*, ICSID Case No. ARB/00/4, Decision on Jurisdiction, 31 July 2001, para. 52. The *Salini* tribunal stated that the requirements under the ICSID Convention cannot be diluted by the consent of the contracting parties.

8 *L.E.S.I. S.p.A. and ASTALDI S.p.A. v. République Algérienne Démocratique et Populaire*, ICSID Case No. ARB/05/3, Decision, 12 July 2006, para. 72; Victor Pey Casado and President Allende Foundation v. Republic of Chile (I), ICSID Case No. ARB/98/2, Award, 8 May 2008, para. 232; *Saba Fakes v. Republic of Turkey*, ICSID Case No. ARB/07/20, Award, 14 July 2010, paras. 110-111, 121; *Quiborax S.A., Non*

Metallic Minerals S.A. and Allan Fosk Kaplún v. Plurinational State of Bolivia, ICSID Case No. ARB/06/2, Decision on Jurisdiction, 27 September 2012, paras. 211, 219-220. Some commentators have also opine that

9 *Joy Mining Machinery Limited v. Arab Republic of Egypt*, ICSID Case No. ARB/03/11, Award on Jurisdiction, 6 August 2004, para. 53.

10 *Malaysian Historical Salvors, SDN, BHD v. The Government of Malaysia*, ICSID Case No. ARB/05/10, Decision on the Application for Annulment, 16 April 2009, paras. 73-74, 79;

11 *Romak S.A. (Switzerland) v. The Republic of Uzbekistan*, UNCITRAL, PCA Case No. AA280, Award, 26 November 2009, para. 207.

12 *Aguas del Tunari, S.A. v. Republic of Bolivia*, ICSID Case No. ARB/02/3, Decision on Respondent's Objections to Jurisdiction, 21 October 2005, para. 264.

13 Dolzer, Kriebaum and Schreuer, *Principles of International Investment Law*, 70.

14 *United Utilities (Tallinn) B.V. and Aktsiaselts Tallinna Vesi v. Republic of Estonia*, ICSID Case No. ARB/14/24, Award, 21 June 2019, para. 420.

15 *Caratube International Oil Company LLP v. Republic of Kazakhstan* (I), ICSID Case No. ARB/08/12, Decision on the Annulment Application of Caratube International Oil Company LLP, 21 February 2014, paras. 272-273; *United Utilities (Tallinn) B.V. and Aktsiaselts Tallinna Vesi v. Republic of Estonia*, ICSID Case No. ARB/14/24, Award, 21 June 2019, para. 369.

16 Dolzer, Kriebaum and Schreuer, *Principles of International Investment Law*, 114.

17 McLachlan, Shore and Weiniger, *International Investment Arbitration*, 247.

18 *Siemens A.G. v. The Argentine Republic*, ICSID Case No. ARB/02/8, Decision on Jurisdiction, 3 August 2004, para. 137; *Ioannis Kardassopoulos v. The Republic of Georgia*, ICSID Case No. ARB/05/18, Decision on Jurisdiction, 6 July 2007, paras. 123-124; *Venezuela Holdings, B.V., et al v. Bolivarian Republic of Venezuela*, ICSID Case No. ARB/07/27, Decision on Jurisdiction, 10 June 2010, para. 165.

19 *Standard Chartered Bank v. The United Republic of Tanzania*, ICSID Case No. ARB/10/12, Award, 2 November 2012, paras. 230-232.

20 *Inceysa Vallisoletana S.L. v. Republic of El Salvador*, ICSID Case No. ARB/03/26, Award, 2 August 2006, para. 207; *Fraport AG Frankfurt Airport Services Worldwide v. The Republic of the Philippines*, ICSID Case No. ARB/03/25, Award, 16 August 2007, para. 306. "[I]t is possible that an economic transaction that might qualify factually and financially as an investment (*i.e.* be comprised of capital imported by a foreign entity into the economy of another state which is party to a BIT), falls, nonetheless, outside the jurisdiction of the tribunal established under the pertinent BIT, because *legally* it is not an "investment" within the meaning of the BIT". Also see *Metal-Tech Ltd. v. Republic of Uzbekistan*, ICSID Case No. ARB/10/3, Award, 4 October 2013, para. 373. "Article 1(1) of the BIT defines investments to mean only investments implemented in compliance with local law. Accordingly, the present dispute does not come within the reach of Article 8(1) and is not covered by Uzbekistan's consent. This means that this dispute does not meet the consent requirement set in Article 25(1) of the ICSID Convention. Accordingly, failing consent by the host state under the BIT and the ICSID Convention, this Tribunal lacks jurisdiction over this dispute".

21 *Saba Fakes v. Republic of Turkey*, ICSID Case No. ARB/07/20, Award, 14 July 2010, para. 119.

22 Salacuse, *The Law of Investment Treaties*, 187; McLachlan, Shore and Weiniger,

International Investment Arbitration, 239-240.

23 *Tokios Tokelés v. Ukraine*, ICSID Case No. ARB/02/18, Decision on Jurisdiction, 29 April 2004, para. 86; *Quiborax S.A., Non Metallic Minerals S.A. and Allan Fosk Kaplún v. Plurinational State of Bolivia*, ICSID Case No. ARB/06/2, Decision on Jurisdiction, 27 September 2012, para. 280.

24 *Achmea B.V. v. Slovak Republic*, UNCITRAL, PCA Case No. 2008-13, Award, 7 December 2012, para. 166.

25 *Ibid.*, paras. 170-171.

26 *Ibid.*, paras. 175-177.

27 *Yukos Universal Limited (Isle of Man) v. Russian Federation*, UNCITRAL, PCA Case No. 2005-04/AA227, Final Award, 18 July 2014, para. 1349. "The Tribunal notes that there is support in the decisions of tribunals in investment treaty arbitrations for the notion that, even where the applicable investment treaty does not contain an express requirement of compliance with host State laws (as is the case with the ECT), an investment that is made in breach of the laws of the host State may either: (a) not qualify as an investment, thus depriving the tribunal of jurisdiction; or (b) be refused the benefit of the substantive protections of the investment treaty".

28 *Phoenix Action, Ltd. v. The Czech Republic*, ICSID Case No. ARB/06/5, Award, 15 April 2009, para. 101. "In the Tribunal's view, States cannot be deemed to offer access to the ICSID dispute settlement mechanism to investments made in violation of their laws. If a State, for example, restricts foreign investment in a sector of its economy and a foreign investor disregards such restriction, the investment concerned cannot be protected under the ICSID/BIT system. These are illegal investments according to the national law of the host State and cannot be protected through an ICSID arbitral process. And *it is the Tribunal's view that this condition – the conformity of the establishment of the investment with the national laws – is implicit even when not expressly stated in the relevant BIT*". (emphasis added)

29 *Gustav F W Hamester GmbH & Co KG v. Republic of Ghana*, ICSID Case No. ARB/07/24, Award, 18 June 2010, paras. 123-124.

30 Salacuse, *The Law of Investment Treaties*, 174-175; McLachlan, Shore and Weiniger, *International Investment Arbitration*, 156; Lim, Ho and Paparinski, *International Investment Law and Arbitration*, 299-300.

31 To be more precise, the legal personality of SOEs is governed by the domestic law of the place of their incorporation (Article 4(2) of the ILC Articles). See also *Ahmadou Sadio Diallo (Republic of Guinea v. Democratic Republic of the Congo), Preliminary Objections, Judgment, I.C.J. Reports 2007*, p. 582, para. 61: "In determining whether a company possesses independent and distinct legal personality, international law looks to the rules of the relevant domestic law".

32 IMF, *IMF Fiscal Monitor. Chapter 3. State-Owned Enterprises: The Other Government*, April 2020, 47; United Nations Conference on Trade and Development, *2014 World Investment Report*, 2014, 20-22.

33 *Ceskoslovenska Obchodni Banka, A.S. v. The Slovak Republic*, ICSID Case No. ARB/97/4, Decision of the Tribunal on Objections to Jurisdiction, 24 May 1999, para. 27; *Beijing Urban Construction Group Co. Ltd. v. Republic of Yemen*, ICSID Case No. ARB/14/30, Decision on Jurisdiction, 31 May 2017, para. 33. Also, Salacuse, *The Law of Investment Treaties*, 211-222.

34 The ICSID Convention does not offer a state-to-state dispute resolution

mechanism and, therefore, it may be arguable that SOEs acting as agents of a state or engaging in governmental activities cannot bring an investment claim under the ICSID Convention. See *Ceskoslovenska Obchodni Banka, A.S. v. The Slovak Republic*, ICSID Case No. ARB/97/4, Decision of the Tribunal on Objections to Jurisdiction, 24 May 1999, para. 17; *Beijing Urban Construction Group Co. Ltd. v. Republic of Yemen*, ICSID Case No. ARB/14/30, Decision on Jurisdiction, 31 May 2017, para. 31: "It is common ground that Article 25(1) of the ICSID Convention is not a State-to-State dispute resolution mechanism and is not open to State-owned companies as claimants when acting as agents of the State or when engaged in activities where they exercise governmental functions. It is common ground that in such circumstances State-owned enterprises are barred from bringing a claim under Article 25(1)".

35 *Plama Consortium Limited v. Republic of Bulgaria*, ICSID Case No. ARB/03/24, Decision on Jurisdiction, 8 February 2005, para. 162. "In the Tribunal's view, therefore, *the object and purpose of the ECT suggest that the right's exercise should not have retrospective effect*. A putative investor, properly informed and advised of the potential effect of Article 17(1), could adjust its plans accordingly prior to making its investment. If, however, the right's exercise had retrospective effect, the consequences for the investor would be serious. The investor could not plan in the "long term" for such an effect (if at all); and indeed such an unexercised right could lure putative investors with legitimate expectations only to have those expectations made retrospectively false at a much later date". (emphasis added.) See also *Liman Caspian Oil BV and NCL Dutch Investment BV v. Republic of Kazakhstan*, ICSID Case No. ARB/07/1, Award, 22 June 2010, para. 225.

36 *Ulysseas, Inc. v. The Republic of Ecuador*, UNCITRAL, Interim Award, para. 173. "A further question is whether the denial of advantages should apply only prospectively, as argued by Claimant, or may also have retrospective effects, as contended by Respondent. *The Tribunal sees no valid reasons to exclude retrospective effects*. In reply to Claimant's argument that this would cause uncertainties as to the legal relations under the BIT, it may be noted that since the possibility for the host State to exercise the right in question is known to the investor from the time when it made its the investment, it may be concluded that the protection afforded by the BIT is subject during the life of the investment to the possibility of a denial of the BIT's advantages by the host State". (emphasis added.) Also see *Pac Rim Cayman LLC v. Republic of El Salvador*, ICSID Case No. ARB/09/12, Decision on the Respondent's Jurisdictional Objections, 1 June 2012, paras. 4.83-4.85.

37 Salacuse, *The Law of Investment Treaties*, 247. The same view was adopted by the Supreme Court of British Columbia in its review of the *Metalclad* award. The Court held that, in using the words 'international law', NAFTA Article 1105 refers to customary international law, which is developed through the common practices of countries. *The United Mexican States v. Metalclad Corporation*, 2001 BCSC 664, Reasons for Judgment of the Honourable Mr. Justice Tysoe, 2 May 2001, para. 62.

38 Salacuse, *The Law of Investment Treaties*, 245-251; Lim, Ho and Paparinski, *International Investment Law and Arbitration*, 331-334.

39 *L.FAY H. NEER AND PAULINE NEER (USA) V. UNITED MEXICAN STATES*, Mexico-United States Claims Commission, Decision, 15 October 1926.

40 *Alex Genin, Eastern Credit Limited, Inc. and A.S. Baltoil v. The Republic of Estonia*, ICSID Case No. ARB/99/2, Award, 25 June 2001, para. 367. Also see *Rusoro Mining Ltd. v. Bolivarian Republic of Venezuela*, ICSID Case No. ARB(AF)/12/5, 22 August 2016, para. 520.

41 Dolzer, Kriebaum and Schreuer, *Principles of International Investment Law*, 191-194; Lim, Ho and Paparinski, *International Investment Law and Arbitration*, 340-350; Thomas J. Westcott, "Recent Practice on Fair and Equitable Treatment", *Journal of World Investment & Trade* 8, no. 3 (June 2007): 414-415. See also *Azurix Corp. v. The Argentine Republic*, ICSID Case No. ARB/01/12, Award, 14 July 2006, para. 372: "It is also understood that the conduct of the State has to below international standards but those are not at the level of 1927".

42 *CMS Gas Transmission Company v. The Republic of Argentina*, ICSID Case No. ARB/01/8, Award, 12 May 2005, para. 208; *Azurix Corp. v. The Argentine Republic*, ICSID Case No. ARB/01/12, Award, 14 July 2006, para. 372: "Except for *Genin*, there is a common thread in the recent awards under NAFTA and *Tecmed* which does not require bad faith or malicious intention of the recipient State as a necessary element in the failure to treat investment fairly and equitably".

43 *Saluka Investments B.V. v. The Czech Republic*, UNCITRAL, Partial Award, 17 March 2006, para. 296.

44 Salacuse, *The Law of Investment Treaties*, 249.

45 For instance, *Saluka Investments B.V. v. The Czech Republic*, UNCITRAL, Partial Award, 17 March 2006, paras. 286-287.

46 Salacuse, *The Law of Investment Treaties*, 250.

47 *Impregilo S.p.A. v. Argentine Republic*, ICSID Case No. ARB/07/17, Award, 21 June 2011, para. 289; *Murphy Exploration & Production Company International v. Republic of Ecuador*, PCA Case No. 2012-16, Partial Final Award, 6 May 2016, para. 206: "This debate is more theoretical than substantial. It is clear from the repeated reference to "fair and equitable" treatment in investment treaties and arbitral awards that the FET treaty standard is now generally accepted as reflecting recognisable components, such as: transparency, consistency, stability, predictability, conduct in good faith and the fulfilment of an investor's legitimate expectations. The precise application of these components, and the stringency of the standard applicable, may vary from case to case depending on the terms of the clause and the specific circumstances of the case. Notwithstanding, the function of the FET clause in investment treaties is broadly the same: it ensures the stability and predictability of the legal and business framework in the State party subject to any qualifications otherwise established by the treaty and under international law". See also *Rusoro Mining Ltd. v. Bolivarian Republic of Venezuela*, ICSID Case No. ARB(AF)/12/5, 22 August 2016, para. 520: "[I]ncorporation of the CIM Standard *[customary international minimum standard]* into the definition of the FET does not provoke a major disruption in the level of protection: the CIS Standard has developed and today is indistinguishable from the FET standard and grants investors an equivalent level of protection as the latter. The whole discussion of whether Art. II.2 of the BIT incorporates or fails to incorporate the CIS Standard when defining FET has become dogmatic: there is no substantive difference in

the level of protection afforded by both standards".

48 Article 1.2 of the BIT, Article 1(2) of the TIT, and Article 12.1 of the FTA. Note, however, that under the Korea-US Free Trade Agreement (KORUS FTA), a protected investor includes an entity that attempts to make an investment in a host state, thereby extending its protection to the pre-establishment phase (Article 11.28 of the KORUS FTA).

49 Article 1(5) of the TIT and Article 12.1 of the FTA.

50 Article 2.1 of the BIT ("Each Contracting Party shall ... admit such investments in accordance with its laws and regulations".), Article 2.2 of the TIT ("Each Contracting Party shall, subject to its rights to exercise powers in accordance with the applicable laws and regulations, including those with regard to foreign ownership and control, admit investment of investors of another Contracting Party".), and Article 12.2(2) of the FTA ("Each Party shall, subject to its rights to exercise powers in accordance with the applicable laws and regulations, including those with regard to foreign ownership and control, admit investment of investors of the other Party".).

51 *Emilio Agustín Maffezini v. The Kingdom of Spain*, ICSID Case No. ARB/97/7, Decision of the Tribunal on Objections to Jurisdiction, 25 January 2000, para. 56; *Siemens A.G. v. The Argentine Republic*, ICSID Case No. ARB/02/8, Decision on Jurisdiction, 3 August 2004, paras. 102-103; *RosInvestCo UK Ltd. v. The Russian Federation*, SCC Case No. V079/2005, Award on Jurisdiction, 1 October 2007, para. 133; *Impregilo S.p.A. v. Argentine Republic*, ICSID Case No. ARB/07/17, Award, 21 June 2011, paras. 99-103.

52 *Salini Costruttori S.p.A. and Italstrade S.p.A. v. The Hashemite Kingdom of Jordan*, ICSID Case No. ARB/02/13, Decision on Jurisdiction, 9 November 2004, para. 119; *Plama Consortium Limited v. Republic of Bulgaria*, ICSID Case No. ARB/03/24, Decision on Jurisdiction, 8 February 2005, para. 227; *Wintershall Aktiengesellschaft v. Argentine Republic*, ICSID Case No. ARB/04/14, Award, 8 December 2008, para. 197; *ICS Inspection and Control Services Limited (United Kingdom) v. The Republic of Argentina (I)*, UNCITRAL, PCA Case No. 2010-9, Award on Jurisdiction, 10 February 2012, paras. 296, 309; *Daimler Financial Services AG v. Argentine Republic*, ICSID Case No. ARB/05/1, Award, 22 August 2012, para. 278.

53 The first tribunal to examine the effects of an umbrella clause held that such a clause does not confer jurisdiction over the contractual claims. See *SGS Société Générale de Surveillance S.A. v. Islamic Republic of Pakistan*, ICSID Case No. ARB/01/13, Decision of the Tribunal on Objections to Jurisdiction, 6 August 2003, paras. 163-171. However, this view appears to be minority position and has not been widely adopted by subsequent tribunals.

54 To be clear, even in the absence of an umbrella clause, the contractual relationship between an investor and a host state may still be relevant in investment arbitration. For instance, the host state may engage in conduct that breaches not only contractual obligations but also treaty obligations. In such a case, the investor may file a claim against the host state under the investment dispute settlement mechanism, regardless of whether an umbrella clause exists.

55 Investment arbitral awards are divided on whether an umbrella clause allows an investor to invoke it for violations of domestic laws or other general regulatory commitments when the wording of the relevant treaty does not limit its

applicability, as seen in the BIT. The annulment committee in *CMS* case held that such obligations under an umbrella clause must be specific and it does not cover general requirements imposed the laws of the host state. *CMS Gas Transmission Company v. The Republic of Argentina*, ICSID Case No. ARB/01/8, Decision of the ad hoc Committee on the Application for Annulment of the Argentine Republic, 25 September 2007, para. 95(a). Some other tribunals have adopted the same view: *BayWa r.e. Renewable Energy GmbH and BayWa r.e. Asset Holding GmbH v. Spain*, ICSID Case No. ARB/15/16, Decision on Jurisdiction, Liability and Directions on Quantum, 2 December 2019, para. 442. On the contrary, other tribunals have opined that host state's obligations under its domestic law and regulation may become obligations under an umbrella clause. See *LG&E Energy Corp., LG&E Capital Corp., and LG&E International, Inc .v. Argentine Republic*, ICSID Case No. ARB/02/1, Decision on Liability, para. 175: "These laws and regulations became obligations within the meaning of Article II(2)(c), by virtue of targeting foreign investors and applying specifically to their investments, that gave rise to liability under the umbrella clause".

56 The TIT and the BIT also adopt the same definition of an investment dispute (Article 15.1 of the TIT and Article 9.1 of the BIT). However, due to the presence of an umbrella clause, a host state's breach of contractual obligations may also constitute a violation of the TIT or the BIT, thereby allowing the investor to seek recourse through the dispute settlement mechanism under the TIT or the BIT.

57 Lim, Ho and Paparinski, *International Investment Law and Arbitration*, 467-473; Caroline Henckels, "Whither Security? The Concept of 'Essential Security Interests' in Investment Treaties' Security Exceptions", *Journal of International Economic Law* 27 (2024): 114-129.

58 Dolzer, Kriebaum and Schreuer, *Principles of International Investment Law*, 309-310.

59 Article 25 of the Draft Articles on Responsibility of States for Internationally Wrongful Acts (the "ILC Articles").

60 James Crawford, *Brownlie's Principles of Public International Law*, 9th Edition (Oxford: Oxford University Press, 2012), 550.

61 For instance, *Bernhard von Pezold and Others v. Republic of Zimbabwe*, ICSID Case No. ARB/10/15, Award, 28 July 2015, paras. 624-668.

62 *Total S.A. v. The Argentine Republic*, ICSID Case No. ARB/04/01, Decision on Liability, 27 December 2010, paras. 483-484; *Hochtief AG v. Argentine Republic*, ICSID Case No. ARB/07/31, Decision on Liability, 29 December 2014, para. 301; *Bernhard von Pezold and Others v. Republic of Zimbabwe*, ICSID Case No. ARB/10/15, Award, 28 July 2015, para. 668.

63 *LG&E Energy Corp., LG&E Capital Corp., and LG&E International, Inc .v. Argentine Republic*, ICSID Case No. ARB/02/1, Decision on Liability, 3 October 2006, para. 266. However, the *LG&E* tribunal emphasized that once the state of necessity was over, the state could no longer invoke the defense from that moment onward.

64 For instance, *Saluka Investments B.V. v. The Czech Republic*, UNCITRAL, para. 225; *Chemtura Corporation v. Government of Canada*, PCA Case No. 2008-01, Award, 2 August 2010, para. 266; *Philip Morris Brands Sàrl, Philip Morris Products S.A. and Abal Hermanos S.A. v. Oriental Republic of Uruguay*, ICSID Case No. ARB/10/7, para. 295.

65 Article 3.4(b) of the BIT provides that most-favoured-nation treatment does not

apply in the context of international agreements relating to taxation. However, this does not entirely exempt taxation measures from the application of the BIT.

66 *Hulley Enterprises Limited (Cyprus) v. The Russian Federation*, PCA Case No. 2005-03/AA226, Final Award, 18 July 2014, para. 1407; *Yukos Universal Limited (Isle of Man) v. The Russian Federation*, PCA Case No. 2005-04/AA227, Final Award, 18 July 2014, paras. 1430-1433.

67 *EnCana Corporation v. Republic of Ecuador*, LCIA Case No. UN3481, Award, 3 February 2006, para. 142(1): "It is in the nature of a tax that it is imposed by law. Tax authorities are not robber barons writ large, and an arbitrary demand unsupported by any provision of the law of the host State would not qualify for exemption under Article XII".

68 *RosInvestCo UK Ltd. v. The Russian Federation*, SCC Case No. V079/2005, Final Award, 12 September 2010, para. 628.

69 *EnCana Corporation v. Republic of Ecuador*, LCIA Case No. UN3481, Award, 3 February 2006, para. 173.

70 *Plama Consortium Limited v. Republic of Bulgaria*, ICSID Case No. ARB/03/24, Decision on Jurisdiction, 8 February 2005, para. 161.

71 *Liman Caspian Oil BV and NCL Dutch Investment BV v. Republic of Kazakhstan*, ICSID Case No. ARB/07/14, Award, 22 June 2010, para. 225; *Anatolie Stati, Gabriel Stati, Ascom Group SA and Terra Raf Trans Traiding Ltd v. Kazakhstan (I)*, SCC Case No. V 116/2010, Award, 19 December 2013, para. 745.

72 *Pac Rim Cayman LLC v. Republic of El Salvador*, ICSID Case No. ARB/09/12, Decision on the Respondent's Jurisdiction Objections, 1 June 2012, paras. 4.83-4.92; *Guaracachi America, Inc. and Rurelec PLC v. The Plurinational State of Bolivia*, UNCITRAL, PCA Case No. 2011-17, Award, 31 January 2014, para. 376.

73 *NextEra Energy Global Holdings B.V. and NextEra Energy Spain Holdings B.V. v. Kingdom of Spain*, ICSID Case No. ARB/14/11, Decision on Jurisdiction, Liability and Quantum Principles, 12 March 2019, paras. 262. 271.

74 A number of awards or decisions issued by investment tribunals have discussed, at least briefly, these interpretive principles. For example, see *Metalclad Corporation v. The United Mexican States*, ICSID Case No. ARB(AF) /97/1, Award, 30 August 2000, paras. 70-71; *Técnicas Medioambientales Tecmed, S.A. v. The United Mexican States*, ICSID Case No. ARB (AF)/00/2, Award, 29 May 2003, para. 155; *LG&E Energy Corp., LG&E Capital Corp., and LG&E International, Inc. v. Argentine Republic*, ICSID Case No. ARB/02/1, Decision on Liability, 3 October 2006, paras. 122-124.

75 In most investment arbitration cases, "treaty shopping" occurs when an investor structures its investment through intermediary entities. For instance, if an investor from Country A invests in Country B by establishing intermediary entities in Countries C and D, the investor may choose among multiple treaties – such as those between A and B, B and C, and D and B – when initiating investment arbitration against Country B. The investor would strategically select the most favorable treaty among them. However, in the case of Korea and China, "treaty shopping" can occur even without a layered investment structure, as three different treaties exist between the two nations. This unique situation allows investors to choose among multiple legal frameworks without the need to restructure their investments across different jurisdictions, potentially influencing the outcome of investment disputes.

76 This conclusion may be supported by real-world cases. Two investment disputes have involved investment treaties between Korea and China: *Ansung Housing Co., Ltd. v. People's Republic of China* (ICSID Case No. ARB/14/25) and *Fengzhen Min v. Republic of Korea* (ICSID Case No. ARB/20/26). In both instances, the claimants opted to invoke the BIT rather than the other agreements, likely due to the stronger investor protections it offers compared to the TIT and FTA. Ultimately, both tribunals ruled in favor of the respondent state - the former case was dismissed for lack of jurisdiction, while the latter was decided on the merits.

77 The FTA, however, may influence the interpretation of the BIT. According to Article 31.3(c) of the VCLT, when interpreting a treaty, any relevant rules of international law applicable in the relations between the parties must be taken into account, along with with the treaty's context. Given that the FTA is a legally binding instrument between Korea and China, it may constitute such relevant rules of international law in disputes arising under the BIT. This means that provisions of the FTA, particularly those related to investment protection could inform the interpretation of the BIT, potentially influencing the scope of investor rights and state obligations. However, despite this interpretative interplay, the fundamental principle of treaty interpretation remains that the ordinary meaning of the treaty's terms should prevail. Unless explicitly incorporated into the BIT, the FTA's provisions should not override or distort the clear language and intent of the BIT. Instead, they might serve as supplementary interpretative tools to clarify ambiguities or resolve interpretative uncertainties.

KYIL

International Divorce in Korea: Legal Framework and Practical Issues

Yunjeong HWANG
Attorney at Korean Law
Lawyer Hwang Law Office[1]

Abstract

This article examines the legal framework and practical issues of international divorce in Korea, focusing on procedural aspects and private international law. Under Korean law, divorce may be obtained either by agreement or through judicial proceedings. Divorce by agreement is relatively simple and becomes legally effective upon registration, but it may not be recognized in foreign jurisdictions due to the absence of a court-issued judgment. Judicial divorce is governed by a fault-based system.

Following the amendment to Korea's Act on Private International Law in 2022, special jurisdiction provisions for international family cases were introduced. In addition, the rules for determining the applicable law differ depending on the specific legal issue—such as divorce, asset division, and parental rights and obligations—requiring careful analysis of both jurisdiction and governing law in each case. The discussion also addresses the issue of international litigation concurrence and the application of the public policy exception.

The article concludes by emphasizing the need for further legislative and judicial development to effectively address the evolving realities of Korea's increasingly multicultural society.

Keywords

International marriage, International divorce, divorce by agreement, judicial divorce, international jurisdiction, habitual residence, principle of nationality

1. International Divorce in Korea

Korea has traditionally been regarded as an ethnically homogeneous nation with a relatively low number of immigrants. However, over the past decades, the steady increase in immigration and the growing number of international marriages have contributed to the emergence of multicultural families as a visible and significant demographic in Korean society.

According to national statistics, a total of 222,412 marriages were registered in Korea in 2024, of which 20,759 were international marriages. During the same year, there were 91,151 cases of divorce, including 6,022 international divorces. As the number of immigrants continues to rise, along with increases in international divorces, legal disputes arising from cross-border divorce are becoming increasingly prominent in Korean family law.

This article seeks to explore the legal framework dealing with international divorces in Korea, with particular emphasis on issues of international court jurisdiction, applicable law, and related procedural and substantive challenges. Both theoretical discussions and practical considerations will be examined to provide a comprehensive understanding of this evolving area of law.

2. Legal Procedures for Divorce in Korea: Divorce by Agreement and Judicial Divorce

2-1. Introduction

Under Korean law, there are two legal procedures for divorce: divorce by agreement and judicial divorce. These legal procedures originated in the late Joseon Dynasty and during the Japanese colonial period, when the Joseon Civil Ordinance introduced both the divorce by agreement system and the judicial divorce system. Both divorce systems continue to exist today.

The divorce by agreement process is procedurally very simple; however, the parties may only agree on the intention to divorce, parental rights and obligation matters. Matters such as division of property and spousal compensation (damages) must be resolved through a separate agreement between the parties or through additional legal proceedings. Furthermore, a divorce by agreement takes legal effect only upon registration in accordance with the Act on Registration of Family Relations,[2] and not through court procedures. As a result, in cases of international divorce, there is a disadvantage in that a divorce by agreement, although effective in Korea, may not be recognized in the foreign spouse's home country when registering the divorce. On the other hand, with respect to judicial divorce, Korea adheres to the fault-based principle, meaning that one can only file for judicial divorce if the other party is at fault, which poses a limitation.

The following sections provide a brief overview of both divorce by agreement and judicial divorce under the Korean legal system.

2-2. Divorce by Agreement

2-2-1. Historical Development of the Divorce by Agreement System

Article 834 of the Civil Act provides that "[h]usband and wife may get a divorce by agreement". This Article was provided in the original version of the Civil Act. The review system for reporting a divorce agreement was introduced in 1963, and the confirmation system for mutual intent to divorce was introduced in 1977, which formally incorporated the court's involvement in the process. However, as the court's confirmation procedure was often merely a formality, issues arose such as inadequate protection for children and instances where one party was unilaterally divorced without proper safeguards. To address these concerns, a mandatory cooling off period and counseling recommendation system were introduced on June 22, 2008, along with a revised divorce by agreement system requiring the submission of a written agreement on child custody and parenting matters. This reformed system remains in effect to this day. Unlike judicial divorce, the divorce by agreement system reflects elements of the no-fault principle.[3]

2-2-2. Procedure of divorce by Agreement

Article 836-2 of Civil Act states the procedure of divorce by agreement as follows:

Article 836-2 (Procedure of Divorce)

(1) Any person who intends to get a divorce by agreement shall have a guidance on divorce provided by the Family Court and, if necessary, the Family Court may recommend to take counsel with a professional counselor who has expertise and experiences in

counseling.

(2) The party who filed an application for the confirmation of intention to divorce with the Family Court may have the confirmation of intention to divorce after the periods, prescribed by the following subparagraphs, have passed since the day of having such guidance referred to in paragraph (1):

1. Three months, if the party has any child to take care of (including an unborn child; hereafter the same shall apply in this Article);
2. One month, if not falling under subparagraph 1.

(3) The Family Court may exempt the party from or reduce the period under paragraph (2), when there are such urgent circumstances to proceed a divorce as the party's unbearable suffering may be expected due to domestic violence.

(4) The party who has any child to take care of shall submit the documents of agreement on fostering under Article 837 and decision of custody under Article 909 (4) or the original copy of adjudication of the Family Court under Articles 837 and 909 (4)

(5) The Family Court shall establish a child support order to confirm the details of child support agreed between parties. In such cases, with respect to the effect of the child support order, Article 41 of the Family Litigation Act shall apply mutatis mutandis. <Newly Inserted on May 8, 2009>

[This Article Newly Inserted on Dec. 21, 2007]

As stipulated in the above Article, a divorce by agreement under Korean law may be completed without the assistance of legal counsel, as the parties themselves may submit an application for confirmation of divorce by agreement. After a relatively short cooling-off period prescribed by law—one month in cases without minor children, and three months when minor children are involved—the parties must appear before the court to confirm their mutual intent to divorce. Upon completion of the divorce registration with the local government office, the divorce becomes final.

2-2-3. Cooling off Period

During an international legal conference held several years ago, I had the opportunity to participate in comparative discussions with foreign legal professionals regarding the divorce systems of various jurisdictions. They expressed notable interest in the fact that Korea's cooling-off period for divorce by agreement is limited to a maximum of three months. In contrast, many foreign jurisdictions require a separation period of two to three years to establish the irretrievable breakdown of the marriage. From a comparative perspective, Korea's system may therefore appear to be relatively straightforward and accessible. However, if a party engages in a romantic relationship with another person during the cooling-off period, such conduct may be constituted as infidelity, and the party may be held liable for damages for mental suffering. The purpose of the cooling-off period is not to establish that the marriage has irretrievably broken down, but to allow time for the spouses to reflect and possibly restore the marital relationship.[4]

2-2-4. Legal Requirements for the Effectiveness of Divorce by Agreement: Recognition Issues in Foreign Jurisdictions

One of the most distinctive features of the Korean divorce by agreement system lies in the timing at which the divorce becomes legally effective. Unlike judicial divorce, which takes effect upon the court's final judgment, a divorce by agreement becomes legally effective upon registration with the local government office. This structural distinction has significant implications, particularly in the context of international divorces, where recognition of the divorce in foreign jurisdictions may depend on the procedural framework under which it was obtained. Article 836 of the Civil Act states as follows:

> **Article 836 (Taking Effect of Divorce and Method of Reporting)**
>
> (1) Divorce by agreement shall take effect upon reporting in accordance with the Act on the Registration, etc. of Family Relationship after obtaining the confirmation of the Family Court. <Amended on Dec. 31, 1977; May 17, 2007>
>
> (2) The report as mentioned in paragraph (1) shall be filed in writing with joint signatures of both parties and two adult witnesses.

According to the above Article, even when the court confirms the parties' intent to divorce, the divorce does not take legal effect immediately. Pursuant to the Act on Registration of Family Relations, the divorce becomes legally effective only upon submission of the divorce registration. The relevant provision of the Act on Registration of Family Relations concerning the registration of a divorce by agreement is as follows:

> **Article 75 (Confirmation of Divorce by Agreement)**
>
> (1) Where a person intends to divorce by agreement, he or she shall file a report with confirmation of the Family Court having jurisdiction over the person's place of registration or address: Provided, That where the person does not reside in the State, such confirmation shall be made at the Seoul Family Court.

(2) The report referred to in paragraph (1) shall be filed within three months from the date on which a certified copy of confirmation is issued or delivered by the family court, attaching the certified copy of the confirmation thereto.
(3) Where the period specified in paragraph (2) has elapsed, the confirmation by the family court shall be invalid.
(4) Necessary matters concerning the procedure of confirmation by a family court and filing a report shall be prescribed by the Supreme Court Regulations.

According to the abovementioned provisions, even after the court confirms the parties' intent to divorce by agreement, the divorce does not take legal effect unless it is registered within three months in accordance with the Act on Registration of Family Relations. In practice, there are cases in which the parties fail to complete the divorce registration after obtaining court confirmation, resulting in the nullification of the legal effect of the divorce.

This raises an important issue when one of the parties is a foreign national. Since the family relations register contains entries only for citizens of the Republic of Korea, the legal effect of a divorce by agreement involving a foreign national spouse can only be verified through the Korean ex-spouse's certificate of family relations. In such cases, the foreign national is recorded as the ex-spouse in the Korean national's family relations certificate. As a result, the legal effect of the divorce is not evidenced by a court-issued document, but rather by the entry in the Korean family registry. Due to this system, some foreign jurisdictions do not recognize the legal validity of a Korean divorce by agreement.

In this regard, I always advise foreign clients who are considering a divorce by agreement in Korea to first verify whether such a divorce will be recognized in their home country. In one recent consultation, I encountered a case in which a foreign national had gone through a divorce by agreement with a Korean spouse several years earlier, only to find that the divorce was not recognized in his home jurisdiction. The court of that country declined to recognize the divorce on the grounds that the legal effect of the divorce could not be confirmed through a court-issued document.

Thus, while Korea's divorce by agreement system is procedurally simple and convenient, it poses potential risks for foreign nationals, as the divorce may not be recognized in their home countries. In light of the increasing number of international divorces in Korea, the Korean court should provide advance notice of this issue to foreign parties at the time of submission of the application for confirmation of intent to divorce by agreement.

2-3. Judicial Divorce

2-3-1. Principle of Prefixing Conciliation

With respect to judicial divorce in Korea, there are two available procedures: divorce mediation and divorce trial. Article 50 of the Family Litigation Act provides that a petition for divorce must first be submitted for mediation. If a party initiates a divorce trial without first applying for mediation, the Family Court is required to refer the case to mediation.

However, there are exceptions where the case may proceed directly to trial without resorting to mediation first. The second sentence of Article 50(2) sets forth such exceptional circumstances as follows:

Article 50 (Principle of Prefixing Conciliation)
(1) A person who intends to institute a litigation or to request an adjudication to the family court for family litigation cases of Categories B and C and family

non-litigation cases of Category E, shall first make a request for conciliation.

(2) When a litigation has been instituted or an adjudication has been requested without making a request for conciliation on any case under paragraph (1), the family court shall refer the relevant case to conciliation: Provided, That the same shall not apply if deemed that it is impossible to summon one side or both of the parties unless resorting to a service by public notice, or that it is impossible to constitute a conciliation even if the relevant case is referred to conciliation.

[This Article Wholly Amended on Mar. 31, 2010]

2-3-2. Causes for Judicial Divorce

Article 840 of the Civil Act sets forth the grounds for judicial divorce as follows:

Article 840 (Causes for Judicial Divorce)

Either husband or wife may apply to the Family Court for a divorce in each case of the following subparagraphs: <Amended on Jan. 13, 1990>

1. If the other spouse has committed an act of unchastity;
2. If one spouse has been maliciously deserted by the other spouse;
3. If one spouse has been extremely maltreated by the other spouse or his/her lineal ascendants;
4. If one spouse's lineal ascendant has been extremely maltreated by the other spouse;
5. If the death or life of the other spouse has been unknown for three years;
6. If there exists any other serious cause for making it difficult to continue the marriage.

Under Korean law, divorce claims brought by the at-fault spouse are not accepted. The Supreme Court first adopted this principle in a decision rendered in 1965, and has since consistently held that a party who bears responsibility for the breakdown of the marriage is, in principle, precluded from seeking a divorce.[5]

However, subparagraph 6 of Article 840 is sometimes interpreted as partially incorporating elements of the irretrievable breakdown theory. While the fault-based approach has long been the prevailing standard in Korean divorce law, in recent years, the Supreme Court has issued decisions that suggest a partial shift toward accepting the irretrievable breakdown of the marriage as a basis for divorce in exceptional cases.

Each subparagraph of Article 840 is generally regarded as constituting an independent legal ground for claiming judicial divorce, and moreover, a party may assert multiple grounds simultaneously. However, the court is limited to examining only those grounds that have been explicitly raised by the parties.

Notably, subparagraph 1, which refers to "unchastity", is considered a broader concept than "adultery", and therefore, the term "infidelity" is often viewed as a more accurate translation. Even in the absence of a sexual relationship, repeated emotional intimacy or the exchange of romantic messages with another person may be deemed as infidelity. In such cases, the aggrieved spouse may seek damages for mental suffering (e.g., spousal compensation), and may bring a separate civil claim for damages against the third party involved in the affair based on article 750 of the Civil Act.

3. International Jurisdiction and Applicable Law in Divorce and Related Matters under Korean Law

3-1. Introduction

Following the comprehensive revision of Korea's Act on Private

International Law in 2022 (hereafter referred to as the "2022 Act"), specific articles were introduced to address jurisdictional issues and the applicable law in international divorce proceedings. The following discussion will focus on legal and practical issues regarding jurisdiction and choice of law in matters related to divorce, including the division of marital property, parental authority, and custody.

3-2. Judicial Divorce

3-2-1. International Jurisdiction

Before the 2022 Act was introduced, only Article 2 provided general principles regarding international court jurisdiction in divorce cases. The 2022 Act now establishes specific rules governing international court jurisdiction in such matters.

3-2-1-1. General Principles

The general rules governing international jurisdiction under the 2022 Act are set forth as follows:

Article 2 (General Principles)

(1) The court of the Republic of Korea (hereinafter referred to as "court") shall have international jurisdiction where a party or a case in dispute has a substantial connection with the Republic of Korea. In determining whether any substantial connection exists, the court shall adopt reasonable principles, compatible to the ideology of the allocation of international jurisdiction, which aims to achieve impartiality between the parties, and appropriateness, speediness, and economy of adjudication.

> (2) Where there is no provision regarding international jurisdiction in this Act or in any other statutes or regulations, or treaties of the Republic of Korea, the court shall determine whether it has international jurisdiction, in consideration of the provisions of the domestic laws on jurisdiction, but shall give full consideration to the special nature of international jurisdiction, in light of the purport of paragraph (1).

The above Article serves as a declaration of the general principle governing international jurisdiction under the Act on Private International Law. In the absence of specific provisions on international jurisdiction in the 2022 Act—and in cases where there are no territorial jurisdiction rules under domestic law—the court may recognize jurisdiction based solely on the existence of a substantial connection, pursuant to Article 2(1).

However, as expressly stated in Article 2(2), this Article is supplementary in nature and is to be applied only where no provision regarding international jurisdiction exists in this Act, or in any other statutes, regulations, or treaties of the Republic of Korea. Accordingly, the applicability of Article 2(2) must be strictly construed, and its use should be limited to cases that clearly meet this threshold.[6]

3-2-1-2. Special Jurisdiction

The 2022 Act introduced a newly established Article on special jurisdiction with respect to divorce, as follows:

> **Article 56 (Special Jurisdiction over Cases Regarding Marital Relationships)**
>
> (1) The court shall have international jurisdiction over cases regarding a marital relationship, in any of the following

> cases:
> 1. Where one of the spouses has his or her habitual residence in the Republic of Korea, and the last common habitual residence of the spouses was in the Republic of Korea;
> 2. Where a plaintiff, and all or some of the minor children have their habitual residence in the Republic of Korea;
> 3. Where both of the spouses are nationals of the Republic of Korea;
> 4. Where a plaintiff who has habitual residence in the Republic of Korea as a national of the Republic of Korea files a lawsuit only for the purpose of terminating the marital relationship.
>
> (2) The court shall have international jurisdiction over a case regarding a marital relationship involving both of the spouses, in any of the following cases:
> 1. Where the habitual residence of one of the spouses is in the Republic of Korea;
> 2. Where one of the spouses is dead and the habitual residence of the surviving spouse is in the Republic of Korea;
> 3. Where both of the spouses are dead and the last habitual residence of one of the spouses was in the Republic of Korea;
> 4. Where both of the spouses are nationals of the Republic of Korea.

According to the above provision, Korean courts have jurisdiction over divorce proceedings between a Korean national residing in Korea and a foreign spouse. In matters of jurisdiction, the concept of habitual residence is of primary significance, while nationality is not determinative. Accordingly, Korean courts may also exercise jurisdiction over divorce cases between two foreigners having different nationalities whose habitual residence is in Korea.

However, Korea adopts the principle of nationality (*jus sanguinis*) in determining personal status. From this perspective, it may be appropriate to apply jurisdiction based on nationality, considering various factors such as the parties' interest in litigating in a court geographically close to them, the relevance of the Korean family relations register, and the importance of accurately disclosing a Korean national's legal status through official records.

Nonetheless, under the 2022 Act, the application of nationality-based jurisdiction is interpreted conservatively and is recognized only when both spouses are Korean nationals.[7] In addition, Article 56(1), subparagraphs 2 and 4 of the 2022 Act adopt the *forum actoris* principle under certain conditions. This reflects the recognition that family law matters have a profound impact on an individual's personal status and overall life circumstances, and thus, particular consideration must be given to the plaintiff's position to ensure appropriate legal relief.[8]

As will be further discussed below, where both spouses are foreign nationals sharing the same nationality, the Korean Family Court will adjudicate the divorce under the foreign law of their common nationality.

An additional question arises as to whether jurisdiction by agreement and jurisdiction by pleading may be permitted in family law matters under the 2022 Act. There are several persuasive arguments against allowing such forms of jurisdiction in this context.

First, family law cases, unlike property or commercial disputes, are characterized by a higher degree of public interest, which warrants stricter limitations on the parties' freedom to determine jurisdiction unilaterally or by mutual agreement. Second, the 2022 Act already provides multiple bases for jurisdiction in marital matters, thereby reducing the practical necessity of recognizing additional grounds through agreement or appearance that would confer jurisdiction on foreign courts. Third, from a comparative perspective, the Brussels II *bis* and Brussels II *ter* Regulations of the

European Union also do not permit jurisdiction by agreement or appearance in family law cases. Thus, maintaining the current restrictive stance in Korean private international law would serve to promote international consistency and coherence in the handling of cross-border family disputes.[9] As stipulated in Article 13 of the 2022 Act, jurisdiction by agreement and jurisdiction by pleading are, in principle, not permitted. Nevertheless, as will be discussed in a later section, an exception applies in the case of maintenance-related proceedings.

Notably, as previously explained, the family relations register in Korea is kept exclusively for Korean nationals. Therefore, in order for a marriage to be recorded in the register, at least one of the spouses must be a Korean citizen. If both spouses are foreign nationals, the marriage registration is merely received by the relevant Korean authority without being recorded in the family relations register.

For example, in one of the cases I handled, the parties were foreign nationals of different nationalities who had reported their marriage solely in Korea. After the breakdown of the marriage, both parties left Korea and established residence in different countries. Although this case did not fall within the scope of special jurisdiction under Article 56 of the 2022 Act, the Korean court accepted general jurisdiction and granted the divorce.

Given the increasing complexity of international marriages—particularly the diverse combinations of nationalities and habitual residences—there is a pressing need for more detailed legal consideration in determining jurisdiction. It may also be desirable for the Act on Private International Law to more fully reflect the wide variety of factual patterns arising in cross-border divorce cases.

3-2-1-3. Jurisdiction over Divorce Mediation

Regarding the jurisdiction over family mediation cases, the 2022 Act provides as follows, just as jurisdiction is established for a divorce trial, the same jurisdiction shall be deemed to exist for divorce conciliation proceedings as well.

> **Article 62 (Jurisdiction over Family Mediation Cases)**
> Where the court has international jurisdiction over a case pursuant to Articles 56 through 61, it shall also have international jurisdiction over the mediation case.

3-2-2. Governing Law

The 2022 Act did not introduce any new provisions regarding the governing law applicable to divorce. According to the relevant articles cited below, Korean law is generally applied in most international divorce cases filed in Korean family courts. However, there are circumstances in which foreign law may be applicable. Therefore, it is essential to conduct a careful review of each case to determine the appropriate governing law in international divorce matters.

3-2-2-1. Relevant Articles and Common Types

The Articles of the 2022 Act the applicable law in international divorces as follows:

> **Article 66 (Divorce)**
> Article 64 shall apply mutatis mutandis to divorce: Provided, That where one of the spouses is a national of the Republic of Korea, with his or her habitual residence in the Republic of Korea, the divorce shall be governed by the law of the

Republic of Korea.

Article 64 (General Effects of Marriage)

The general effects of marriage shall be governed by the laws in the following order:

1. The same law of the nationality of the spouses;
2. The same law of the habitual residence of the spouses;
3. The law of the place to which the spouses are most closely related.

The most common type of international divorce in Korea involves a Korean national and a foreign national residing in Korea. In such cases, pursuant to Article 64, subparagraph 2 of the 2022 Act, Korean law is designated as the applicable law. Even when both parties are foreign nationals residing in Korea, Korean law is likewise applied as the governing law.

3-2-2-2. Application of Foreign Law

In less common cases where both spouses are foreign nationals of the same nationality residing in Korea, the law of their common nationality will apply. As a result, the Korean court will designate foreign law as the applicable law in the divorce proceeding.

According to Article 18 of the 2022 Act, when foreign law is designated as the governing law under the Act, the court is obligated to investigate and apply the content of that foreign law *ex officio*. This means that the court must ascertain and apply the relevant provisions of foreign law, regardless of whether the parties raise such claims.[10] The relevant Article of the 2022 Act is as follows:

Article 18 (Application of Foreign Law)

The court shall examine and apply, *ex officio*, the details of the foreign law determined to be the applicable law under this Act and may request a party's cooperation for the purpose.

3-2-2-3. Applicable Law Based on Religious Affiliation

In certain foreign jurisdictions, the law applicable to divorce varies depending on the parties' religion. For example, in India, different laws such as the Hindu Marriage Act, the Indian Christian Marriage Act, and the Special Marriage Act govern divorce depending on religious affiliation.

I once handled a judicial divorce case involving an Indian couple of the Hindu faith, in which the Hindu Marriage Act was applied as the governing law. This raises a hypothetical but significant question: how would the Act the 2022 Act apply if the two spouses had belonged to different religions?

Given the growing number of foreign residents in Korea from diverse religious backgrounds, careful consideration must be given to the issue of religion-based designation of applicable law in the context of private international law. The evolving demographics of Korean society call for a more nuanced approach in addressing such matters within the existing legal framework.

3-3. Division of Property

3-3-1. International Jurisdiction

In the course of legislative deliberations on the amendment, there was debate as to whether a special jurisdiction rule should be established for matrimonial property regimes. However, the amended Act ultimately did not introduce any such provision. As the 2022 Act does not contain a separate jurisdictional rule for matters concerning matrimonial property, the jurisdictional rules applicable to marital relations are, by default, applied to disputes involving matrimonial property. Consequently, jurisdiction by agreement and jurisdiction by pleading are not permitted in such cases.[11]

3-3-2. Governing Law

With respect to the division of property upon divorce, the majority view holds that Article 65(1) of the 2022 Act—rather than Article 66, which governs the applicable law for divorce—should be applied.[12] Article 65(1) of the 2022 Act, along with the applicable provision by reference, Article 64, are as follows:

> **Article 65 (Matrimonial Property Regime)**
> (1) Article 64 shall apply mutatis mutandis to the matrimonial property regime.
>
> **Article 64 (General Effects of Marriage)**
> The general effects of marriage shall be governed by the laws in the following order:
> 1. The same law of the nationality of the spouses;
> 2. The same law of the habitual residence of the spouses;
> 3. The law of the place to which the spouses are most closely related.

3-3-3. Division of Property under Civil Act

The 1990 amendment to the Korean Civil Act introduced the statutory right to claim division of property upon divorce. To that end, Article 839-2 of the Civil Act was newly enacted, as follows:

> **Article 839-2 (Claim for Division of Property)**
> (1) One of the parties who have been divorced by agreement,

may claim a division of property against the other party.
(2) If no agreement is made for a division of property as referred to in paragraph (1), or if it is impossible to reach an agreement, the Family Court shall, upon a request of the parties, determine the amount and method of division, considering the amount of property acquired by cooperation of both parties and other circumstances.
(3) The claim for division of property as referred to in paragraph (1) shall be extinguished after two years have passed from the date of divorce.
[This Article Newly Inserted on Jan. 13, 1990]

The legal basis for the claim for division of property upon divorce is generally understood to involve both liquidation and supportive elements. The liquidation aspect is grounded in the idea that marital property accumulated through the joint efforts of both spouses during the marriage should be equitably divided based on the respective contributions of each party. The supportive aspect arises from the view that the duty of mutual support between spouses does not necessarily terminate upon divorce and may, in certain cases, continue to justify post-divorce financial adjustment. The Korean Supreme Court adopts a hybrid approach, characterizing the division of property upon divorce as a system that primarily serves to liquidate jointly acquired property, while also incorporating elements of post-marital support for the economically weaker spouse.[13] However, it is important to note that Korean law does not recognize a separate system of alimony, understood in many jurisdictions as ongoing financial support payments to a former spouse after divorce.

The procedure for division of property under Korean law generally proceeds as follows:

(1) Submission of property lists by both the plaintiff and the defendant;
(2) If necessary, a party may request an official inquiry into the

other party's assets;
(3) All assets held by both parties are totaled;
(4) The proportion of division is determined by taking into account the duration of the marriage and the respective contributions of each party;
(5) The party whose share exceeds the amount to which they are entitled, based on the determined division ratio, must pay the difference to the other party.

In principle, assets acquired prior to the marriage, or assets acquired by inheritance or gift during the marriage, are categorized as peculiar property and are excluded from the marital property subject to division. However, if the other spouse has made contributions to the formation, maintenance, or appreciation of such separate property, those contributions may be considered in determining the final division of property.

In cases where assets are located abroad, Korean courts do not have the authority to compel foreign banks or institutions to produce financial documents. Consequently, the court must rely primarily on the voluntary disclosure of information by the parties.

In general, under Korean law, a spouse who has served as a full-time homemaker during a marriage of 20 years may be awarded 50% of the property subject to division, reflecting the presumption of equal contribution.

3-4 Parental Rights and Obligations

3-4-1. International Jurisdiction

Where a Korean court has jurisdiction over a divorce case, it may also exercise jurisdiction over incidental matters arising from the divorce, such as the designation of parental authority and custodial rights, as well as claims for child support. The relevant Article of the

2022 Act addressing this issue is set forth below:

Article 6 (Jurisdiction over Connected Cases)

(1) Where the court has international jurisdiction over one of multiple claims that are closely related to one another, a single lawsuit including such multiple claims may be filed with the court.

(2) Where the court has general jurisdiction under Article 3 over one of the co-defendants, and where there is a close connection between a claim against the defendant and another claim against the other co-defendants, a single lawsuit against the co-defendants may be filed with the court, only to avoid the risk of conflicting judgments.

(3) Where the court has international jurisdiction over the main claim of the following cases pursuant to Articles 56 through 61, a lawsuit involving claims incidental to the main claim, such as the designation of a person with parental authority or a caregiver for a child, and the payment of support may also be filed with the court:

1. Cases regarding a marital relationship;
2. Cases regarding a biological parental relationship;
3. Cases regarding an adoptive relationship;
4. Cases regarding a parent-child relationship;
5. Cases regarding a support relationship;
6. Cases regarding guardianship.

(4) Where the court has international jurisdiction only over claims incidental to the main claim of a case under the subparagraphs of paragraph (3), no lawsuit on such main claim may be filed with the court.

Where a party files a claim solely concerning parental authority, custody, or visitation rights, without filing for divorce, a special jurisdiction rule applies, as set forth in the Article below.

Article 60 (Jurisdiction over Cases Regarding Support)

(1) The court shall have international jurisdiction over cases regarding support, where a person entitled to support has his or her habitual residence in the Republic of Korea.

(2) Even where the parties enter into an agreement on international jurisdiction over a case regarding support under Article 8, such agreement shall not be effective in any of the following cases:

1. Where a person entitled to support is a minor or a ward: Provided, That the same shall not apply where the person entitled to support, either a minor or a ward, is allowed to file a lawsuit not only with the court, but also with a foreign court under the relevant agreement;
2. Where a country designated by agreement is not or slightly related to the issue.

(3) Article 9 shall not apply, where a case regarding support falls under any of the following:

1. Where a person entitled to support is a minor or a ward;
2. Where the Republic of Korea is not or slightly related to the issue.

As seen above, jurisdiction by pleading may be applied in maintenance-related cases. However, where the maintenance creditor is a minor, such jurisdiction does not apply. Accordingly, in cases involving claims for child support for a minor, jurisdiction by pleading is not recognized.

3-4-2. Governing Law

The applicable law governing matters such as the designation of parental authority and child custody is set forth as follows:

Article 72 (Parent-Child Legal Relationship)
Where both parents and a child have the same law of nationality, the parent-child legal relationship shall be governed by the same law of nationality, but in other cases, the law of the habitual residence of the child shall govern.

In addition, the following Article applies to matters concerning child support.

Article 73 (Support)
(1) Support obligations shall be governed by the law of the habitual residence of a person entitled to support: Provided, That where the person entitled to support cannot obtain support from a person with support obligations under the relevant law, the law of the common nationality of the parties shall govern. (2) Where a divorce is completed or approved in the Republic of Korea, the support obligations between the divorced parties shall be governed by the law under which the divorce is granted, notwithstanding paragraph (1). (3) With respect to support obligations among collateral relatives by blood or relatives by marriage, the alleged obligor may contend, against the person who claims to be entitled to support, that he or she has no support obligations under the law of the common nationality of the parties, and where such law does not exist, he or she may contend that no support obligations arise under

the law of his or her habitual residence.

(4) Where both a person with support obligations and a person entitled to support are nationals of the Republic of Korea, and where the habitual residence of the former is in the Republic of Korea, the law of the Republic of Korea shall govern.

As can be seen from the above Article, the law of the child's habitual residence takes precedence in order to protect the child's rights. However, paragraph 4 introduces nationality as a relevant connecting factor, providing that if the person with support obligations has habitual residence in Korea, Korean law shall apply, thereby enhancing the parties' reliance interest and foreseeability in legal outcomes.[14]

In cases of international divorce, the husband and wife often have different nationalities, and children born to such couples may acquire dual nationality. Under the Nationality Act, which adheres to the principle of *jus sanguinis* (nationality by descent), a child automatically acquires Korean nationality if either parent is a Korean national, regardless of the place of birth, as seen the following article of the Nationality Act.

Article 2 (Acquisition of Nationality by Birth)

(1) Any of the following persons shall be a national of the Republic of Korea at birth:

1. A person whose father or mother is a national of the Republic of Korea at the time of the person's birth;
2. A person whose father was a national of the Republic of Korea at the time of the father's death, if the person's father died before the person's birth;
3. A person who was born in the Republic of Korea, if both of the person's parents are unknown or have no nationality.

> (2) An abandoned child found in the Republic of Korea shall be deemed born in the Republic of Korea.
>
> [This Article Wholly Amended on Mar. 14, 2008]

The 2022 Act provides that in cases involving dual nationals, if one of the nationalities is Korean, Korean law shall take precedence when determining the applicable law based on nationality. The relevant Article is as follows:

> **Article 16 (Law of Nationality)**
>
> (1) Where a party having two or more nationalities is required to be governed by the law of the nationality, the law of the country most closely related to the party shall be the law of his or her nationality: Provided, That where the nationalities the party holds include the Republic of Korea, the law of the Republic of Korea shall be the law of nationality.
>
> (2) Where a party has no nationality, or his or her nationality cannot be identified, the law of the country of his or her habitual residence (hereinafter referred to as "law of habitual residence") shall govern, and where the habitual residence cannot be identified, then the law of the country of his or her residence shall govern.
>
> (3) Where a party has nationality of a country which has varying laws depending on the territorial unit, the law designated under the optional provisions of the law of the country shall govern and, in the absence of such provisions, the law of a territorial unit most closely related to the party shall govern.

Accordingly, where a child possesses dual nationality, including Korean nationality, and resides outside of Korea, but the non-custodial parent responsible for child support is a Korean national with habitual residence in Korea, the applicable law governing child support will be the Korean Civil Act. Where Korean law is applied, child support is determined based on the combined income of the parents, the age of the child, and other relevant economic and special circumstances. The Family Court provides guidance to the parties by referring to the Child Support Guidelines Table, which serves as a standardized reference for calculating appropriate support amounts.

4. International Litigation Concurrence

In cases of international divorce, it is not uncommon for both parties to initiate divorce proceedings in two different jurisdictions. This may occur as a form of forum shopping, where one party attempts to obtain a more favorable outcome by selecting a jurisdiction perceived to be more advantageous.

When divorce actions are filed in two jurisdictions, the relevant Article of the 2022 Act applies. Under this Article, if certain conditions are met, the Korean court may suspend the proceedings, and if a final and binding judgment is subsequently rendered by the foreign court, the Korean action will be dismissed.

In determining whether to suspend the proceedings, the chronological order of filing is a key factor—specifically, the court will consider which action was filed first.

Article 11 (International Litigation Concurrence)

(1) Where a lawsuit over the same case pending in a foreign court between the same parties is filed with the court, and where a judgment rendered by the foreign court is expected to be approved in the Republic of Korea, the court may, by decision, suspend the legal

proceedings *ex officio* or upon the application of a party: Provided, That the same shall not apply in any of the following cases:

1. Where the court has international jurisdiction, in accordance with an agreement on exclusive international jurisdiction;
2. Where it is obvious that the court is more apt to render a judgment on the relevant case than its foreign counterpart.

(2) A party may file an immediate appeal against the court's suspension decision under paragraph (1).

(3) Where a judgment rendered by a foreign court meets the requirements for approval in accordance with the statutes or regulations, or treaties of the Republic of Korea, but where the same lawsuit between the same parties is filed with the court, the court shall dismiss such lawsuit.

(4) Where a foreign court fails to take measures necessary for rendering a judgment on the merits, or where a foreign court fails to or is not expected to pronounce a judgment on the merits within a reasonable period, the court, upon the receipt of an application by the parties, may continue to review the suspended case under paragraph (1).

(5) Where a decision is made on whether to suspend the legal proceedings under paragraph (1), the order of lawsuits filed shall be determined based on the date of filing.

As previously explained, under the Korean Civil Act, a spouse at fault is not permitted to file for divorce, and the non-fault spouse is entitled to claim compensation for mental suffering (damages) against the at-fault spouse. Consequently, an at-fault spouse may seek to initiate divorce proceedings in a jurisdiction that adheres to the no-fault principle, in an effort to circumvent the restrictions imposed by Korean law.

However, even if the judicial divorce is filed abroad by the at-fault spouse prior to the action filed in Korea, a claim for damages (such as spousal compensation) is treated as a separate cause of action under Korean law. Therefore, the non-fault spouse may still bring a claim for damages before the Korean courts.

In such a situation—where the non-fault spouse files both a divorce and damages claim in Korea, but the at-fault spouse files for divorce first in a foreign court and obtains a final judgment—the Korean court would likely dismiss the divorce claim due to the existence of the prior foreign judgment, but may nevertheless proceed to hear and adjudicate the damages claim independently.

5. Public Policy

Under the Act on Private International Law, even when a foreign law is designated as the applicable law, its application may be refused if the result would be manifestly incompatible with the fundamental principles of Korean law, including core moral convictions, essential values, or basic notions of justice. This is referred to as the defensive or restrictive function of the public policy clause. Article 23 of the 2022 Act provides that foreign law shall not be applied if its application would contravene the public order of Korea, as set forth below.

Article 23 (Provisions of Foreign Law Contrary to Social Order)

Where a foreign law shall govern but the application of the provisions of the foreign law is clearly contrary to good morals and other public order of the Republic of Korea, the provisions shall not apply.

The application of the public policy clause in divorce cases is extremely rare. One notable case in which the clause was applied involved the application of Philippine law, which categorically prohibits divorce. The Korean court refused to apply Philippine law on the grounds that such a blanket prohibition on divorce was inconsistent with Korea's public policy, which broadly recognizes both divorce by agreement and judicial divorce. Accordingly, Korean law was applied instead.

One potential area in which public policy considerations may arise in relation to divorce is same-sex marriage. Since same-sex marriage is not legally recognized under Korean law, questions may arise where a foreign same-sex couple, who lawfully married in a jurisdiction that permits same-sex marriage, seeks to obtain a divorce in Korea after entering the country. A divorce petition presupposes the legal validity of the marriage. Therefore, in order for the court to adjudicate the petition, it would need to recognize the underlying same-sex marriage as valid. Whether such recognition would be denied under Article 23 of the 2022 Act on the grounds of being contrary to Korean public policy remains an open question.

6. Conclusion

Although international marriages and divorces are on the rise in Korea and attracting increasing social attention, the characteristics of Korea's divorce system remain relatively unknown abroad. In particular, in the case of divorce by agreement, the likelihood of recognition in foreign jurisdictions is low, yet Korean courts and administrative authorities provide insufficient guidance to the parties involved.

In addition, the Act on Private International Law was amended in 2022 to introduce special jurisdiction provisions applicable to family law matters, marking a meaningful development in the legislative framework. However, the amended Act still fails to fully reflect the diverse and complex nature of international divorce cases. For example, in situations where the applicable law for marriage and divorce may differ depending on the parties' religion, the Act does not offer a clear solution for determining the governing law.

Moreover, in practice, Korean courts do not always engage in a sufficiently detailed analysis of the Act on Private International Law when adjudicating international divorce cases. As the number of immigrants in Korea continues to grow, international divorce is increasingly becoming a routine aspect of family life.

Given this context, there is a pressing need for both legislative and judicial efforts to ensure that parties undergoing changes in their personal status through marriage and divorce do not face legal uncertainty or procedural barriers, and that their status can be clearly and effectively registered and recognized across jurisdictions. A more comprehensive and inclusive approach to international divorce is necessary to address the evolving realities of a more diverse Korean society.

References

[1] Cho, Kyungae. (2019). A Study on the Amendment and Development Process of the Divorce by Consent System in Korea - With Suggestions for Institutional Improvement -. Anam Law Association. vol., no 59.

[2] Suk, Kwang-Hyun. (2022) International Adjudicatory Jurisdiction Law. PYbook.

[3] Suk, Kwang-Hyun.(2024). Candid Advice to Korean Lawyers dealing with International Family Cases. Korean Journal of Family Law. vol 30. No. 1.

[4] Suk, Kwang-Hyun. (2025). Private International Law: Applicable Law. PYbook.

[5] Yune, Jinsu. (2023). Lectures on Family and Succession Law, PYbook.

[6] https://kostat.go.kr/board.es?act=view&bid=204&list_no=435601&mid=a10301010000&utm

[7] Busan Family Court Judgment of February 14, 2020, 2018Deudan205427

[8] Supreme Court of Korea, September 21, 1965, 65Meu37

Notes

1 www.lawyerhwang.com
2 Unless otherwise indicated, all legal references in this article pertain to the laws of the Republic of Korea.
3 Cho, Kyungae. (2019). A Study on the Amendment and Development Process of the Divorce by Consent System in Korea - With Suggestions for Institutional Improvement -. Anam Law Association. vol., no 59. 75-76.
4 Busan Family Court Judgment of February 14, 2020, 2018Deudan205427
5 Supreme Court of Korea, September 21, 1965, 65Meu37
6 Suk, Kwang-Hyun. (2022) International Adjudicatory Jurisdiction Law. PYbook. 66-67.
7 Ibid., 253.
8 Ibid., 251-252.
9 Ibid., 254.
10 Suk, Kwang-Hyun. (2025). Private International Law: Applicable Law. PYbook. 120.
11 Suk, Kwang-Hyun. International Adjudicatory Jurisdiction Law. 256.
12 Suk, Kwang-Hyun.(2024). Candid Advice to Korean Lawyers dealing with International Family Cases. Korean Journal of Family Law. vol 30. No. 1. 13.
13 Yune, Jinsu. (2023). Lectures on Family and Succession Law, PYbook. 119.
14 Suk, Kwang-Hyun. Private International Law: Applicable Law. 791.

SPECIAL REPORTS

Ecologically or Biologically Significant Marine Areas (EBSAs) in the Convention on Biological Diversity and the Issue of Dokdo*

Jinwoong SEO
Research Fellow of Dokdo Reserch Institute,
Northeast Asian History Foundation (Seoul, Republic of Korea)

Abstract

In the Convention on Biological Diversity (CBD), efforts are being made to introduce the Ecologically or Biologically Significant Marine Areas (EBSAs) system for the protection of marine areas. Considering the nature of the CBD, an environmental convention, discussions like this should be welcomed. However, although the CBD regulates matters within the jurisdiction of the parties, there are parts that deviate from this in the discussion of EBSAs.

Both Republic of Korea and Japan have not been able to achieve maritime delimitation in the East Sea, and in particular, Japan continues to protest unreasonable territorial sovereignty over Dokdo. In this situation, if the EBSAs system is adopted on the same basis as the current standard, the problem of territorial disputes regarding sovereign rights over the East Sea, especially the waters near Dokdo, may arise.

This article examines the current trends in EBSAs discussions and potential issues that could arise if Korea or Japan applies for EBSAs. In conclusion, it suggests a new negotiation strategy to address these issues.

Key Words

Convention Biological Diversity, Ecologically or Biologically Significant Marine Areas (EBSAs), Dokdo, maritime boundary delimitation, Island Sovereignty Dispute

1. Introduction

The 15th Conference of the Parties ("COP") to the Convention on Biological Diversity ("CBD") was held in Montreal, Canada, from December 7 to 19, 2022. The 10th Meeting of the Parties ("MOP") to the Cartagena Protocol on Biosafety ("CP"), an annex to the CBD, and the 4th Meeting of the Parties to the Nagoya Protocol ("NP") were held concurrently. The Kunming-Montreal Declaration was adopted.[1]

The agenda consists of four goals and 22 targets. The Convention on Biological Diversity is generally understood as an environmental protection treaty. Therefore, it is likely to be understood as having no relation to Dokdo sovereignty. However, at the 15th CBD General Assembly, an agenda called "Ecologically or Biologically Significant Marine Areas" ("EBSAs") was reviewed.

This discussion encapsulates the discussions that have taken place since the CBD/COP/DEC/IX/20 in 2008, when the CBD decided to identify and describe "ecologically or biologically significant marine areas" based on a set of scientific criteria covering areas within national jurisdiction and beyond national jurisdiction.[2] Given the possibility that this agenda could be misused for the East Sea name and Dokdo dispute, the need for future research in the aspects of maritime law and territorial sovereignty is raised.

However, no conclusion was reached on EBSAs at this CBD COP. Although the EBSAs-related document was adopted at the plenary session,[3] CBD/COP/15/L.14, the document only contains the full text and nine articles from the original proposed negotiation text, CBD/COP/15/WG2/CRP8, and was carried over to the next CBD COP without reviewing all 12 annexes.

This article will examine the issues to be considered in future EBSA discussions, focusing on the issues that the author thought about while participating in the EBSA negotiations during the 15th COP of the CBD. However, the author would like to clarify that this is his personal opinion and is separate from the official position of the CBD 15th COP negotiation team. As for the non-paper materials, which are the first documents used in the EBSAs negotiations, they are unofficial drafts and the author will review the trends in the EBSAs discussions based on CBD/COP/15/WG2/CRP8, which is the public document used by revising the non-paper in the EBSAs negotiations, and then examine the influence that these trends in discussions may have on Dokdo.

2. Trends in Discussion of EBSAs under the Convention on Biological Diversity

2-1. Concept and Legal Status of EBSAs

2-1-1. Concept of EBSAs

EBSAs are marine areas that are ecologically or biologically important, for example, by providing important habitats, feeding grounds and breeding areas, including both the water column and the seabed.[4] The EBSA concept includes the following seven scientific criteria for identifying EBSAs, as discussed under the CBD 9th COP in 2008.[5] These criteria were also reaffirmed at the CBD 15th COP.[6] Additionally, each scientific criterion is defined as follows:[7]

(1) **Uniqueness or rarity**: Area contains either (i) unique ("the only one of its kind"), rare (occurs only in few locations) or endemic species, populations or communities, and/or (ii) unique, rare or distinct, habitats or ecosystems; and/or (iii) unique or unusual geomorphological or oceanographic features;
(2) **Special importance for life-history stages of species:** Areas that are required for a population to survive and thrive;
(3) **Importance for threatened, endangered or declining species and/or habitats:** Area containing habitat for the survival and recovery of endangered, threatened, declining species or area with significant assemblages of such species;
(4) **Vulnerability, fragility, sensitivity, or slow recovery:** Areas that contain a relatively high proportion of sensitive habitats, biotopes or species that are functionally fragile (highly susceptible to degradation or depletion by human activity or by natural events) or with slow recovery;
(5) **Biological productivity:** Area containing species, populations or communities with comparatively higher natural biological productivity;
(6) **Biological diversity:** Area contains comparatively higher diversity of ecosystems, habitats, communities, or species, or has higher genetic diversity;
(7) **Naturalness:** Area with a comparatively higher degree of naturalness as a result of the lack of or low level of human-induced disturbance or degradation.

Between 2011 and 2019, the CBD Secretariat, with considerable input from scientific experts worldwide and in collaboration with governments and international organizations, convened 15 regional workshops that addressed 321 areas that met the EBSAs criteria, including areas within national jurisdiction and beyond national jurisdiction. In several cases, States were asked to designate marine protected areas where EBSAs were located within national jurisdiction.[8]

At the 12th CBD COP in 2014, it was decided to initiate a process to further strengthen the scientific methodology and approach to the description of areas that meet the EBSAs criteria.[9] However, EBSAs are still under discussion.

2-1-2. EBSAs Legal Status

The CBD COP stated that "the description of a marine area" meeting the criteria of an ecologically or biologically significant marine area is a "strictly scientific and technical act, without economic or legal significance, of a State, territory, city or region or of its authorities, or of its frontiers or boundaries",[10] and is therefore understood to have no legal effect. EBSA descriptions are assessed as having no legal significance in themselves, but may have important legal significance in providing scientific justification for subsequent legal measures to protect the ecosystems, habitats and species described.

This was reflected in Article 4[11] of the main text and Article 2 of Annex 1[12] of the negotiation text CBD/COP/15/WG2/CRP8, which was first proposed at the 15th CBD COP, but Article 4 of the main text was deleted in CBD/COP/15/L14 adopted at the 15th CBD COP, and Annex 1 was not adopted. Given that the description of the legal status of EBSAs was not included, there is a need to continuously monitor future trends in discussions regarding the legal status of EBSAs.

2-2. EBSAs Proposal and Modification Procedures

2-2-1. EBSAs Proposal Procedures

Annex IX of CBD/COP/15/WG2/CRP8 provides for the following instances in which proposals for EBSA descriptions may be submitted, under the headings supporting descriptions of ecologically or biologically important marine areas:

(1) **Proposed EBSAs within national jurisdiction:** the country within the jurisdiction in which the proposed area is located;
(2) **Proposed EBSAs beyond national jurisdiction:** any country and/or competent intergovernmental organization;
(3) **Proposed EBSAs within and beyond national jurisdiction:** the country(ies) within the jurisdiction in which the proposed area is partially located.

In addition, those proposing for EBSAs are encouraged to collaborate with relevant knowledge holders, including traditional knowledge, when preparing their proposals.

The evaluation process for the submitted proposals as mentioned above was not discussed at this COP. It presents a rough workflow of the process adopted at the previous 10th COP, and it is understood that the new EBSAs proposal will also follow this process.

According to this process, intergovernmental regional workshops are used to describe potential areas that meet the EBSAs criteria. The "scientific and technical data and information and results collected through the workshops" are shared with relevant agencies, organizations and partners and compiled into a report that is forwarded to the next CBD Advisory Committee on Science and Technology ("SBSTTA"). The SBSTTA then recommends specific EBSAs descriptions for inclusion in the synthesis report to the COP, which considers the synthesis report and the EBSAs described and decides whether to "endorse" them. The final approved EBSAs descriptions are entered into the CBD EBSAs repository and submitted to the UN General Assembly, Parties, other governments and other relevant international organizations.[13]

2-2-2. EBSAs Modification Procedures

2-2-2-1. Reasons for Modifying EBSAs Descriptions

According to Annex 3, the following seven reasons are mentioned as reasons for modifying the text description of an EBSAs, modifying the area ranking for the EBSAs criteria, and/or modifying the description of the location, shape, depth, and/or size of an EBSA:

(a) Newly available/accessible knowledge, including scientific and traditional knowledge, on features associated with an EBSA;
(b) Change in the information that appears in the current description of an EBSA, including its name;
(c) Change in the ecological or biological feature(s) of an EBSA;
(d) Scientific error(s) identified in an EBSA description;
(e) Modification(s) to the EBSA criteria, to guidance in the application of the EBSA criteria or to the template[14] used to describe EBSAs;
[(f) Land and/or maritime boundary disputes;]
[(g) Editorial errors in an EBSA description.]

Although the annex 3 containing the above content itself was not adopted, it is expected that the most acute problem will arise among the 7 reasons mentioned above, namely, 'land and/or maritime boundary disputes'. However, the relevant part is currently bracketed and will be further discussed during the review of the Annex III, and its inclusion has not been decided yet.

Although the EBSA is a non-legally binding initiative, the guidance in Annex I of the "Decision adopted by the Conference of the Parties to the Convention on Biological Diversity on October 30, 2024" adopted by COP 16 states that "[n]othing in the present modalities shall prejudice the rights, jurisdiction and duties of States under the United Nations Convention on the Law of the Sea, including in respect of the exclusive economic zone and the continental shelf within and beyond 200 nautical miles".[15] Considering the effectiveness of recommendations under international law, it is questionable how effective the recommendations under the Initiative will be.

2-2-2-2. Proponents of the Modification of Descriptions of EBSAs

Annex IV provides for the following entities who may submit proposals for modifications to the EBSAs description, if there is a reason to do so: modify the textual description of the EBSAs, modify the ranking of areas with respect to the EBSAs criteria, and/or modify the description of the location, shape, depth, and/or size of the EBSAs:[16]

> (a) **For a modification within national jurisdiction:** the State(s) within whose jurisdiction(s) the modification is proposed;
> (b) **For a modification in areas beyond national jurisdiction:** any State(s) and/or competent intergovernmental organization(s), with provision of notice to all States;
> (c) **For a modification in areas both within and beyond national jurisdiction(s):** the State(s) within whose jurisdiction(s) the area subject to a modification proposal is partially located;

2-2-2-3. Procedure for Modifying EBSAs Descriptions

Modification of existing EBSAs descriptions is divided into 1) EBSAs for editorial reasons, 2) EBSAs within national jurisdictions, including EBSAs straddling multiple national jurisdictions and, 3) EBSAs of Areas Beyond National Jurisdiction ("ABNJ"), and 4) EBSAs straddling areas both within and beyond national jurisdiction.[17]

3. Review of Dokdo Issues Related to EBSAs

3-1. Possibility of EBSAs designation

In the East Asia region, there are 24 EBSAs regions under consideration at the CBD COP.[18] In the case of Korea, the Nanjido Ecological Park is included.[19] However, as shown in the map below, in the East Sea region, only some coastal areas of Japan are included in the area that currently meets the EBSA criteria, and there are no areas in the East Sea region that are considered to meet the EBSA criteria. In addition, there are no EBSAs under consideration by the CBD COP in this region. However, the East Sea, especially the water columns around Dokdo, are one of the areas with internationally valuable natural values and importance, and Dokdo and the water column around it are known as areas with great need for biodiversity conservation as they are home to rare marine species that have important habitats in the East Sea.[20]

Dokdo and its surrounding water columns are the northernmost islands in the East Sea, and are located at the point where the cold northern current and the warm southern current from the south meet. Due to these geographical conditions, Dokdo and its surrounding water columns provide an environment suitable for various marine species to inhabit. Dokdo and its surrounding waters are home to a variety of marine species, including seaweed, fish, and invertebrates. In particular, the area called 'Dokdo Pin', which has a narrow habitat area, is home to dozens of large invertebrate species, and Dokdo and its surrounding water columns are one of the areas with the largest number of loaches and tunas in Korea and the East Sea region. In addition, internationally valuable species are found in Dokdo and its surrounding waters. For example, Dokdo and its surrounding water columns are one of the only areas in the East Sea where red forest crabs are distributed. In addition, rare marine species, such as white crabs, oriental sword clams, and oriental sunfish, inhabit Dokdo and

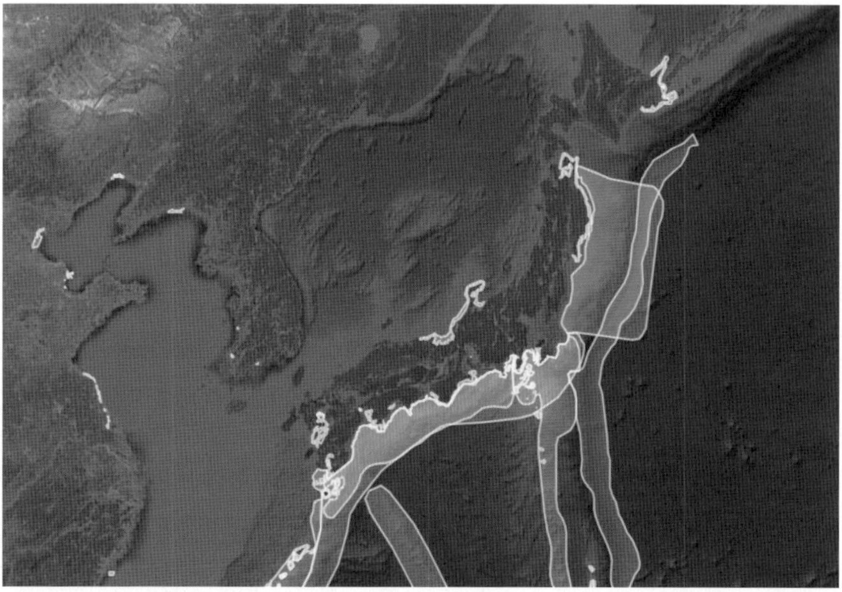

[Figure 1] Status of areas meeting EBSA criteria near the Korean Peninsula (Source: https://www.cbd.int/ebsa/)

its surrounding water columns.[21] In particular, endemic species that are only distributed in Dokdo and the surrounding water columns include Dokdoaemulgae, Dokdo enchovy, red tree coral, yellowtail and etc.[22]

As can be seen in the figure below,[23] which is a result of a study conducted in Japan on whether the East Asian water columns of Japan meet the EBSAs criteria, it can be confirmed that the East Sea meets the EBSAs criteria.

The table above is the data analyzing the East Asian water columns by integrating the seven criteria of EBSA. Image A is displayed based on the integration by the sum of the seven criteria, Image B is displayed based on the number of "high" evaluations for each grid, Image C is displayed based on the integration by the sum of the seven criteria by selecting 10% of the study area, and Image D is displayed as the integration by complementary analysis by selecting 10% of the study area.

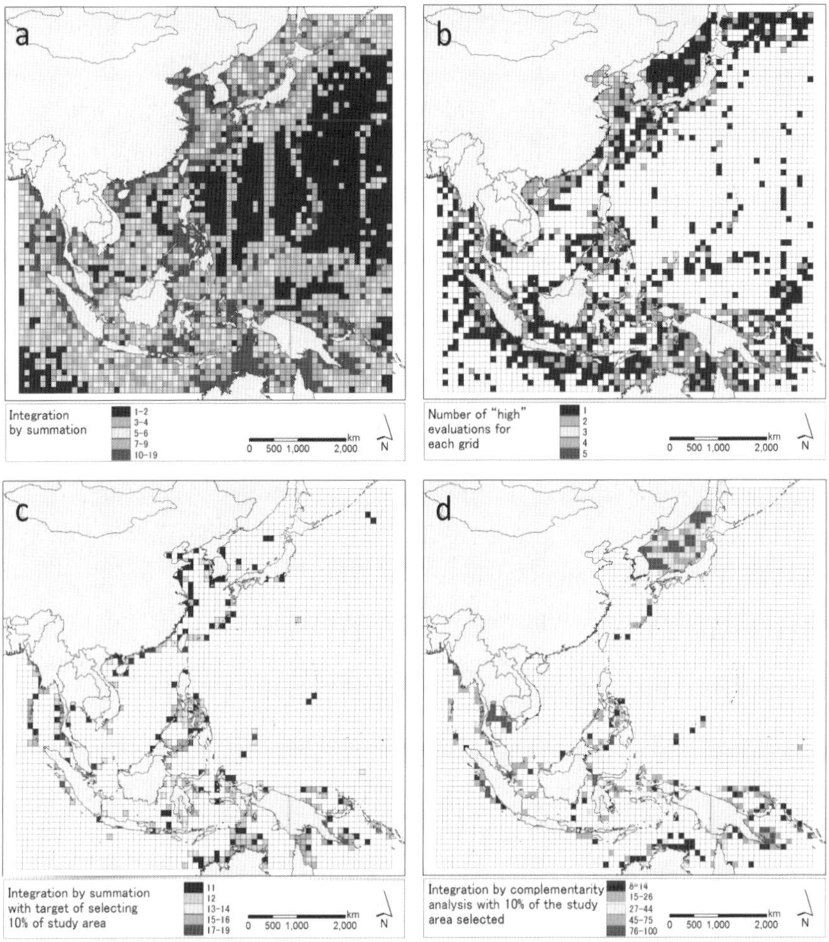

[Figure 2] Integration of EBSA's seven criteria

3-2. EBSAs Proposal and Dokdo issue

The EBSAs proposal itself can be understood as an act of establishing a marine protected area based on scientific and technical matters. In addition, as previously examined, the EBSAs proposal or the modification of the description assumes various cases.

It is noteworthy that it is necessary to consider cases where an EBSA proposal including Dokdo is made or where a modification of the description is requested thereafter. Specifically, this should be reviewed by dividing it into case where the Republic of Korea proposes for an EBSA in a water column including Dokdo and case where Japan proposes for an EBSA in a water column including Dokdo.

3-2-1. In the case of the Republic of Korea Proposing for EBSA in a Water Column including Dokdo

Although the Republic of Korea has territorial sovereignty over Dokdo, the surrounding water columns are areas where maritime boundaries with Japan have not been undelimited. Therefore, if we hypothetically consider proposals for EBSA, including Dokdo and it's surrounding water columns, it is difficult to determine whether it is an EBSA proposed within the national jurisdiction of the Republic of Korea or a case where it spans the jurisdictions of multiple countries. Considering the diplomatic relationship between Republic of Korea and Japan, it is reasonable to assume that if the government of the Republic of Korea proposes for EBSA, including Dokdo and it's surrounding water columns, it will only include water columns within the jurisdiction of the Republic of Korea.

However, in this case, there are two things to consider. First, there is the issue of the name of the sea, and second, there is the possibility of a territorial dispute over Dokdo. Accordingly, if the Republic of Korea proposes for an EBSA including the Dokdo and it's surrounding water columns, Japan's response is expected to be twofold. First, based on EBSA Annex III, paragraph 1(b), it can be argued that the name East Sea is an error and should be written as Sea of Japan. Second, it can be argued that the EBSA designation by the Republic of Korea is an infringement on its own jurisdiction, as it is understood to be a case where it crosses the jurisdiction of several countries, according to EBSA Annex VI. Such arguments are likely to be raised including the issue of Dokdo sovereignty. In such a case, it is possible that it will raise an international issue that contradicts the position that Dokdo is not a disputed area and that Dokdo sovereignty is firmly vested in the Republic of Korea.

3-2-2. In the case of the Japan Proposing for EBSA in a Water Column including Dokdo

It is necessary to assume that Japan proposes for EBSA in water columns, including Dokdo. In this case, the most notable point is that the current procedure does not clearly identify whether Japan's EBSA application is proposed in an area within national jurisdiction under Article 9(a) of the EBSAs or in an area within and outside national jurisdiction under Article 9(c).

Whether Japan's EBSA proposal is under Article 9(a) or (c), it is problematic in that it will ultimately infringe upon the territorial sovereignty of the Republic of Korea, and in this case, there is a high possibility that the name of the East Sea will be exclusively designated as the Sea of Japan.

In this case, if Republic of Korea raises an objection based on the revision or parallel listing of the name of the sea or the sovereignty over Dokdo, Japan is highly likely to use this as an opportunity to turn Dokdo into a disputed area. In particular, if we base it on reason (f) of the explanation in Annex III, it is predicted that the possibility of Dokdo becoming a disputed area will increase even more.

3-2-3. Review

If an EBSA is proposed for water columns, including Dokdo, it may cause political and diplomatic problems regardless of whether the EBSA proposal is made by Japan or Republic of Korea. This is an issue that does not need to be considered if a maritime boundary delimitation has been made between Republic of Korea and Japan. However, the possibility of a maritime boundary delimitation in the East Sea between Republic of Korea and Japan is currently pretty slim, and considering the current situation in which Japan is attempting to make Dokdo as a disputed area, it can be assessed that the EBSA proposal highly likely to escalate into an exclusive economic zone and territorial issue rather than a scientific and technical act.

It cannot be concluded that this problem is unique to Republic of Korea. As of now, only about 1/3 of areas has had a maritime boundary delimited and it is necessary to consider the fact that there are also many territorial disputes over the islands.

Article 2 of Annex I of the EBSA stipulates that EBSA is a scientific and technological exercise and should not have any influence on territorial sovereignty or maritime boundary delimitation. However, considering the reality of international relations, it can be said that the proposal for EBSAs in water columns with maritime boundaries non-delimitation has limitations that inevitably lead to diplomatic friction.

4. Conclusion

As discussed above, the current EBSAs discussions are more likely to cause disputes in maritime boundary delimitation water columns than to be dealt with as scientific and technical issues. This is a problem with the current EBSAs approach. The current EBSAs system is problematic in that it allows a country with jurisdiction over even a part of the relevant water columns to unilaterally propose for EBSA.

If we examine the EBSAs system only in terms of scientific and technical issues, it may be an appropriate system for the conservation and sustainable use of the ocean. However, considering the maritime boundary un-delimitation water columns and territorial dispute areas in the international community, the EBSA is likely to become a catalyst for international disputes. This was examined through the relationship between Republic of Korea and Japan.

The solution to the anticipated limitations of EBSA can also be found in these limitations. In water columns where maritime boundaries have been delimitated, it is reasonable to assume that EBSAs proposes are clearly identified and unlikely to become a catalyst for disputes. Considering this, it is necessary to change the negotiation response strategy for EBSAs. It should be approached in two tracks, depending on whether maritime boundaries have been delimited.

In other words, in the case of maritime boundary delimited each country should be able to freely propose for EBSAs based on its sovereign rights within its jurisdictional water columns. And in the case of maritime boundary non-delimitation zones, proposals by one of the interested countries should be restricted. In the latter case, EBSA proposals should be restricted so that interested countries can only propose for EBSA upon all interested countries joint agree.

In addition, in the case of areas beynd national jurisdiction, the UN is currently preparing a legal document related to BBNJ, and it is necessary to consider that MPA deals with similar content during the discussion. In addition, considering that CBD itself deals with the scope of jurisdiction of the contracting parties, in the case of areas beyond national jurisdiction, it should be left as an issue of MPA in the BBNJ legal document.

If this approach were reflected in the current EBSA discussion, it would be a way to overcome the problems identified in this article.

Notes

* This Article has been written with some updates and changes based on the author's Korean Article, "The trend of discussion regarding Ecologically or Biologically Significant Marine Areas (EBSAs) in the Convention on Biological Diversity and the issue of Dokdo" in the *Journal of Legal Studies* vol.31 no.2, 2023 published by Gyeongsang National University.

1 CBD/COP/DEC/15/4
2 CBD/COP/DEC/IX/20
3 CBD/COP/15/L.14
4 David E. Johnson *et, al.*, "Reviewing the EBSA process: Improving on success". *Marine Policy* vol.88, 2018, pp. 75-85.
5 CBD/COP/DEC/IX/20
6 CBD/COP/15/L.13
7 Johnson, *op. cit.*, p. 76.
8 Daniel C. Dunn *et. al.*, "The Convention on Biological Diversity's Ecologically or Biologically Significant Areas: Origins, development, and current status". *Marine Policy* vol.49, 2014, pp. 137-145.
9 CBD/COP/DEC/XII/22
10 *Ibid.*.
11 CBD/COP/15/WG2/CRP.8 para.4

[4. [Endorses]/[Takes note of] the annexes to the present decision addressing modalities for modifying descriptions of ecologically or biologically significant marine areas (EBSAs) and for describing new areas, invites Parties and other Governments to implement these modalities, <u>while fully respecting the sovereignty, sovereign rights and jurisdiction of States</u> and requests the Executive Secretary to facilitate the implementation of these modalities;,] (Added emphasis by author)

12 CBD/COP/15/WG2/CRP.8 Annex I General considerations in the modification of descriptions of ecologically or biologically significant marine areas and the description of new areas, para. 2.

[2. The description of marine areas meeting the criteria for ecologically or biologically significant marine areas <u>does not imply the expression of any opinion whatsoever concerning the legal status of any country, territory, city or area or of its authorities, or concerning the delimitation of its frontiers or boundaries, nor does it have economic or legal implications.</u> It is strictly a scientific and technical exercise. No action or activity taken on the basis of this document shall be interpreted or considered as prejudicing the position of States on a land or maritime sovereignty dispute or a dispute concerning the delimitation of maritime areas.] (Added emphasis by author)

13 CBD. Decision X/29
14 http://www.cbd.int/doc/meetings/mar/ebsaws-2015-01/other/ebsaws-2015-01-template-en.dot
15 CBD/COP/DEC/16/16, Annex Ⅰ, para. 1.
16 CBD/COP/15/WG2/CRP.8, Annex Ⅳ, para. 1.
17 *see* more details: CBD/COP/15/WG2/CRP.8, Annex Ⅴ.~ Annex Ⅷ.
18 *see* https://www.cbd.int/ebsa/ebsas
19 *Ibid.*.

20 see Jeong, H. Y. *et. al,*, "Distributional patterns of benthic macroalgae in the coastal waters of Dokdo, Korea". *Ocean Science Journal*, vol.47(3), 2012; Kim, Y. H. *et. al.*, "A review of the ichthyofaunal diversity in Korean waters". *Journal of Ecology and Environment*, vol.37(1), 2014; Lee, S. H. *et. al.*, "Diversity and distribution of benthic macrofauna in the coastal waters of Dokdo, Korea". *Korean Journal of Environmental Biology* vol.29(2), 2011.

21 UNESCO-IOC, *Ecological and biological characteristics of sea areas adjacent to Dokdo/Takeshima*, Republic of Korea/Japan, IOC Technical Series, No. 120 (2016).

22 *see* Kim, J. H., *et. al.*, "A new species, Patinapta ooplax sp. nov. (Dictyotales, Phaeophyceae), from Korea, based on morphological observations and DNA barcode data" *Phycologia* vol.55(2), 2016; Kang, E. J., *et. al.*, "Genetic diversity and population structure of a Korean endemic fish, the Dokdo anchovy (Engraulis japonicus koreanus), inferred from microsatellite marker analyses", *Genetics and Molecular Biology* vol.36(4), 2013; Lee, C. H., *et. al.*, "Fish community structure in the waters around Dokdo, Korea", *Ocean and Polar Research* vol.34(2), 2012; Kang, J. H., *et. al.*, "Red tree coral, Primnoa pacifica, in Korean waters", *Journal of Ecology and Environment* 34(3) (2011).

23 Takehisa Yamakita *at. al.*, "Identification of important marine areas using ecologically or biologically significant areas (EBSAs) criteria in the East to Southeast Asia region and comparison with existing registered areas for the purpose of conservation", *Marine Policy* vol. 81 (2017), p. 279.

KYIL

Victims of Japanese Forced Labor & Its Approach By the Transitional Justice of the UN Human Rights Committee in the ICCPR[1]

Jang-Hie LEE
Professor Emeritus, Law School, Hankuk University of Foreign Studies

Abstract

Koreans suffered from wartime forced labor during the Japanese colonial occupation (1910-1945). Nevertheless, revised Japanese textbooks distorted the truth. The Japanese government on March 28, 2023, approved school textbooks whitewashing the forced mobilization of Koreans to labor in factories during World War II.

Meanwhile, victims of Japanese forced labor have resisted numerous temptations and endured hardships for decades in order to receive apologies for the illegal acts of Japanese colonial rule and to restore their reputation. In 2018, the Korean Supreme Court ruled in favor of victims of forced labor for the first time.

Unfortunately, the enforcement of the Korean Supreme Court's ruling in favor of compensation for victims of forced labor during the Japanese colonial rule has been delayed and complete due to the former government's preference to a third-party compensation scheme rather than a direct enforcement of the Court's ruling, in addition to the instigation of the Japanese government to the war criminal companies. Therefore, the issue of victims of forced labor under Japanese colonial rule cannot be left solely to the Korean government, but it is appropriate and effective for individual victims of Japanese forced labor to file transitional justice complaints directly to the UN Human Rights Committee based on the individual notification system after meeting the conditions for completion of domestic relief in accordance with the ICCPR and its Optional Protocol to which Korea is a party.

Key Words

Victims of Japanese Forced Labor, Transitional Justice, UN Human Rights Committee to ICCPR.

1. Introduction

Koreans suffered from wartime forced labor during the Japanese colonial occupation (1910-1945). Nevertheless, revised Japanese textbooks distorted the truth. The Japanese government on March 28, 2023, approved school textbooks whitewashing the forces mobilization of Koreans to labor in factories during World War II.[2]

In some of textbooks, publishers deleted the expression "forced mobilization", which was previously used to describe Koreans who were mobilized to work in Japanese factories during Japan's 1910-1945 occupation of Korea.[3]

In response, the Korean Ministry of Foreign Affairs protested over Japan's latest attempt to whitewashing its history, which came less than two weeks after the first summit between former President Yoon and Japanese Prime Minister Fumio Kishida on March 16, 2023. The Japanese government refused to pay compensation for victims of forced labor and refused to restore the honour of the Pacific war & Japanese colonial rule in 1945.[4]

Meanwhile, victims of Japanese forced labors have resisted numerous temptations and endured hardships for decades in order to receive apology for the illegal acts of Japanese colonial rule and to restore their reputation. They attempted to file lawsuits for legal damages and their honour against the Japanese and Korean government. They lost almost all lawsuits.

However, in 2018, the Korean Supreme Court ruled in favor of victims of forced labor for the first time.

Unfortunately, the enforcement of the Korean Supreme Court's ruling in favor of compensation for victims of forced labor during the Japanese colonial rule has been delayed and remains incomplete due to the Korean government's preference for a third-party compensation payment plan rather than pursing a direct enforcement of the Court's ruling, in addition to the instigation of the Japanese government to the war criminal companies. The attitude of the two governments in Korea and Japan in the execution of the Supreme Court's favorable ruling in 2018 goes beyond the restoration of the victims' honor and compensation and legitimizes Japan's past colonial rule, and also undermines the core values of the Constitution of the Republic of Korea and destroys historical justice in Korean-Japan history.

Fortunately, on January 18, 2024, the Gwangju District Court ruled that Japan's Mitsubishi Heavy Industries, a war criminal company, should pay partial damages to Mrs. Jeong In-Yeong, a victim of forced mobilization. Surviving forced labor victims are refusing third-party reimbursement from the Korean government. Increasingly, the government's third-party reimbursement is becoming ineffective both practically and legally.

2. Legal Issues between Korea and Japan regarding Japanese Forced Labor Victims

Japan views, from its legal perspective, that Japan's forced labor issue was "completely and finally resolved" under Article 2 of the 1965 Korea-Japan Claims Agreement and Article 1, which provides a payment of 500 million U.S. dollars. Japan protests that Korea does not comply with the 1965 international treaty.[5] On the other hand, the Korean government has demanded compensation and honour restoration of victims of forced labor from Japan, claiming that Japan bears remaining state responsibility since the disclosure of diplomatic documents from the Korea-Japan negotiations in 2005 to the Yoon Seok-yeol administration in May 2021. Under international law, the "complete and final resolution" under the Korea-Japan Claims Agreement is nothing more than the Korean government's waiver of diplomatic protection rights for its citizens. This means that the individual right to claim victims violations of forced labor cannot be deprived by the international treaty between Korea and Japan (1965).

As is well known, forced labor under Japanese colonial rule is a serious violation of human rights resulting from crimes against humanity and a violation of *jus cogens*[6] in international law. Crimes that violate *jus cogens* norms, such as forced labor, crime against humanity, genocide and the prohibition of the use of force, cannot be set aside by any international treaty, including those between Korea and Japan.

Compensations for damages arising from *jus cogens* violations has no statute of limitations and can not be extinguished by international treaties between states. International treaties can not take away individual rights of claim of forced labor, an *jus cogens* norm. What the victims want is not just monetary money, but a true apology and compensation for war crimes against humanity. The four Korean surviving victims and their bereaved families revealed through content certification in March 2023 that they could not accept Japan's admission of war crimes and third-party compensation without apology.

Basically, Japan and Korea have completely different legal perspectives on forced labor. Based on the 1952 San Francisco Peace Regime and its subordinate system, the 1965 Korea-Japan Agreement, Japan views Japanese colonial rule itself as legal and Japanese forced labor also as legal. Therefore, it is argued that forced labor issues were finally and completely resolved through Article 1 (Payment of $500 million, both free and paid) and Article 2 (Final/Complete Resolution) of the 1965 Korea-Japan Claims Agreement.

Additionally, the Japanese government is trying to abuse the theory of state immunity[7] under international law as impunity for the issue of victims of forced labor.

On the other hand, the Korean government views Japan's forced annexation in 1910 as illegal. Since the disclosure of Korea-Japan diplomatic documents in 2005, forced labor under Japanese colonial rule has been illegal, and the 1965 Claims Agreement is nothing more than a waiver of the country's right to diplomatic protection. The compensation of individual victims of forced labor was not included in the 1965 Korea-Japan Claims Agreement, and it is believed that individual compensation can be claimed against the Japanese government at any time.

3. Change of the Korean Government's Position Since May 2022 Regarding Victims of Forced Labors

The Japanese government's previous position remains the same even upon a change in administration by the former Yoon administration in May 2022. In other words, meaning that all issues related to Korea-Japan past history were resolved finally and completely through the 1965 Korea-Japan Agreement. Japan continues to argue that Korea is not complying with international law, particularly with the the 1965 Korea-Japan Agreement. Of course, the Japanese government strongly opposed the Supreme Court's ruling held in October 2018, which was one of the primary causes of the strain in Korea-Japan relations. The Japanese government insisted on filing a complaint with the International Court of Justice arguing that Korea violated the 1965 Korea Japan Agreement.

However, the position of the former Yoon administration was completely different from the position of the previous Korean administrations. Viewing the historical issues between Korea and Japan from a Mahayana perspective, the administration accepted

Japan's position and attempted to normalize Korea-Japan relations as a priority. Former President Yoon emphasized normalizing diplomatic relations with Japan and sought a diplomatic resolution to the issue of forced labor compensation through a third-party compensation scheme. However, the administration encountered strong resistance from victims of Japanese forced labor and those who advocated the liquidation of colonial crimes and historical justice. In particular, regarding the issue of forced mobilization damage, the Ministry of Foreign Affairs oversaw and rather advocated for alternative means other than enforcement of the Court's ruling, such as through third-party reimbursement plans.

However, despite the alternative approach taken by the former Yoon administration which lacks adequate historical basis, the Korean court in 2023 has been doing its best to protect the honor of forced labor victims. Nevertheless, the former Korean administration pressed ahead to promote third-party compensation rather that direct enforcement of the Court's decision pursuant to Article 469 of the Korean Civil Code, without a direct apology or compensation from the Japanese companies who committed the acts of forced labor.

To elaborate, the former Korean government's alternative solution —third-party compensation—sidesteps the judicially recognized rights of forced labor victims and risks undermining their human rights and dignity. By promoting an executive-led scheme that delays the enforcement of Supreme Court judgments, it may seem that the administration may be encroaching upon the constitutional principle of separation of powers, which may raise serious concerns about the former administration's respect for judicial independence and the rule of law enshrined in the Korean Constitution.

Victims of forced labor who lost in the first and second trials were the first to win a reverse victory at the Supreme Court in 2012, but after a reversal and reconsideration in 2013, the former government's allegedly judicial manipulation continued for five years until the

Korean Supreme Court's final and final ruling on October 30, 2018. The 2018 Supreme Court ruling recognized the right of victims of forced labor to claim personal alimony, and the final ruling stipulated that Nippon Steel (defendant) should pay 100 million won each to the victims of forced labor. Accordingly, the Pohang Branch of the Daegu District Court ordered on January 9, 2019, the seizure of Nippon Steel's assets in Korea and their conversion into cash. However, enforcement has been delayed for over five years, largely due to diplomatic considerations and the former administration's promotion of an alternative third-party compensation mechanism, which has drawn criticisms for undermining judicial independence and victims' rights. Accordingly, as of November 16, 2023, three out of four plaintiffs have died and only one remains alive, with no compensation made due to the delay in enforcement of the judgment. Diplomatic efforts, such as the Ministry of Foreign Affairs' submissions of opinions to courts and the promotion of a third-party compensation scheme, may have contributed to the postponement asset seizures under Supreme Court rulings, although not judicially deemed unlawful. Also, at the instigation of the Japanese government, Mitsubishi, a war criminal company, deliberately ignored court orders even though it had sufficient ability to repay.

Moreover, following the 2023 Korea-Japan Summit, held on March 16-17, 2023, the former Yoon administration adopted a third-party repayment plan—funded by Korean businesses—as part of its strategy to improve bilateral relations. The Korean government attempted to implement third-party repayment by reimbursing the compensation primarily through the Korea Foundation for Victims of Forced Mobilization. The former administration also expressed public criticism of ongoing enforcement efforts. While some reports indicate that the government allocated 420 million won in the 2024 budget related to legal affairs involved forced labor litigation, it remains unclear whether this was specifically intended to oppose the victims' claim.[8]

4. Strategy through the Transitional Justice of the UN Human Rights Committee

Therefore, looking at the administrative actions that the Korean and Japanese governments have taken on the issue of forced labor, the restoration of fair rules, the correct interpretation of history, and the sincerity of transitional justice to implement them should not be left to the two governments alone. Rather, in order to objectively restore the honor and compensation for victims of forced labor, an approach to transitional justice according to the UN Human Rights Committee (Article 28(1) of the ICCPR must be taken. The complaint procedures and individual notification system of the UN Human Rights Council[9] under the General Assembly, established in June 2006, which replaced the UN Commission on Human Rights under the Economic and Social Council, are very effective. The UN Human Rights Committee is composed of 18 experts and maintains independence without receiving instructions from the countries to which it belongs.[10]

Since the creation of the United Nations in 1945, human rights issues have moved from a domestic issue to an international issue. However, there has been persistent interference by member countries in redress for individual human rights violations through international organizations under the pretext of interference with sovereignty.

However, it can be argued that Korea and Japan's act of interfering with this is a violation of the 1966 International Covenant on Human Rights, to which both countries have joined, especially Article 8(3)(a) (Prohibition of Forced Labor) of the ICCPR.

Japan's neglect and interference with the issue of victims of forced labor is a war crime resulting from the colonial war, a violation of the Treaty on Prohibition of Forced Labor, which Japan joined in 1938, and a violation of Article 8 of the International Covenant on Civil and Political Rights, which it is currently a party to.

At the same time, the Korean government's lack of support for, and political opposition to the 2018 Supreme Court's ruling in favor of forced labor victims raises serious concerns about its commitment to judicial independence and victims' rights, and also raises concerns with its obligations to comply with the ICCPR, such as Article 8 and Article 2(3) concerning forced labor and remedies, respectively. In addition, third-party reimbursement under Article 469 of the Korean Civil Act may undermine justice when used to bypass judicial rulings and pressure victims into accepting alternatives with their full and voluntary consent.

According to the International Human Rights Covenant(1966), there are three ways to protect human rights in case of human rights violations. One is the national reporting system known as the Universal Periodic Review ("UPR"). Countries that have signed the Covenant regularly submit regular reports to the Human Rights Council every four years on their country's human rights situation (Article 40 of the ICCPR), and after receiving counter-reports from private organizations, both are reviewed simultaneously. The second is the cross-border reporting system, which is a system in which Contracting States report violations of the rules by other Contracting States (Article 41 of the ICCPR). The third is the individual national reporting system, also known as the "individual notification system" (Optional Protocol B, introduced in 2007). An individual or organization submits a complaint to the Human Rights Committee regarding a violation of the Human Rights Covenant by the country to which it belongs. The country that received a complaint must submit an explanation within six months. The Human Rights Committee reviews both reports in private and notifies the Contracting States and individuals of the Human Rights Committee's final opinion. A Korean example of the application of the ICCPR Protocol is the Kim Geun-tae National Security Law case (September 27, 1993). Here, after the Supreme Court ruling or the Constitutional Court ruling on the National Security Law, "local remedies" were completed and other conditions were met, effective relief measures were requested on the grounds that the punishment of Mr. Kim Geun-tae under the National Security Law was a violation of freedom of expression (Article 19(2) of the ICCPR). The Human Rights Committee provided an affirmative recommendation relating to this case.

In conclusion, since its inauguration, the former Yoon administration has prioritized strengthening the ROK-US military alliance and normalizing Korea-Japan relations, while sidelining the rights of victims of forced labor during the colonial period by promoting a third-party compensation scheme that avoids direct enforcement of the 2018 Korean Supreme Court ruling. Therefore, the issue of victims of forced labor under Japanese colonial rule cannot be left solely to the Korean government, but it is appropriate and and effective for individual victims of Japanese forced labor to file a transitional justice complaint to the UN Human Rights Committee based on the individual notification system after meeting the conditions for completion of domestic relief in accordance with the ICCPR and its Optional Protocol to which Korea is a party.

Notes

1 International Covenant on Civil and Political Rights (1966)(the B Covenant on Human Rights), Adopted by UNGA Resolution 2200 A(XXI) of 16/12/66.ELF 23/3/76.
2 March 28, 2023. The Korea Times.
3 Ibid.
4 Ibid.
5 https://www.kr.emb-japan.go.jp/relation/history_issues_QnA.html
6 Ian Brownlie, Principles of Public International Law, Fourth Edition, Clarendon Press, Oxford, pp.512-515.
7 Malcolm N.Shaw,International Law, Fifth Edition, Cambridge University, 2003, pp.625-628.
8 www.hani.co.kr; www.pressian.com
9 Linda Fasulo, An Insider Guide to the UN, Third Edition, Yale University Press, New Haven and London 2015, pp.161-165.
10 "The members of the Committee shall be elected and shall serve in their personal capacity", Article 28, Paragraph 3, International Covenant on Civil and Political Rights (1966).

KYIL

Application of Korean Data Privacy Regulations to Foreign Business Operators

Ju Eun LEE
Attorney at law
Bae, Kim & Lee, Seoul, Korea

Abstract

This article examines the extraterritorial application of Korea's Personal Information Protection Act (PIPA) to foreign business operators. Amid increasing enforcement by the Personal Information Protection Commission (PIPC), including recent high-profile sanctions, the article analyzes the legal basis for such application, focusing on the Guidelines issued in 2024 by the PIPC. It further outlines key compliance obligations under the PIPA, including privacy policy disclosures, designation of a domestic representative, notification duties, and cross-border transfer requirements. While the Guidelines improve practical understanding, their non-binding nature and the lack of a clear statutory provision on extraterritoriality raise concerns about legal certainty and enforceability. Compared to the EU General Data Protection Regulation (GDPR), which establishes a firm legislative basis for extraterritorial reach, Korea's reliance on administrative guidance highlights the limitations of its current framework in ensuring predictability and regulatory effectiveness for foreign entities subject to Korean data privacy law.

Key Words

Data privacy, data protection, scope of application, Personal Information Protection Act, Personal Information Protection Commission, foreign business operator

1. Introduction

With the widespread proliferation of global online services, instances in which foreign business operators process personal information of Korean data subjects have grown rapidly. Correspondingly, there has been a notable increase in cases involving personal information infringements by such operators. In the Republic of Korea, the regulatory framework governing personal information is primarily structured around two major statutes: the Personal Information Protection Act (the "PIPA") and the Act on Promotion of Information and Communications Network Utilization and Information Protection (the "IT Network Act"). The Personal Information Protection Commission (the "PIPC") is the chief data protection regulator, having full scope of authority under the PIPA to administer and enforce the framework of restrictions and safeguards; and the Korea Communications Commission (the "KCC") is in charge of privacy-related rules (affecting smartphone data access settings, and marketing-related messaging) under the IT Network Act. This article focuses particularly on the regulatory framework established under the PIPA and the position of the PIPC, in order to examine the application of Korean data privacy regulations to foreign business operators.

Recently, the PIPC has adopted a more proactive stance toward violations of the PIPA by foreign business operators, and there has been a noticeable increase in the number of cases where such violations have resulted in actual enforcement measures. In

September 2022, the PIPC imposed over USD 70 million total in fines on Google and Meta for collecting their users' third-party behavioral information ("3P BI") without due consents (i.e., informed, optional consent). The PIPC found that Google and Meta, in gathering their users' 3P BI via tracking tools distributed by the companies, failed to obtain user consents based on sufficiently clear disclosures. Fines of KRW 69 billion (approx. USD 53.5 million) for Google, and KRW 31 billion (approx. USD 24 million) for Meta based on Korean user-derived revenues, represent the first cases of sanctions directed to behavioral data collection for personalized advertising in Korea.[1]

Also, in July 2024, the PIPC imposed administrative fines exceeding USD 1.4 million on Alibaba for its failure to comply with the statutory notification obligations concerning cross-border transfers of personal information, as well as for its failure to disclose the designation of a domestic representative, as required under the PIPA.[2] In a separate case, DeepSeek voluntarily suspended its services in Korea as of February 15, 2025, in order to enhance its compliance with the PIPA. The suspension followed an official inquiry initiated by the PIPC in response to the launch of DeepSeek's large language model (LLM)-based AI chatbot service. Following heightened public scrutiny and concerns raised by domestic media outlets regarding the potential privacy risks associated with the chatbot, the PIPC conducted a preliminary analysis and identified issues related to third-party data transfers and a lack of transparency in the company's privacy policy. As a result, the PIPC announced that it would closely monitor DeepSeek's compliance measures throughout the suspension period to ensure alignment with the requirements of the PIPA and to address outstanding privacy concerns prior to the company's resumption of service in the Korean market.[3]

Against the backdrop of the PIPC's increasingly assertive stance on enforcing personal information regulations against foreign business operators, it is noteworthy that in April 2024, the PIPC announced the publication of a guidance document (the "Guidelines"[4]) aimed at clarifying legal obligations that foreign business operators have either previously neglected or may easily overlooked under the amended law. The Commission stated that the Guidelines reflect expert consultations as well as feedback gathered during an on-site roundtable held in January 2024 with foreign business operators.

The PIPC further published the Guidelines in English and shared them with major overseas supervisory authorities. Emphasizing that "in a globally connected environment where online services are ubiquitous, the PIPA applies equally to both domestic and foreign business operators", the PIPC expressed its hope that the Guidelines will help foreign businesses gain a deeper understanding of and comply with Korea's legal requirements, thereby contributing to the effective protection of Korean data subjects' personal information.[5]

Based on the content of the Guidelines, this article will, in Section 2, examine the legal basis and criteria for applying the PIPA to foreign business operators, and in Section 3, analyze the specific obligations that the PIPC has highlighted as requiring particular attention in light of the unique characteristics of such operators.

2. Criteria for Application of the PIPA to Foreign Business Operators

In today's highly information-driven society, the processing of personal data occurs across time and space, transcending traditional physical boundaries. Therefore, distinguishing the applicability of personal information protection laws based solely on national borders is neither logical nor practically sound. In particular, if PIPA applies only to domestic business operators—even when the relevant business or service is conducted within Korea or impacts Korean data subjects—issues of fairness may arise, as foreign business operators could enjoy a comparative advantage without being subject to the same legal obligations. This highlights the strong need to establish clear criteria for applying the PIPA to foreign business operators.

However, applying Korean administrative regulations to foreign business operators inherently raises the issue of "extraterritorial application". Extraterritorial application refers to the application of a country's laws to foreign individuals or entities located outside its territory, or to acts committed beyond its national borders—in other words, an extension of a state's jurisdiction beyond its territorial limits. The core concept in extraterritorial application is state jurisdiction, which encompasses the authority a state may exercise over persons, objects, resources, or conduct. As a rule, the territorial scope of state jurisdiction corresponds to the state's physical territory. Thus, extraterritorial application necessarily involves extending jurisdiction over individuals, objects, or acts situated within the territory of another sovereign state, thereby raising potential conflicts or overlaps between state jurisdictions.[6] It is therefore essential to establish a strong legal basis for extraterritorial application. In this context, the Guidelines begin by introducing the criteria for applying the PIPA to foreign business operators.

The Guidelines explain that the fact that the PIPA does not limit its scope and applicability to Korean nationals or legal persons within Korea serves as the basis for its application to foreign entities. Article 2 of the PIPA provides the definition of "personal information controller"[7] and "data subject"[8] without limiting its scope to Korean nationals or entities within Korea. Under such legislation, the Guidelines provided the criteria for the PIPC when determining the applicability of the PIPA as follows: (1) whether the foreign business operator provides goods or services to the Korean Data Subjects, (2) the impact of the foreign business operators' data processing on Korean nationals and the Korean Data Subjects, and (3) whether the foreign business operator's place of business is located in Korea, together with the general principles of international law, pursuant to which Korean laws are applicable to foreign business operators.

2.1 Criterion (1) Provision of Goods or Services to Data Subjects in Korea

The Guidelines first state that a foreign business operator must comply with the PIPA, provided that it provides goods or services to a Korean data subject. Whether the business operator provides goods or services to Korean data subjects shall be determined in consideration of the language, the currency, and the form and manner used or supported to provide goods or services. Examples of such cases are as follows:

(a) Where a foreign business operator specifies South Korea as one of the supported countries and territories while providing services globally;
(b) Where a foreign business operator provides global services using a separate domain for Korea in its Internet address (e.g., "ko-kr.xxx.com" or "www.xxx.com/ko-kr");
(c) Where a foreign business operator develops an app and releases it to a Korean app store, or releases it to a global app store and sets the default language as Korean; and
(d) Where a foreign business operator provides service in Korean (even if it states that only the laws of a particular country apply to the provision of their service)

Furthermore, supplementary considerations—such as whether the foreign business operator collects the data subject's address in Korea for delivery purposes, offers customer support services in Korean via telephone or online chat, designates a dedicated point of contact for Korean data subjects, or engages in targeted advertising directed at Korean individuals—may also be taken into account in assessing the operator's intention to offer goods or services to data subjects in

Korea.

Nevertheless, the PIPC has clarified that the mere provision of goods or services to Korean nationals does not, in itself, trigger the applicability of the PIPA. For instance, the PIPA would not apply where a Korean individual utilizes goods or services offered offline in a foreign jurisdiction by a foreign business operator, or accesses online services notwithstanding the fact that the foreign operator has explicitly excluded Korea from the list of supported countries or territories.[9]

2.2 Criterion (2) Impact of Data Processing on Data Subjects in Korea

The PIPC articulates its position that, even in cases where foreign business operators do not directly offer goods or services to Korean data subjects, they may nonetheless fall within the scope of the PIPA if their processing of personal information pertaining to Korean data subjects has a direct and substantial impact on those individuals, and if the effects and nature of such processing activities are reasonably foreseeable.

This standard is particularly salient in assessing the relationship between foreign business operators and their Korean counterparts. For instance, the PIPA may be deemed applicable where a foreign business operator serves as either the entrusting or entrusted party in relation to the processing of personal information of Korean data subjects on behalf of a Korean business operator, or where it receives such personal information from a Korean business operator for the purpose of pursuing its own business interests.

The Guidelines further illustrate this principle through specific examples: (i) where a foreign business operator does not directly obtain or access the personal information of Korean data subjects, but instead outsources the processing to another entity and receives only the resulting output, it remains subject to the PIPA's provisions governing entrustment; and (ii) where a foreign business operator receives and processes personal information—including learning data—for the purpose of developing an artificial intelligence model, the PIPA applies in full.[10]

2.3 Criterion (3) Place of Business Located within Korea

The Guidelines explain that the PIPA applies to foreign business operators providing goods or services with a business presence in Korea. The form of the presence includes not only corporations, but also individual offices, liaison offices, and business establishments of people entrusted. However, even if the foreign business operator maintains a business presence in Korea, if the processing of personal information in the provision of goods or services is unrelated to the activities of the business establishment in Korea, the PIPA may not be applicable. For instance, if a foreign business operator maintains a sales organization in Korea for software sales and maintenance but separately operates an online shopping mall outside Korea without offering services to Korean data subjects, then the online shopping mall may not be subject to the PIPA.[11]

2.4 Analysis on the Legal Basis of the Criteria

Under current Korean law, certain statutes explicitly stipulate extraterritorial application. These include the Monopoly Regulation and Fair Trade Act (MRFTA), the Financial Investment Services and Capital Markets Act (FSCMA), and the Foreign Exchange Transactions Act.[12] [13] The relevant provisions are based on the effect doctrine, which allows for the extraterritorial application of domestic law when an act committed by a foreign national outside the territory has an immediate and substantial effect on the domestic legal order.

The Korean Supreme Court has also affirmed this principle in the context of the MRFTA. In a 2004 decision (Supreme Court Decision 2004Du11275), the Court held that "even if a foreign business entity enters into an agreement with another entity abroad to restrict competition, the MRFTA shall apply to the extent that the agreement targets the Korean market and has effects therein". This judgment clearly recognizes the extraterritorial application of the MRFTA based on the effect doctrine.

In the digital domain, provisions for extraterritorial application were newly introduced in 2018 into the Telecommunications Business Act, which governs the communications sector, and in 2020 into the IT Network Act, which regulates information and communications services.[14] However, the PIPA still lacks an explicit provision regarding extraterritorial application. Therefore, the PIPC has, over time, clarified the applicability of the PIPA to individual foreign business operators through a series of administrative decisions. In July 2023, the PIPC published the results of its investigation of an AI service provider and, in doing so, presented specific criteria for determining the applicability of domestic law.[15] The PIPC concluded that the provider was subject to Korean law, citing factors such as the explicit inclusion of South Korea among the countries and regions where the service is available, the indication in technical documentation that the AI system achieved a 77% accuracy rate in Korean, and the presence of a significant number of Korean users. Based on these elements, the Commission determined that the AI service was effectively being offered to Korean users.

This case is particularly noteworthy in the context of generative AI services, which are inherently global in nature and capable of being translated into multiple languages, including Korean. Even in the absence of a dedicated Korean-language site or a localized interface specifically targeting Korean users, the PIPC signaled that Korean law may still apply if the service is accessible to Korean users and has a tangible presence in the Korean market. Subsequently, in April 2024, the PIPC released the Guidelines based on its prior decisions. These Guidelines are expected to enhance legal predictability for foreign service providers until an explicit provision for extraterritorial application is introduced into the PIPA.

However, the PIPC's decision to issue applicability standards in the form of non-binding Guidelines, rather than through a formal legislative provision on extraterritoriality, raises significant concerns. Although the PIPC is the primary regulatory authority for data privacy in Korea, publishing the criteria of PIPA application that can lead to administrative sanctions—such as fines, administrative penalties, and corrective orders—on foreign entities through a document lacking legal force undermines legal certainty and predictability.

A particularly problematic aspect of the Guidelines lies in the second criterion for determining applicability: whether the relevant data processing "has a direct and substantial impact on Korean data subjects". This standard mirrors the effect-based provisions codified in other Korean statutes that recognize extraterritorial application and, as such, arguably constitutes a mandatory rule under international law.[16] Had this criterion been explicitly codified in the PIPA, it could have served as a legal basis for applying Korean data protection law to disputes involving foreign entities—even in cases where the governing law was otherwise agreed to be foreign—under Article 20 of Korea's Private International Law.[17] However, because the standard was articulated in a non-legally binding document rather than in statutory form, its legal status and enforceability remain ambiguous. This lack of clarity diminishes the authority of the Guidelines and leaves foreign service providers uncertain about their legal obligations under Korean law.

From a comparative legal perspective, the European Union's General Data Protection Regulation (the "GDPR") offers a clear statutory basis for the territorial scope of the regulation in Article 3.

Article 3(1) governs the application of the GDPR within the EU, and Article 3(2) provides for its extraterritorial application. Specifically, Article 3(1) states that the Regulation "applies to the processing of personal data in the context of the activities of an establishment of a controller or a processor in the Union, regardless of whether the processing takes place in the Union or not". Furthermore, Article 3(2) stipulates that the Regulation "applies to the processing of personal data of data subjects who are in the Union by a controller or processor not established in the Union, where the processing activities are related to: (a) the offering of goods or services, irrespective of whether a payment of the data subject is required; or (b) the monitoring of their behaviour as far as their behaviour takes place within the Union".

The European Data Protection Board ("EDPB") Guidelines[18] provide further clarification on these provisions. The Guidelines emphasize that the phrase "data subjects who are in the Union" is not limited by the data subject's citizenship, residence, or any other legal status. In addition, the EDPB elaborates on what constitutes an "offering of goods or services", identifying relevant elements for assessment, and offers detailed interpretations of what types of processing activities may be considered "monitoring of behavior", referencing not only the Recitals to the GDPR but also providing practical examples.

This legislative structure—wherein the statute clearly defines the scope of extraterritorial application and the Guidelines serve to interpret and supplement statutory provisions with practical illustrations—ensures both legal certainty and predictability. It also enhances the effectiveness of GDPR compliance by foreign entities. From this standpoint, the Korean regulatory framework would have been more rational and effective if it had adopted a similar model: enacting an explicit statutory basis for extraterritorial application under the PIPA, and then using Guidelines to provide interpretive support and practical examples, rather than attempting to establish core applicability standards solely through non-binding administrative guidance.

In conclusion, the PIPC's effort to address the issue of regulatory parity between domestic and foreign service providers—by issuing the Guidelines and, for the first time, articulating the scope of the PIPA—represents a meaningful regulatory development. Nonetheless, setting forth such standards through non-binding guidance, rather than through a formal legislative amendment, raises concerns regarding the legal basis and normative clarity of such measures. Particularly, the adoption of a criterion based on whether the processing of personal data produces effects on data subjects in Korea implicates the doctrine of mandatory rules under private international law. Given the potential legal implications, it would be more appropriate to codify such standards explicitly within the text of the PIPA, rather than rely on interpretive administrative documents.

Furthermore, as foreign service providers potentially subject to Korean law typically operate globally across multiple jurisdictions, the risk of overlapping and conflicting regulatory obligations is substantial. In this regard, any framework governing the extraterritorial application of data protection laws should account for the broader international context and consider the burdens placed on multinational entities. In the long term, addressing issues of regulatory overlap may require enhanced international cooperation, intergovernmental coordination mechanisms, and the development of harmonized global norms to ensure legal certainty and promote effective cross-border data governance.[19]

3. Specific Compliance Requirements for Foreign Business Operators Subject to the PIPA

While the Guidelines affirm that foreign entities subject to the

PIPA are required to comply with all obligations prescribed therein, they also emphasize certain specific requirements in light of the unique operational characteristics of foreign business operators.

3.1 Disclosure of the Privacy Policy

When foreign business operators establish and disclose a privacy policy pursuant to the PIPA in relation to the goods or services they offer, the policy must be provided in the Korean language to ensure that Korean data subjects can readily comprehend the details concerning the processing of their personal information. Furthermore, the PIPC underscores that such a privacy policy should not merely constitute a translated version of a policy prepared in accordance with foreign legal regimes, but rather must be specifically tailored and disclosed in compliance with the substantive and procedural requirements set forth under the PIPA, thereby enhancing the accessibility and convenience for data subjects.

A common legal deficiency observed in the privacy policies of foreign business operators is the failure to clearly differentiate between third-party provision and entrustment, with both often being described collectively under the vague term "sharing". Under the PIPA, personal information controllers are obligated to make a clear distinction between third-party provision and entrustment within their privacy policies.

With respect to the cross-border transfer of personal information, it is advisable to disclose such transfers separately from disclosures concerning third-party provision or entrustment. However, if separate disclosures result in unnecessary redundancy that impairs the readability and user-friendliness of the privacy policy, it is permissible to include information regarding third-party provision or outsourcing within the broader context of cross-border transfer disclosures. In such instances, the relevant information must nonetheless be presented in a clear and comprehensible manner to ensure that data subjects can easily understand the implications of the processing activities.

In cases where goods or services are provided uniformly across multiple jurisdictions, the identity of the personal information controller may vary depending on the country. Accordingly, the privacy policy must explicitly specify the entity responsible for processing the personal information of Korean data subjects. Furthermore, if the processing takes place outside of Korea, the policy must clearly indicate that such processing occurs overseas, identify the specific country where the processing is conducted, and disclose the name of the business operator that performs the processing.

In certain instances, foreign business operators opt to disclose a globally applicable privacy policy while omitting specific elements required under the PIPA, instead supplementing such deficiencies by providing Korea-specific provisions or an addendum on a separate webpage. However, it is recommended that, to the extent practicable, the privacy policy made accessible to Korean data subjects integrate all PIPA-mandated disclosures within a single webpage. Where the policy references additional information via hyperlinks, such design should not impair the accessibility of the information by requiring data subjects to navigate through multiple layers of links. It is also essential to manage these links on a regular basis to ensure that they direct users to the intended content, and any linked pages must be available in the Korean language.[20]

Pursuant to Article 30(2) of the PIPA—a provision newly introduced in March 2023—the PIPC is authorized to conduct evaluations of privacy policies and, where deemed necessary based on the results of such evaluations, may issue recommendations for their improvement. The scope of evaluation is determined based on a holistic assessment of various factors, including the type and revenue scale of the personal information controller, the nature and volume of personal information processed, the legal grounds and methods of processing, any history of legal violations, and characteristics of the data subjects, such as whether they include children or adolescents.

The evaluation criteria consist of three core elements: (i) appropriateness, referring to whether the policy adequately addresses all legally required components; (ii) clarity, assessing whether the content is presented in an easily understandable manner; and (iii) accessibility, evaluating whether the policy is disclosed in a manner that enables data subjects to readily locate and review the relevant information.

In 2024, the PIPC conducted its first evaluation of privacy policies pursuant to the selection criteria outlined in Article 4 of the *Notification on the Evaluation of Privacy Policies*, which came into effect in February 2024. A total of 49 companies across seven industry sectors were selected for evaluation, and the assessment was carried out throughout the year. Given that foreign businesses received markedly lower scores compared to their domestic counterparts, the PIPC convened a consultation meeting on the Privacy Policy Evaluation System with 14 foreign business operators in March 2025. During the meeting, the PIPC explained that the lower evaluation results for foreign businesses were primarily attributable to (i) insufficient clarity regarding data handling practices and the rights of data subjects, (ii) privacy policies characterized by overly literal translations and unnecessarily lengthy text, and (iii) policies that were ambiguously labeled or difficult to locate.

Recognizing the critical role that well-drafted and legally compliant privacy policies play in ensuring data protection accountability—particularly for foreign business operators—the PIPC announced its intention to revise and enhance the drafting guidelines for privacy policies. Taking into account the findings of the 2024 evaluation and the challenges identified in relation to foreign entities, the updated guidelines are expected to be issued within the year.

3.2 Domestic Representative

A foreign business operator with neither an address nor a place of business in Korea is required to designate a domestic representative if the operator's sales[21] or the volume of personal information it retains[22] exceeds a specified threshold, or where the PIPC requests the submission of information and subsequently deliberates and determines that the designation of a domestic representative is necessary. The determination of whether a foreign business operator has a business presence in Korea may be based on factors such as the manner in which complaints from Korean data subjects are addressed and how regulatory enforcement is executed in the event of a personal information infringement.

Even where a foreign business operator has established a local corporation in Korea, such presence will not be regarded as an "address or place of business" under the PIPA if the corporation does not act as the personal information controller. In cases where the foreign business operator is obligated to designate a domestic representative and has either established a Korean subsidiary or exercises substantial influence over a local corporation—such as through control over executive appointments and operational decisions—it is advisable to designate that corporation as the domestic representative.

A domestic representative may be either a natural person or a legal entity with an address or place of business in Korea. In the case of a natural person, Korean nationality is not a prerequisite; however, the individual must be fluent in Korean, as the role involves handling complaints from Korean data subjects and submitting accurate information and documentation to regulatory authorities. The designation must be made in writing, and the following information must be disclosed in the foreign business operator's privacy policy: the name (and in the case of a corporation, the name of the entity and its representative), address (the business office location for a corporation), telephone number, and email address of the domestic representative.

If multiple domestic representatives are designated, information for each must be included in the privacy policy. Any changes to the designated representative must be promptly reflected through revisions to the policy. The telephone number disclosed must be a Korean domestic number. While this does not need to be the personal mobile number of the representative, it must be a contact line through which complaints and inquiries related to personal information protection can be effectively managed.

The domestic representative is required to perform the duties of a personal information controller on behalf of the foreign business operator, including the handling of grievances, the facilitation of remedies for damages, and other matters related to the processing of personal information. The domestic representative may also be responsible for notifying data subjects in the event of a loss, theft, or unauthorized disclosure of personal information, as well as for submitting the relevant reports concerning such incidents. In addition, where the PIPC requests the submission of documents, data, or other relevant materials, the domestic representative must expeditiously carry out the necessary procedures in accordance with applicable laws and regulations, acting on behalf of the foreign business operator. Accordingly, it is incumbent upon the foreign business operator to promptly provide the domestic representative with the necessary information and support to ensure the effective performance of these responsibilities.

Moreover, complaints and requests for remedies filed by Korean data subjects in relation to personal information processing must be addressed in a practical and responsive manner. If the foreign business operator only provides recorded messages instructing data subjects to submit inquiries via email or web-based forms, without having personnel available to directly respond, or if the assigned personnel lack the capacity to address such complaints and remedies appropriately, it may be deemed that a domestic representative has not been properly designated to act on behalf of the personal information controller.[23]

In March 2025, the National Assembly passed an amendment to the PIPA aimed at strengthening the local representative system applicable to foreign business operators. The amendment is expected to come into effect in the near future. Originally, the local representative system was introduced to ensure the effective protection of the personal information of Korean data subjects and to facilitate appropriate remedial measures in cases involving foreign entities. The recent legislative revision introduces several significant enhancements designed to improve the system's efficacy and practical enforcement. In particular, to prevent the system from being implemented merely as a procedural formality, the amendment mandates that where a foreign business operator has an incorporated entity in Korea, that entity must be designated as the local representative. Furthermore, the foreign headquarters is now expressly obligated to oversee and supervise the activities of its designated local representative. The amendment also introduces new enforcement mechanisms. Specifically, if a foreign business operator fails to fulfill its supervisory obligations, neglects to designate a local representative in accordance with statutory requirements, or does not disclose essential contact information—such as the representative's telephone number—administrative fines may be imposed.

3.3 Notification and Reporting of Divulgence of Personal Information

The loss, theft, or divulgence (hereinafter referred to as "divulgence") of personal information refers to situations in which personal information becomes accessible to an unauthorized third party due to the personal information controller's loss of control or oversight, absent a lawful basis or intentional authorization. Under Article 34(1) and (3) of the PIPA, once a divulgence of personal information is identified, the personal information controller is obligated to notify the affected data subjects within 72 hours. Such notification must include the following information: (1) the specific items of personal information that were divulged; (2) the time and method of the divulgence; (3) guidance on measures that data subjects may take to mitigate potential harm; (4) the countermeasures adopted by the personal information controller and the available remedial procedures; and (5) contact information, including a help desk, through which data subjects may report damages or seek assistance.

In cases where the divulgence affects 1,000 or more individuals, involves sensitive or personally identifiable information, or results from unlawful external access, the incident must also be reported to the PIPC or the Korea Internet & Security Agency (KISA) within 72 hours. Notably, the mere awareness that unauthorized third parties may have accessed the personal information is considered sufficient to constitute recognition of a divulgence.

The PIPC acknowledges that foreign business operators may face uncertainty in determining whether they are subject to the reporting obligations under the PIPA. In response, the Guidelines clarify that a foreign operator is deemed to have become aware of a divulgence involving Korean data subjects' personal information once the occurrence of the divulgence is confirmed and the operator does not maintain data systems that segment personal information by the nationality or country of the data subjects. This holds true even if the full extent of the divulgence is not yet ascertained. However, where it is confirmed—through internal analysis conducted within 72 hours—that no personal information pertaining to Korean data subjects was included in the incident, the reporting obligation may not apply.

Furthermore, where the divulgence of personal information is discovered through internal monitoring mechanisms, communications from hackers, or inquiries received via customer service channels—but without a full understanding of the specific details of the incident, such as the categories of personal information involved, the timing, or the circumstances of the divulgence—the personal information controller is still required to report the incident and notify the affected data subjects without delay. In accordance with Article 40(1) and (2) of the Enforcement Decree of the PIPA, the notification must include the fact of the divulgence, the information confirmed at the time, and any other relevant details available for disclosure to the data subjects. Such reports may be filed through the Privacy Portal (privacy.go.kr) or by submitting a completed reporting form via email (118@kisa.or.kr). The reporting obligation may also be fulfilled by a designated domestic representative acting on behalf of the foreign business operator.

In situations where reporting within the statutory 72-hour period is infeasible due to *force majeure* events such as natural disasters or other uncontrollable circumstances, the report must be submitted without undue delay once such circumstances have been resolved. Additionally, under Article 40(1) of the Enforcement Decree of the PIPA, if it is confirmed that the path of divulgence has been identified and the exposed information has been either retrieved or deleted, thereby significantly reducing the risk of harm to the data subjects, the reporting requirement may be waived. In such cases, however, the personal information controller must retain objective evidence substantiating the retrieval or deletion of the divulged information and the corresponding mitigation of risk.[24]

3.4 Entrustment and Third-party Provision

Under the PIPA, there are two types of data transfers: (i) “entrustment”, which involves sharing PI for the data controller’s own purposes, such as outsourcing data processing (i.e., analogous to controller-to-processor transfers), and (ii) “third-party provision”, which involves sharing personal data for the recipient’s purposes (i.e., analogous to controller-to-controller transfers). This distinction originates from a Supreme Court decision, which held that the difference between entrustment and provision to a third party depends on whether the transfer of personal information goes beyond the original purpose of its collection and use, and whether it is made for the recipient’s own business operations and interests (*Supreme Court Decision 2016Do13263*).

If a foreign business operator transfers personal information to a third party in order to perform its obligations under an agreement with the data subjects in connection with the provision of goods or services to the data subjects, such transfer can be deemed as entrustment of personal information processing. In this case, the foreign business operator can be held liable for the damages to the data subjects. On the contrary, if a foreign business operator transfers personal information to a third party beyond the scope of the agreement with the data subject or to provide services that connect the data subject with a third party beyond the scope of the agreement with the data subjects, such transfer can be deemed provision of personal information to a third party. In this case, the foreign business operator must have a valid legal basis for providing personal information to a third party.

For entrustment, only a disclosure in the privacy policy is required, whereas for third-party provision, both obtaining consent and making a disclosure in the privacy policy are necessary. When obtaining consent for third-party provision of the data, the following matters must be notified to the data subject: (i) the recipient of the data; (ii) the PI recipient's purpose of use of the data; (iii) the items of data to be provided; (iv) the data recipient's period for retaining and using the data; (v) the fact that the data subject has a right to refuse consent, and, in case of any disadvantage following refusal of consent, particulars of the disadvantage.

For reference, the personal information controller is exempt from having to obtain a separate consent if personal information is provided to a third-party within the scope reasonably related to the original purposes of collection. However, unlike the consent for collection/use of personal information, it is not considered unlawful to obtain a 'mandatory' consent for these cases of third-party provision that fall under this exception.

Further, it must be noted that the PIPA applies, *mutatis mutandis,* to the person entrusted; therefore, the entrusted entity can be penalized for its violation of the PIPA as well. In this case, if a personal information controller who entrusted data processing is deemed to have been negligent in its obligation to supervise the person entrusted, it can also be penalized for the violation of its obligation under PIPA.[25]

3.5 Cross-border Transfer

Cross-border transfer of personal information refers to cross-border provision (including inquiry), entrusted processing, or storage. The PIPA forbids cross-border transfer of personal information, but allows it in any one of these cases: (i) separate consent is obtained from the data subject; (ii) it is separately governed by statute or international treaties or conventions; (iii) it is necessary to entrust the processing and storage of personal information in order to conclude and perform a contract with the data subject; (iv) the recipient of personal information obtains certification determined and publicly notified by the PIPC; (v) the PIPC recognizes that the country or international organization to which the personal information is to be transferred has the equal level of personal information protection as in the PIPA in aspects of personal information protection system, the scope of guarantee of the rights of the data subject, and the procedures for damage relief, and etc. (Article 28-8(1) of the PIPA).

Foreign business operators shall comprehensively verify the legal basis of personal information processing for the goods or services they provide; relevant statutes and regulations; related certificates; whether the country where personal information is to be transferred to has been recognized by the PIPC, and then prepare for lawful ways of transferring personal information.

The Guidelines specifically highlights that the foreign business operators shall be aware that the PIPC can order to suspend their cross-border transfer of personal information in cases of them failing to comply with the PIPA such as: (i) their transfer does not fulfill condition(s) for allowed cross-border transfer; (ii) they fail to set up the prescribed protection measures; (iii) they fail to guarantee the prescribed rights of the data subjects.[26]

Furthermore, any cross-border transfer requires specific consent and disclosures. The personal information controller must obtain separate consent for personal information collection and processing. However, if the cross-border transfer is only (a) for the purpose of data storage and/or entrustment of data processing, and (b) necessary for the execution and performance of a contract, obtaining consent may be substituted with disclosing related details in the privacy policy. When obtaining consent for overseas transfer of PI, the following matters must be notified to the data subject: (i) the items of PI to be transferred; (ii) the country to which the PI will be transferred, and the timing and method of transfer; (iii) the name of the recipient of the transfer of PI (that is, in the case of a company, the company's name); (iv) the transfer recipient's purposes of use of the PI, and periods for retention and use; and (v) method and procedure for refusing the transfer of PI, and effect of such refusal (Article 28-8 (2) of the PIPA).

3.6 Guarantee of Data Subject's Rights

The PIPA requires personal information controllers to establish clear methods and procedures through which data subjects may exercise their statutory rights, including the rights to request access to, correction or erasure of, suspension of processing of, and withdrawal of consent regarding their personal information. Moreover, such procedures must be made publicly available in order to ensure that data subjects are fully informed of their rights and how to exercise them.

In this regard, foreign business operators must implement user-friendly procedures that enable Korean data subjects to exercise their rights without undue burden. These procedures should be clearly explained in the Korean language, and appropriate, easily accessible communication channels—such as email or telephone—should be provided. Where feasible, the exercise of rights should also be enabled via internet websites or mobile applications.

Upon receipt of a data subject request, a foreign business operator may deny the request only under limited circumstances, including: (i) where special provisions under other applicable statutes exist or compliance with legal obligations renders fulfillment of the request impossible; (ii) where complying with the request may cause harm to the life or physical safety of a third party or may result in an unjustified infringement upon the property or other legal interests of another individual; or (iii) where the processing of the relevant personal information is essential for the performance of a contract with the data subject, and the data subject has not clearly expressed an intent to terminate the contract.

In the event that a request is denied, the foreign business operator must notify the data subject of such denial within ten (10) business days (as calculated according to Korean business days), and must also inform the data subject of the procedures available for raising an objection to the decision.

Once a domestic representative is designated, foreign business operators are obligated to ensure the prompt and effective handling of complaints and requests from data subjects. This may be achieved either by authorizing the domestic representative to respond to such requests on their behalf or by implementing other appropriate and practicable mechanisms to safeguard the rights of data subjects under the PIPA.

However, foreign business operators may encounter legal or regulatory restrictions under foreign jurisdictions that prohibit the disclosure of personal information in response to a data subject's request. The Guidelines clarify that such foreign legal constraints do not, in themselves, constitute a sufficient basis for rejecting a request submitted pursuant to the PIPA.

In a landmark decision issued on April 13, 2023 (*Supreme Court Decision 2017Da219232*), the Korean Supreme Court held that foreign business operators must undertake a comprehensive assessment before denying a request on such grounds. Specifically, operators are required to evaluate: (i) whether the foreign jurisdiction's non-disclosure obligation is substantively consistent with the Korean Constitution and relevant domestic laws, including in terms of its content and legislative purpose; (ii) whether the necessity of observing the foreign legal obligation significantly outweighs the data subject's right to access and control their personal information; and (iii) whether the operator is, in fact, legally bound by a substantive non-disclosure duty under the foreign legal framework. Only where a justifiable reason for non-disclosure is established through such review may a foreign business operator lawfully deny the request. In such cases, the operator must notify the data subject of the specific reason for the denial or restriction, and must grant access to the personal information without delay once the grounds for denial cease to exist.[27]

3.7 Legal Representatives of Children under 14

Article 22-2 of the PIPA requires personal information controllers to obtain and verify the consent of a legal representative when processing the personal information of children under the age of 14. While the definition of a "child" may vary across jurisdictions, it is important to emphasize that, under the PIPA, individuals under the age of 14 are classified as children. Accordingly, foreign business operators must exercise particular caution to avoid collecting personal information from children without obtaining the legally required consent of their legal representatives—especially when offering goods or services directly to children, or in connection with goods or services that necessitate the collection of children's personal information.

Article 17(2) of the Enforcement Decree of the PIPA prescribes specific methods for verifying whether a data subject is under 14 years of age. In line with this provision, the Guidelines recommend that foreign business operators implement appropriate verification measures, such as requiring the data subject to enter their date of birth or using identity verification services provided by certified Identification Service Agencies, as designated under Article 23(3) of the IT Network Act.

These identity verification services may include authentication through I-PIN, mobile phone, credit card, or accredited digital certificates. Business operators may select the most appropriate method based on the nature and characteristics of the goods or services they provide. Information regarding the current status of designated Identification Service Agencies and the services they offer is available at the Identification Service Support Portal (identity.kisa.or.kr).[28]

3.8 PIPC Investigation and Administrative Measures

In terms of enforcement, the PIPC is the chief regulator to monitor and investigate PIPA compliance.[29] As part of this, the PIPC may demand records from a PI controller where the regulator has received a report or complaint of a violation of the PIPA, or where it otherwise has reason to suspect a violation of the PIPA. Upon failure to comply with such a request, the PIPC may proceed with an on-site inspection of records. Even in the absence of a specific suspicion or complaint, the PIPC may conduct inspections, discretionary in nature, where it sees a significant risk of non-compliance or other need for checking. Such inspections, which are not uncommon, typically target controllers selected based on popularity, and involve a detailed review of their privacy policies and user interfaces.

Violations of the PIPA can result in administrative fines, generally in the range of KRW 10 million to KRW 50 million. The PIPC can also impose corrective or remediation orders, including orders to fix the infringing practice or, at the extreme, to suspend the PI handling activity altogether, pending remediation. Revenue-based penalty surcharges can apply in cases of non-consensual use of personal information and other infractions of a relatively serious kind, such as where the data controller uses or transfers data without due consent, or suffers a data incident attributable to a failure to observe due security precautions. The PIPC is able to impose penalty surcharges of up to 3 percent of the business's total revenues, excluding such revenues as the business is able to show are unrelated to the non-compliance (Article 64-2 of the PIPA).

Criminal penalties, including potential imprisonment and surcharges, are applicable to the more egregious, invasive or impactful types of offences, such as a data controller using personal information or transferring it to a third-party without the data subjects' consent, or a party receiving personal information for a profit-making purpose. Under the PIPA, a range of criminal as well as civil liability implications can extend to offshore persons.

General compliance scrutiny often leads to, first, a stage of one or more warnings and requests for modifications from the monitoring agency called Korea Internet & Security Agency ("KISA"), before possible escalation to the PIPC for review for definitive action.[30]

4. Conclusion and Supplementary Discussion

It is of particular significance that the PIPC has published the Guidelines in both Korean and English, classifying the scope of application into three distinct categories and providing a clear explanation thereof. Furthermore, the separate articulation of the obligations imposed on foreign business operators—along with detailed guidance on the applicable requirements and procedures—may be evaluated as an effective measure in addressing concerns regarding potential reverse discrimination between domestic and foreign entities, as well as in enhancing the enforceability of legal compliance by foreign operators.

Nonetheless, the fact that the scope of application of the PIPA has not been stipulated through explicit statutory provisions, but rather through the non-binding format of the Guidelines, may be regarded as a provisional and limited approach. Accordingly, there remains an ongoing necessity to establish a clear and authoritative legal basis for the Act's extraterritorial application—preferably through formal legislation, or at a minimum, through a Presidential Decree or an official administrative notice.

Meanwhile, the discussion of jurisdiction in this paper has so far focused on legislative jurisdiction; however, further examination is needed from the perspective of enforcement jurisdiction. Enforcement jurisdiction refers to the authority of the executive or judicial branch to physically implement the law through coercive measures.[31] Under international legal theory, exercising enforcement jurisdiction within the territory of another state without that state's consent may constitute a violation of the latter's territorial sovereignty. As a general rule, a state may not exercise its public authority within the territory of another state without explicit consent.[32] Unlike legislative jurisdiction, therefore, enforcement jurisdiction is fundamentally constrained by territorial limits.

This means that even if a state has legislative jurisdiction over foreign entities —enabling it to regulate or penalize them through its laws—whether it can actually enforce such legislation abroad is a separate issue. As administrative legal relationships tend to reflect each state's unique policy priorities and national interests, attempts to exercise enforcement jurisdiction in this area are more likely to be perceived as infringing upon the sovereignty of other nations. Therefore, the issue of enforcement jurisdiction—whether jurisdiction can be effectively exercised—entails complex legal and practical challenges.[33]

Currently, administrative sanctions—such as corrective orders, administrative fines, and penalty surcharges—are being imposed in relation to violations of the PIPA. However, it is also necessary to consider preemptive measures to secure enforceability. Due to the inherently non-substitutable and self-executing nature of administrative regulations imposed on internet service providers, the available means of securing direct effectiveness appear to be limited, typically to measures such as the imposition of compliance fines.

However, in the case of internet services, where violations involving personal information can rapidly escalate as time passes, more proactive and urgent enforcement powers may be required. Accordingly, in the case of foreign business operators, ensuring enforceability through the local representative is likely to be of even greater importance.

As previously discussed, with the passage of the amended PIPA in March 2025, the local representative system is expected to be implemented more effectively. It is anticipated that regulatory authorities and foreign business operators will be able to communicate more efficiently through local representatives, thereby ensuring better compliance with the PIPA and related legal norms. Nevertheless, as noted earlier, there remains a need to further clarify the legal basis for the exercise of legislative jurisdiction, enforcement jurisdiction in cases of extraterritorial application to foreign business operators.

Notes

1 Personal Information Protection Commission, PIPC Sanctions Google and Meta for Illegal Collection of Personal Information (2022), https://www.pipc.go.kr/np/cop/bbs/selectBoardArticle.do?bbsId=BS074&nttId=8221&mCode=C020010000 [Accessed on June 29, 2025]

2 Personal Information Protection Commission, PIPC Imposes KRW 1.978 Billion Fine on AliExpress for Violating the Personal Information Protection Act (2024), https://www.pipc.go.kr/np/cop/bbs/selectBoardArticle.do?bbsId=BS074&mCode=C020010000&nttId=10386 [Accessed on June 29, 2025]

3 Personal Information Protection Commission, "DeepSeek App" to Temporarily Suspend Domestic Service for Improvements and Modifications (2025), https://www.pipc.go.kr/np/cop/bbs/selectBoardArticle.do?bbsId=BS074&mCode=C020010000&nttId=11007 [Accessed on June 29, 2025]

4 Personal Information Protection Commission, *Guidelines on Applying the Personal Information Protection Act to Foreign Business* Operators, PIPC Guidelines, 2024/04.

5 Personal Information Protection Commission, PIPC Publishes "Guidelines on Application of the Personal Information Protection Act to Foreign Business Operators (2024), https://www.pipc.go.kr/np/cop/bbs/selectBoardArticle.do?bbsId=BS074& mCode=C020010000&nttId=10056 [Accessed on June 29, 2025]

6 Haewon Lee, *A Legal Research on the Scope of Application of the Personal Information Protection Act*, Vol.26 No.1, Journal of Information Law, (2022), p. 292.

7 PIPA Article 2 Item 5 A public institution, legal person, organization, or an individual that processes personal information directly or indirectly to operate the personal information files as part of its work (Article 2 Item 5 of the PIPA)

8 PIPA Article 2 Item 3 An individual who is identifiable through the information processed and is the subject of that information

9 Personal Information Protection Commission, *Guidelines on Applying the Personal Information Protection Act to Foreign Business* Operators, PIPC Guidelines, 2024/04, pp. 9-11.

10 Personal Information Protection Commission, *Guidelines on Applying the Personal Information Protection Act to Foreign Business* Operators, PIPC Guidelines, 2024/04, pp. 13-14.

11 Personal Information Protection Commission, *Guidelines on Applying the Personal Information Protection Act to Foreign Business* Operators, PIPC Guidelines, 2024/04, pp. 14-15.

12 MRFTA, Article 3 (Application to Acts Conducted Outside Korea)
This Act shall apply to acts conducted outside Korea if such acts have effects on the domestic market.
FSCMA, Article 2 (Application to Extraterritorial Acts)
This Act shall apply to acts conducted outside Korea if their effects reach the territory of Korea.
Foreign Exchange Transactions Act, Article 2 (Scope of Application)
(1) This Act shall apply in any of the following cases:
2. Transactions, payments, or receipts between the Republic of Korea and foreign countries, and other related acts (including acts conducted abroad that have

effects within the Republic of Korea).

13 Korea Communications Commission, *A Study on the Measures to Secure Execution on Foreign Businesses for Their Violation of Administrative Regulation*, Broadcasting and Telecommunications Policy Research, (2017), pp. 10–11.

14 Telecommunications Business Act, Article 2-2 (Application to Extraterritorial Acts)
This Act shall apply to acts conducted outside Korea if such acts affect the domestic market or users in Korea.
IT Network Act, Article 5-2 (Application to Extraterritorial Acts)
This Act shall apply to acts conducted outside Korea if such acts affect the domestic market or users in Korea.

15 Personal Information Protection Commission, PIPC Imposes Fine and Issues Recommendation for Improvement to OpenAI (2023), https://www.pipc.go.kr/np/cop/bbs/selectBoardArticle.do?bbsId=BS074&mCode=C020010000&nttId=9055#LINK [Accessed on June 29, 2025]

16 Hyun-Ah Kim, *Critical Comments on the Provision for Extraterritorial Application among the Amendments to the E-Commerce Act*, Vol. 28 No.1, Korea Private International Law Journal, (2022), pp. 344-345

17 Private International Law, Article 20 (Application of Mandatory Provisions)
Notwithstanding the provisions of this Act, if there exist mandatory provisions under Korean law that must be applied to a certain case, such provisions shall apply.

18 European Data Protection Board, *Guidelines 3/2018 on the Territorial Scope of the GDPR (Article 3)*, EDPB Guidelines, 2018/11.

19 Kwang-Hyun Seok, Extraterritorial Application of the E-Commerce Act and Consumer Protection under Private International Law (2025), https://www.lawtimes.co.kr/news/171144 [Accessed on June 29, 2025]

20 Personal Information Protection Commission, *Guidelines on Applying the Personal Information Protection Act to Foreign Business* Operators, PIPC Guidelines, 2024/04, pp. 20-21.

21 A person whose total sales for the previous year (referring to the previous business year in the case of a corporation) is at least one trillion won. (Article 32-3 (1) of the Enforcement Decree of the PIPA)

22 A person who has an average of at least one million domestic data subjects whose personal information is stored and managed for the immediately preceding three months as of the end of the previous year. (Article 32-3 (1) of the Enforcement Decree of the PIPA)

23 Personal Information Protection Commission, *Guidelines on Applying the Personal Information Protection Act to Foreign Business* Operators, PIPC Guidelines, 2024/04, pp. 37-38.

24 Personal Information Protection Commission, *Guidelines on Applying the Personal Information Protection Act to Foreign Business* Operators, PIPC Guidelines, 2024/04, pp. 17-18.

25 Personal Information Protection Commission, *Guidelines on Applying the Personal Information Protection Act to Foreign Business* Operators, PIPC Guidelines, 2024/04, p.35.

26 Personal Information Protection Commission, *Guidelines on Applying the Personal Information Protection Act to Foreign Business* Operators, PIPC Guidelines, 2024/04, p.30.

27 Personal Information Protection Commission, *Guidelines on Applying the Personal*

Information Protection Act to Foreign Business Operators, PIPC Guidelines, 2024/04, pp. 23-24.

28 Personal Information Protection Commission, *Guidelines on Applying the Personal Information Protection Act to Foreign Business* Operators, PIPC Guidelines, 2024/04, pp. 28.

29 The PIPA stipulates the PIPC's power of inspection and disposition on the PI protection matters: Request for materials (Article11), Notification and reporting of leakage of PI (Article 34), Erasure and blocking of exposed PI (Article 34-2), Presentation of opinions and recommendations for improvement (Article 61), Reporting on infringements (Article 62), Requests for materials and inspections (Article 63), Corrective measures (Article 64), Accusation and recommendation for disciplinary action (Article 65), Publication of results (Article 66).
Additionally, the PIPC has established the "Regulation on Investigation and Disposition by the PIPC", which outlines the procedures and methods of investigation, as well as dispositions based on the investigation results.

30 Personal Information Protection Commission, *Guidelines on Applying the Personal Information Protection Act to Foreign Business* Operators, PIPC Guidelines, 2024/04, pp. 40-42.

31 Haewon Lee, *A Legal Research on the Scope of Application of the Personal Information Protection Act*, Vol.26 No.1, Journal of Information Law, (2022), p. 303.

32 Jong-Soo Yoon, *A Study on the State Jurisdiction and Extraterritorial Application of Domestic Statutes for the Internet Issues*, Vol.39 No.1, Public Law, (2010), p. 42.

33 Haewon Lee, *A Legal Research on the Scope of Application of the Personal Information Protection Act*, Vol. 26 No.1, Journal of Information Law, (2022), p. 303.

RECENT DEVELOPMENTS

The Framework Act on National Heritage and Related Laws

Gyooho LEE
Chung-Ang University School of Law

Abstract

The Framework Act on National Heritage was enacted on May 16, 2024 and has been effective since May 17, 2024. The Act purports to transform the cultural heritage system into a national heritage system by changing and expanding the name of cultural property, which has a strong commodity nature, to 'heritage', which encompasses the past, present, and future, by subdividing it into cultural heritage, natural heritage, and intangible heritage, aligning it with the international standard UNESCO system, and by adopting the term 'national heritage' as a whole. Along with the enactment of the Framework Act on National Heritage, several laws were enacted and/or revised. They include the Act on Preservation and Utilization of Cultural Heritage, the Act on Protection and Inspection of Buried Heritage, the Act on the Safeguarding and Promotion of Intangible Heritage, the Special Act on Conservation, Management and Utilization of World Heritage, and the Act on the Conservation and Utilization of Lighthouse Heritage.

Key Words

Framework Act on National Heritage, national heritage, cultural heritage, Act on Preservation and Utilization of Cultural Heritage, intangible cultural heritage

1. Introduction

The Framework Act on National Heritage was enacted on May 16, 2024 and has been effective since May 17, 2024.[1]

The purpose of this Act is to prescribe basic matters regarding national heritage policies and to clarify the responsibilities of the State and local governments for the preservation, management, and utilization of national heritage, thereby actively protecting and creatively inheriting national heritage and contributing to improvement of the quality of life through the cultural enjoyment of citizens.[2]

The Korea Heritage Service aims to overcome the limitations of cultural property policies that have been in place for more than 60 years since the enactment of the Cultural Property Protection Act in 1962. Hence, the purpose of the Act is to transform the cultural heritage system into a national heritage system by changing and expanding the name of cultural property, which has a strong commodity nature, to 'heritage', which encompasses the past, present, and future, by subdividing it into cultural heritage, natural heritage, and intangible heritage, aligning it with the international standard UNESCO system, and by adopting the term 'national heritage' as a whole.[3]

Along with the enactment of the Framework Act on National Heritage, several laws were enacted and/or revised. They, including the Framework Act on National Heritage, are illustrated as follows.

2. The Framework Act on National Heritage (2023)[4]

Pursuant to Article 3 of the Framework Act on National

Heritage, the term "national heritage" refers to "the artificially or naturally formed national, ethnic, or universal heritage, which is cultural heritage, or intangible heritage of outstanding historic, artistic, academic, or scenic value".[5] In this regard, the term "cultural heritage" means "a product of the Korean history and traditions, which is the tangible cultural heritage indicating the uniqueness of culture, the identity of the people, and changes in the lives of citizens".[6] The term "natural heritage" is defined as "natural objects, such as animals, plants, topography, and geological features, or any cultural heritage created by interactions with the natural environment".[7] The term "intangible heritage" means "intangible cultural heritage, which is inherited over several generations and is constantly recreated by interactions between communities and groups, and history and environment".[8] The enactments of or the amendments to other statutes, regulations, etc., related to national heritage shall conform to the purpose and fundamental concepts of the Framework Act on National Heritage.[9]

The State and local governments shall ensure that the following matters are realized when formulating and implementing policies to protect national heritage: they shall (i) thoroughly secure and pass down the tangible and intangible value of national heritage; (ii) protect national heritage together with the surrounding natural scenery or a space with outstanding historic and cultural values; (iii) enhance the value of national heritage and promote the creation of its new values through proactive disclosure and utilization of national heritage; (iv) enable citizens to actively participate in and enjoy such policies in daily life through easy and diverse methods; (v) promote the sustainability of national heritage by maintaining harmony and balance between preservation and utilization of national heritage and by achieving harmony between the socioeconomic activities of citizens and other policies and policy measures; and (vi) respect the unique history and diversity of a region and contribute to the vitalization of various communities and regional development.[10]

Moreover, the State and local governments shall endeavor to develop professional human resources for specialized management, such as the survey and research on national heritage, or for daily use and participation thereof.[11] The State and local governments shall implement policies to foster local communities to ensure that national heritage can be a source of regional integration and self-respect.[12] The State and local governments shall continuously manage the current status of national heritage not designated or registered, and shall devise measures to systematically protect it.[13] The State and local governments shall endeavor to proactively protect resources that have the potential to be national heritage in the future.[14]

When it comes to climate change, the State and local governments shall continuously survey the impacts of climate change on national heritage and the vulnerability of national heritage consequent thereon in order to manage national heritage safely from the changes in the natural environment, natural disasters, etc., resulting from climate change.[15] The State and local governments shall examine the details of the surveys and devise measures to respond to such examination.[16]

The State and local governments shall provide diverse programs for enjoyment, such as watching, exhibitions, education, and experience of national heritage, in order to guarantee the cultural life of citizens.[17] The State and local governments shall create an environment necessary for all citizens to enjoy the national heritage.[18]

The State and local governments shall devise support and policy measures necessary for vulnerable people whose enjoyment of national heritage is restricted due to physical, economic, and geographical constraints, etc.[19] The State and local governments may produce, collect, and manage national heritage data by applying and integrating intelligent information technology or other technologies.[20] The State and local governments shall endeavor to manage national heritage information, including the establishment and operation of related platforms, to efficiently manage national heritage data and to enhance citizens' access to information.[21]

The State and local governments shall encourage industries that utilize national heritage to create new added value through the development, production, distribution, etc., of content or goods mediated by national heritage.[22] The State and local governments shall promote employment, business start-up, and etc., in order to create jobs through national heritage, and shall endeavor to stabilize the employment of persons engaged in the field of national heritage.[23]

The Administrator of the Korea Heritage Service may file an application with UNESCO for the registration of Korea's outstanding national heritage as World Heritage, Intangible Cultural Heritage of Humanity, or Memory of the World in accordance with the Convention concerning the Protection of the World Cultural and Natural Heritage, the Convention for the Safeguarding of the Intangible Cultural Heritage, or UNESCO's programs. In such cases, the Administrator of the Korea Heritage Service shall determine the procedures, etc., for selecting national heritage to be applied for registration, in consideration of UNESCO's regulations.[24]

The State and local governments shall actively endeavor to preserve heritage of humanity, in addition to national heritage registered as World Heritage, Intangible Cultural Heritage of Humanity, or Memory of the World in UNESCO (hereafter in this Article referred to as "World Heritage, etc".), and to widely publicize national heritage abroad.[25] The State and local governments shall protect the World Heritage to the level equivalent to the State-designated heritage from the date on which they are registered, and the Administrator of the Korea Heritage Service may order a person who conducts any activity that is likely to affect the World Heritage and its historical and cultural environment to take measures necessary for the protection of the World Heritage and its historic and cultural environment, as prescribed by Presidential Decree.[26] December 9 shall be designated as National Heritage Day to improve citizens' understanding of national heritage and to raise their awareness of protecting national heritage.[27]

The matters necessary for the events to be held on the National Heritage Day may be otherwise determined by the Administrator of the Korea Heritage Service or the Special Metropolitan City Mayor, a Metropolitan City Mayor, a Special Self-Governing City Mayor, a Do Governor, or a Special Self-Governing Province Governor.[28]

3. Act on Preservation and Utilization of Cultural Heritage (2024)[29]

With the enactment of the Act on the Preservation and Utilization of Natural Heritage, the provisions concerning the preservation and management of natural monuments and scenic spots have been amended by deleting the provisions concerning natural monuments and scenic spots as they are stipulated in the Act.

In line with the Framework Act on National Heritage, the term 'cultural property' was replaced with the term 'cultural heritage' under the Act on Preservation and Utilization of Cultural Heritage.

4. Act on Protection and Inspection of Buried Heritage (2025)[30]

As the term 'cultural property' was changed to 'heritage' and its general term was changed to 'national heritage' in accordance with the enactment of the Framework Act on National Heritage, the name of the Act was changed to the Act on the Protection and Investigation of Buried Heritage, and 'cultural property' was included in the terms of 'cultural heritage' and 'national heritage' and 'buried cultural property' was changed to 'buried heritage' to align with the framework of the National Heritage Act.[31]

The Act provides a basis for imposing a fine of not more than

5 million Korean won if a construction project implementer fails to submit a ground survey report or submits a false report.

5. Act on the Safeguarding and Promotion of Intangible Heritage (2025)[32]

As the term 'intangible cultural property' was changed to 'intangible heritage' with the enactment of the Framework Act on National Heritage, the name of the Act was changed to the Act on the Safeguarding and Promotion of Intangible Heritage, and the term 'intangible cultural property' was changed to 'intangible heritage' to align with the framework of the Framework Act on National Heritage.[33]

The Act on the Safeguarding and Promotion of Intangible Heritage of 2025 established new disqualifications for national intangible heritage transmitters and provided grounds for criminal background checks to verify them.

6. Act on Preservation and Utilization of Natural Heritage (2024)[34]

The term "natural heritage" means a natural object or cultural heritage created by interactions with the natural environment, which has a great historic, scenic, or academic value and falls under any of the following:

(a) Animals (including their habitats, breeding grounds, and migratory places);
(b) Plants (including their communities);
(c) Topographical, geological, or biological products, or natural phenomena;
(d) Natural reserves;
(e) Natural landscape: A space recognized for aesthetic value as nature itself;

(f) Historic and cultural landscape: A space or living place that shows a balance between the natural environment and social, economic, and cultural factors;

(g) Complex landscape: A space with the humanistic value added to the excellent scenery of nature.[35]

Natural heritage shall be preserved, managed, and utilized according to the following principles:

(i) Artificial interference shall be excluded to the maximum extent, but the unique characteristics of natural heritage, such as natural changes shall be reflected;

(ii) The preservation and management of natural heritage shall be in harmony with the sustainable use thereof;

(iii) The property rights of citizens shall not be excessively restricted.[36]

The head of the Cultural Heritage Administration, which has been referred to as 'the Administrator of Korea Heritage Service' following its enactment, can designate as natural monuments or scenic spots that have high historical, scenic, or academic value and are in need of preservation after deliberation by the Cultural Heritage Committee.[37]

7. Special Act on Conservation, Management and Utilization of World Heritage (2024)[38]

With the enactment of the Framework Act on National Heritage, the term 'cultural property' was changed to 'heritage' and its general name was changed to 'national heritage', and the term 'cultural property' was changed to 'national heritage' or individual heritage names pursuant to the articles of this Act, and the names of the cited laws were changed to the names of individual laws related to heritage.[39]

8. Act on the Conservation and Utilization of Lighthouse Heritage (2024)[40]

"Lighthouse heritage" refers to lighthouses, lighthouse ancillary facilities, lighthouse equipment, supplies, and lighthouse-related records, etc. designated pursuant to Article 6 of this Act because they have historical, artistic, or academic value or because of their beautiful surrounding scenery and therefore require special measures for conservation and utilization (including private navigation marks installed pursuant to Article 9 (6) of the Aids to Navigation Act, and excluding designated cultural heritages related to lighthouses pursuant to Article 2 (3) of the Act on Conservation and Utilization of Cultural Heritage, natural monuments related to lighthouses pursuant to subparagraph 5 of Article 2 of the Act on Conservation and Utilization of Natural Heritage, and registered cultural heritages related to lighthouses pursuant to subparagraph 2 of Article 2 of the Act on the Conservation and Utilization of Modern and Contemporary Cultural Heritage (hereinafter referred to as "designated cultural heritages, etc".)).[41]

9. Author's Comments

I agree with the direction of enacting or amending the National Heritage Act and related laws. However, the issue of compatibility with international treaties that still use the term 'cultural property' needs to be resolved,[42] and the validity of using the concept of 'national heritage' in cases where cultural property is a private one may be questioned.

Notes

1 Act No. 19409, enacted on May 16, 2023 and effective since May 17, 2024..
2 Article 1 of the Framework Act on National Heritage.
3 Korea Heritage Service, Press Release, *National Heritage Agency launches with a future-oriented approach* (17 May, 2024) < https://www.khs.go.kr/newsBbz/selectNewsBbzView.do?newsItemId=155704794&sectionId=b_sec_1&pageIndex=53&pageUnit=10&strWhere=&strValue=&sdate=&edate=&category=&mn=NS_01_02 (last visited on March 23, 2025)>.
4 Act No. 19409, revised on May 16, 2023 and effective since May 17, 2024.
5 Article 3 subparagraph 1 of the Framework Act on National Heritage.
6 Article 3 subparagraph 2 of the Framework Act on National Heritage.
7 Article 3 subparagraph 3 of the Framework Act on National Heritage.
8 Article 3 subparagraph 4 of the Framework Act on National Heritage.
9 Article 6 of the Framework Act on National Heritage.
10 Article 7 of the Framework Act on National Heritage.
11 Article 12 (1) of the Framework Act on National Heritage.
12 Article 12 (2) of the Framework Act on National Heritage.
13 Article 14 (1) of the Framework Act on National Heritage.
14 Article 14 (2) of the Framework Act on National Heritage.
15 Article 22 (1) of the Framework Act on National Heritage.
16 Article 22 (2) of the Framework Act on National Heritage.
17 Article 23 (1) of the Framework Act on National Heritage.
18 Article 23 (2) of the Framework Act on National Heritage.
19 Article 23 (3) of the Framework Act on National Heritage.
20 Article 24 (1) of the Framework Act on National Heritage.
21 Article 24 (2) of the Framework Act on National Heritage.
22 Article 27 (1) of the Framework Act on National Heritage.
23 Article 27 (2) of the Framework Act on National Heritage.
24 Article 31 (1) of the Framework Act on National Heritage.
25 Article 31 (2) of the Framework Act on National Heritage.
26 Article 31 (3) of the Framework Act on National Heritage.
27 Article 34 (1) of the Framework Act on National Heritage.
28 Article 34 (2) of the Framework Act on National Heritage.
29 Act No. 19248, revised on March 21, 2023 and effective since May 17, 2024. The Cultural Property Protection Act was enacted on January 10, 1962 and took effect on the same date. It was renamed as the “Act on Preservation and Utilization of Cultural Heritage (Act No. 19248)”, which was revised on March 21, 2023 and took effect on May 17, 2024.
30 Act No. 20742, revised on January 31, 2025 and effective since August 1, 2025. The Act on Protection and Inspection of Buried Cultural Property (Act No. 10001) was enacted on February 4, 2010 and took effect on February 5, 2011. It was renamed as the “Act on Protection and Inspection of Buried Heritage (Act No. 19587)”, which was revised on August 8, 2023 and took effect on May 17, 2024.
31 Act No. 19587, revised on August 8, 2023 and effective since May 17, 2024.
32 Act No. 20835, revised on March 25, 2025 and effective since September 26, 2025. The Act on the Safeguarding and Promotion of Intangible Cultural Property (Act No. 13248) was enacted on March 27, 2015 and took effect on March 28, 2016. It was renamed as the “Act on the Safeguarding and Promotion of Intangible Heritage (Act No. 19588)”, which was revised on August 8, 2023

and took effect on May 17, 2024.

33 Act No. 19588, revised on August 8, 2023 and effective since May 17, 2024.

34 Act No. 19251, enacted on March 21, 2023 and effective since May 17, 2024. It was revised on February 13, 2024 and took effect on February 14, 2025 in accordance with Act No. 20284.

35 Article 2, subparagraph 1 of the Act on Preservation and Utilization of Natural Heritage.

36 Article 3 of the Act on Preservation and Utilization of Natural Heritage.

37 Articles 11 and 12 of the Act on Preservation and Utilization of Natural Heritage.

38 Act No. 16932, enacted on February 4, 2020 and effective since February 5, 2021. It was revised on February 13, 2024 and took effect on November 1, 2024 in accordance with Act No. 20309.

39 Act No. 19594, revised on August 8, 2023 and effective since May 17, 2024.

40 Act No. 20126, enacted on January 23, 2024 and effective since January 24, 2025.

41 Article 2, subparagraph 1 of the Act on the Conservation and Utilization of Lighthouse Heritage.

42 Kwang Hyun Suk, *Consistency between the National Heritage Law Regime Implemented in 2024 and the UNESCO System-Focusing on the Concepts of National Heritage, World Heritage, Cultural Heritage, Natural Heritage, and Intangible Heritage*, Korean Journal of International Trade and Business Law, Vol. 33, No. 1, p. 213.

The Possibility of the 2028 Termination of the Korea-Japan Joint Development Agreement on the Continental Shelf and Anticipated Consequences

Minjung CHUNG
Legislative Research Officer
National Assembly Legislative Research Service, Seoul, Republic of Korea

Abstract

The JDZ Agreement, which was concluded between Korea and Japan in 1974 and entered into force in 1978, has been suspended since 1985, and it may be terminated in 2028. However, boundary delimitation based on the median line, which Japan advocates, is unlikely to be immediately applied after the termination of the Agreement. Furthermore, the possibility of dispute regarding the resources among Korea, Japan, and China regarding the Korea-Japan JDZ is an incentive for the concerned parties to maintain the status quo. Therefore, Korea still has an opportunity to take the lead regarding the handling of Agreement-related matters and charter the future of the East China Sea.

As of now, the rational choice between the two countries is to maintain the effect of the agreement even after 2028 and establish a cooperative system that enables practical exploration and development of the continental shelf. To this end, this article is suggesting that if the two governments cannot reach an agreement, either party should be allowed to conduct independent exploration and development or that both parties should establish a separate joint project organization independent of the two governments.

Key Words

Joint Development Zone (JDZ), Continental Shelf, Natural Prolongation, International Court of Justice (ICJ), East China Sea, Block 7, Okinawa Trough

1. Introduction

In 1974, the natural prolongation principle was the prevailing principle in international law regarding the delimitation of the continental shelf. The Agreement between the Republic of Korea and Japan Concerning the Joint Development of the Southern Part of the Continental Shelf adjacent to the Two Countries, signed on January 30, 1974 ("JDZ Agreement" where JDZ means Korea–Japan Joint Development Zone), is relatively favorable to the Republic of Korea ("Korea") because it was concluded based on the natural prolongation principle. However, owing to the International Court of Justice's ("ICJ") application of the equidistance principle rather than the natural prolongation principle, rulings subsequently shifted in a direction unfavorable to South Korea, and this has allowed Japan to suspend joint development activities in the JDZ.

The JDZ Agreement stipulates that either Korea or Japan may unilaterally notify the other party of its intention to terminate the Agreement at any point beginning in the year 2025, and termination will take effect three years later, that is, in 2028 (if notice is given in 2025). This possibility has raised concerns that Japan may terminate the Agreement in 2025. The most foreseeable scenario at present is that after June 2025, Japan will issue a termination notice, which will lead to the establishment of a boundary line on the continental shelf between Korea and Japan based on the so-called

Second Korea–Japan Fisheries Agreement. Thereafter, the delimitation of the continental shelf in the East China Sea can proceed between China and Japan to the exclusion of South Korea.

However, criticisms arose regarding the primacy of the distance criterion, and these criticisms render premature the conclusion that South Korea has no continental shelf rights beyond 200 nautical miles into the East China Sea. Furthermore, some scholars predict the termination of the Agreement could ignite resource disputes among South Korea, China, and Japan regarding certain waters in the JDZ where resource deposit potential and project profitability are known to be high. Japan must be cautious about this implication since it already has territorial disputes in the East China Sea regarding the Senkaku Islands/Diaoyu Islands issue. These factors mean that Korea has variables that it can manage in relation to the future of the JDZ Agreement and the matter of the continental shelf in the East China Sea.

This article examines the Korea–Japan JDZ Agreement regarding the continental shelf. Specifically, the article projects the implications of the termination of the Agreement for matters in the East China Sea and discusses the challenges Korea will face should it attempt to maintain the Agreement.

2. Content of and Problems with the JDZ Agreement

2-1. Background of the JDZ Agreement

The Emery Report, released in 1968, suggested that the continental shelf of the Yellow Sea and the East China Sea contained abundant petroleum reserves. This prompted coastal states to hurriedly designate exploration blocks according to their respective domestic laws. Following the ICJ's 1969 *North Sea Continental Shelf* judgment,[1] Korea declared Block 7 in 1970 and subsequently signed the JDZ Agreement in 1974. This was an encouraging outcome for Korea in terms of effectively interpreting and leveraging the trends of international law.

The 1958 Convention on the Continental Shelf,[2] the first multilateral treaty on the continental shelf, adopted the equidistance/median line principle for maritime boundary delimitation. However, the ICJ's 1969 North Sea continental shelf judgment defined the concept of the continental shelf based on natural prolongation and introduced the equity principle for boundary delimitation.[3] Korea based its decision to establish Block 7 in the direction of the East China Sea on this ruling and on the geographical fact that the continental shelf extends to the Okinawa Trough.[4] Japan, which had been adhering to the median line principle, responded by requesting negotiations with Korea regarding the continental shelf. These negotiations led to the signing of the JDZ Agreement between the two countries in 1974.

2-2. Content of the JDZ Agreement

The preamble of the JDZ Agreement stipulates that the joint development of marine resources is a common benefit and that the purpose and intent of the Agreement serve the ultimate practical resolution of resource development issues. Article 2 of the Agreement designates the waters south of Jeju Island (i.e., the entire area of Block 7 and parts of Blocks 4, 5, and 6-2) as the JDZ, an area where the continental shelf claims of Korea and Japan overlap. This designation reflects full acceptance of Korea's claim that the continental shelf naturally extends to the Okinawa Trough and is skewed towards Japan's side of the median line between Korea and Japan.

Therefore, the Agreement requires both parties to jointly consult and decide on all matters related to exploration and development in the JDZ. Because of this requirement, one party may frustrate the other by adopting a passive attitude regarding joint exploration and development. For example, under the Agreement, if one party refuses to designate a mining concession holder, no operating contract can be concluded, and consequently, the other party cannot engage in substantial exploration or development.

The parties to the Agreement have established the Korea–Japan Joint Commission to facilitate consultations on matters concerning the implementation of the Agreement (Art. 24(1)). The Joint Commission comprises two individuals appointed by government agencies representing the respective parties (Art. 24(2)) and its structure is designed to prevent decision-making by majority vote. Consequently, the Commission has the limitation of ceasing to function if one of the parties takes a passive stance. The Joint Commission has not been convened since 1985.[5] The year 1985 was the year of the ICJ's *Libya-Malta* judgment,[6] which proposed the primacy of the distance criterion regarding the delimitation of the continental shelf. Interested parties suspect that Japan deliberately avoided convening the Joint Commission. They also speculate that the 1985 *Libya-Malta* Judgment played a role in weakening the momentum of the Agreement.[7]

2-3. Implementation and Operational Problems

Since the conclusion of the Agreement, joint development under the Agreement has been at a standstill due to Japan's passive attitude following a shift in international law that has been unfavorable for Korea. The significance of the 1969 ICJ judgment that acknowledged the existence of the continental shelf based on natural prolongation within 200 nautical miles gradually faded, and converse international case law favoring the approach that continental shelf boundary delimitation in areas where the distance between opposing coasts is less than 400 nautical miles should follow the median line began to accumulate. For example, the ICJ's 1985 *Libya-Malta* judgment delineated the continental shelf boundary based on the median line, and the Court did not consider the geological and geomorphological characteristics of the seabed.[8] Thirty-eight years later, the ICJ, in its 2023 *Nicaragua-Colombia* judgment,[9] ruled that a coastal state's continental shelf rights cannot extend into another country's 200 nautical miles of continental shelf and cannot be naturally prolonged. These two ICJ judgments may indicate that Korea cannot naturally extend its continental shelf beyond 200 nautical miles into Japan's 200 nautical miles. Hence, these judgments provide Japan with a legal basis to fully protect its continental shelf within 200 nautical miles.

3. Potential Termination of the JDZ Agreement

3-1. Prospects for the East China Sea After the Termination of the Agreement

If the Agreement is terminated, Korea will have almost no areas in the current Korea–Japan JDZ where it can independently develop the continental shelf. The United Nations Convention on the Law of the Sea ("UNCLOS") obligates its member States "to make every effort to enter into provisional arrangements of a practical nature" and to refrain from "jeopardiz [ing] or hamper[ing] the reaching of the final agreement".[10] The ruling of the arbitral tribunal constituted under Annex VII of UNCLOS deemed the act of undertaking unilateral test drilling in areas where a boundary has not been delimited as a violation of these obligations because drilling could cause permanent physical impacts in the marine environment.[11]

Although the possibility of Korea's independent development is very low after the termination of the Agreement, the likelihood of conflicts among Korea, China, and Japan remains high. The East China Sea is an area of overlap not only for Korea's and Japan's continental shelf claims but also for China's. In fact, China argues that the part of the JDZ Agreement that regulates the Chinese continental shelf is invalid in the context of the negotiations on the delimitation of the maritime boundary between Korea and China.[12] However, if termination of the Agreement leads to the reversion of the area to an undelimited zone, indiscriminate Chinese and Japanese development activity may proliferate. Another possibility is that China, which has taken the lead in the current situation, could start acting unilaterally.

3-2. Advantages of Maintaining the Status Quo

The prevailing expectation for the domestic realm is that after the Agreement expires, the Japanese government will invoke the median line principle as a basis to seek to assert jurisdiction over most of the JDZ. For example, Park Hee-kwon, a former chief negotiator for Korea in the Korea–Japan maritime boundary delimitation negotiations, stated, based on his conversations with Japanese representatives, that Japan's approach is to enforce its jurisdiction over most of the JDZ following the expiration of the Agreement in accordance with the amended delimitation rules.[13] According to this view, once Japan becomes eligible to notify the termination of the Agreement in June 2025, the issue of continental shelf boundary delimitation between Korea and Japan will rapidly emerge as one of the most critical matters in Korea's diplomacy towards Japan.

However, considering the instability that may arise from the cessation of negotiations, Japan also has an incentive to maintain the status quo rather than ending the Agreement. Maintaining the Agreement for the time being would be advantageous for restraining not only Korea's but also China's unilateral resource exploration activities. China opposes the Japan–South Korea continental shelf joint development system, but the country has not yet conducted independent exploration or development in the Korea–Japan JDZ. This indicates that the Agreement effectively restrains China from penetrating the Korea–Japan JDZ. If the Agreement ends, the Korea–Japan JDZ will become a resource development battleground, contentiously populated by Korea, China, and Japan, particularly around subzones 2 and 4, which are considered to have high resource potential. The possibility of China attempting unilateral development in subzone 4, which is adjacent to its Longjing oil and gas development area, remains particularly high.

Above all, the Agreement can be seen as an alliance between Korea and Japan that counters China's expansion into the East China Sea amid the US–China maritime hegemony competition. In this regard, Yang Hee Cheol, Director of the Korea Institute of Ocean Science and Technology, argues that the most realistic alternative at this point is not to amend the Agreement but rather to derive a new implementation agreement within the current framework. Moreover, Professor Kim Suk Kyoon of Hanseo University, who is also the former commissioner general of the Korea Coast Guard, recommends for the necessity of negotiation between the two States for the extension of the Agreement.[14]

4. Anticipated Challenges

Given the difficulties to reach a final agreement on the continental shelf boundary delimitation, as well as the conflicts regarding resources and the instability that will likely arise in East Asia after the termination of the JDZ Agreement, the desirable course of action is for Korea and Japan to work towards establishing a stable cooperation system for the joint development of the continental shelf through negotiation. In this regard, Korea should emphasize to Japan that maintaining the status quo is in its best interest, especially given the concerns about China's involvement, and that continuity would also improve the operational framework of the Agreement to enable real joint development in the JDZ.

4-1. Maintaining the Current Korea-Japan JDZ

The most important and challenging task related to establishing a sustainable cooperation system for the joint development of the continental shelf between Korea and Japan is maintaining and continuing the current JDZ Agreement.[15] This is because Korea will seek to maintain the current marine area, while Japan will aim to reduce the area in the direction of the Korea–Japan median line. Maintaining the JDZ may conflict with Japan's previous position on delimitation, but legally, it would not unacceptably burden Japan. According to UNCLOS, provisional arrangements do not affect the final delimitation (Art. 74(3); Art. 83(3)). Furthermore, Article 28 of the JDZ Agreement stipulates that nothing in the Agreement shall be regarded as determining the question of sovereign rights over all or any portion of the JDZ or as prejudicing the positions of the respective parties with respect to the delimitation of the continental shelf. Thus, Japan may divest itself of any concern that the JDZ will play a certain role in the final delimitation.

Since ICJ rulings have become unfavorable towards Korea as of the conclusion of the JDZ Agreement, Korea could, to maintain the current marine area, consider offering Japan the revenue from more distant subzones or from those with higher potential for resource deposits as a trade-off, which could be achieved by structuring the revenue shares by subzone.[16] As the current JDZ Agreement does not accommodate expert determination of a means to fairly distribute revenue between the two countries, the two States could refer to the

Agreement Concerning Transboundary Hydrocarbon Reservoirs in the Gulf of Mexico,[17] which the United States and Mexico signed in 2012,[18] as a reference to revise the JDZ Agreement. An alternative to stipulating revenue distribution in the treaty is employing an expert determination system to fairly and equitably allocate revenue and acknowledging the legal enforceability of the system (2012 US–Mexico Agreement, Art. 16(9)).

4-2. Improving the Operational System of the JDZ Agreement

The national practices enshrined in the JDZ Agreement can be categorized into three types depending on the party responsible for operations: (1) the single state authority model where one country leads exploration and development and the other participates in profit-sharing, (2) the compulsory joint venture model where exploration and development can proceed only jointly with the involvement of the concerned parties, and (3) the joint authority model where an independent authority jointly established by the concerned parties conducts exploration and development.[19] The current JDZ Agreement is classified under the compulsory joint venture model.[20]

Since the JDZ Agreement has an operational system where both parties jointly decide and implement all matters concerning exploration and development in the Korea–Japan JDZ, if one party is passive regarding joint exploration and development, the attempts of the other party will inevitably be frustrated. If the Agreement is extended beyond 2028, a design that prevents the misuse of the Agreement to freeze resource development will be necessary. The new design should facilitate real exploration and development.[21]

As previously mentioned, the 2012 US–Mexico Agreement is a potential reference for the parties undertaking the redesign. They can consider stipulating a provision that allows for unilateral exploration and development in cases where the Joint Commission fails to reach an agreement. In such cases, under the 2012 US–Mexico Agreement, the United States and Mexico may unilaterally permit their respective mining concession holders to proceed with the development of oil and gas fields (Art. 7(5)). The resulting profits are shared jointly, and the non-participating party bears only minimal costs. Another option for the redesign of the operational system of the JDZ Agreement is transitioning from the current compulsory joint venture model to a joint authority model. A joint implementation authority can be established separately from the parties and can therefore independently conduct exploration and development.[22]

5. Conclusion

The JDZ Agreement, which was concluded in 1974 and entered into force in 1978, has been suspended since 1985, and it may be terminated in 2028. However, boundary delimitation based on the median line, which Japan advocates, is unlikely to be immediately applied after the termination of the Agreement. Furthermore, the possibility of dispute regarding the resources among Korea, Japan, and China regarding the Korea–Japan JDZ is an incentive for the concerned parties to maintain the status quo. Therefore, Korea still has an opportunity to take the lead regarding the handling of Agreement-related matters and charter the future of the East China Sea.

At this point, the rational choice for both Korea and Japan is to maintain the current JDZ, as per the existing Agreement, after 2028 and establish a cooperation system that allows for real exploration and development of the continental shelf. South Korea could also consider offering Japan the revenue from more distant subzones or from those with higher potential for resource deposits as a trade-off in return for maintaining the current JDZ. This would entail structuring the revenue shares by subzone.

Moreover, the operational system of the Agreement is in urgent need of a revision that will transform it into one that allows for actual resource development. The redesigned system could, for example, allow either Korea or Japan, in the event that the two governments fail to reach an agreement, to conduct exploration and development independently. Alternatively, a revised system could establish a separate joint authority that is independent of both governments.

References

1. Articles

Kim, J., "Scope and Limitations of Exercising Jurisdiction in Areas of Overlapping Maritime Claims between Korea and Japan", 20, *Japan Space*, (2016), pp.151-177.

Kim, J., "International Legal Regime on Joint Development of Offshore Oil and Gas in Areas of Overlapping Claims: Reconsideration of the Korea-Japan Joint Development Agreement", 60(2), *Korean Journal of International Law*, (2015), pp.67-98.

Kim, M., "Revisiting the ICJ's 1985 Libya/Malta case and the Primacy of the Distance Criterion under the Continental Shelf Regime: Implications and Prospects for the 1974 Korea–Japan Joint Development Agreement and the East China Sea", 65, *Korea International Law Review*, (2023), pp.37-77.

Lee, S., "A Legal Study on Joint Development of Shared Marine Resources", 56(2), *Pusan National University Law Studies*, (2015), pp.93-127.

Yiallourides, Constantinos, "Joint Development of Seabed Resources in Areas of Overlapping Maritime Claims in Areas of Overlapping Maritime Claims: An Analysis of Precedents in State Practice", 31, *U.S.F. Maritime Law Journal*, (2018-2019), pp.129-174.

2. Articles in Collections

Kim, M., "Will the Japan–South Korea Joint Development Agreement on the Continental Shelf Be Sustainable after 2028?" in *Reading the World through International Law*, 229 (Korean Society of International Law ed., Parkyoungsa, 2020).

3. Newspaper Articles

Park, H., *[Editorial] The Termination of the Korea-Japan Continental Shelf Agreement: Urgent Need for a Response Strategy*, Korea Economic Daily, February 2, 2022.

4. Working Papers and Reports

KEEI, Agreement between the United States of America and the United Mexican States Concerning Transboundary Hydrocarbon Reservoirs in the Gulf of Mexico, World Energy Market Insight, 2013/17.

National Assembly Research Service, Implementation and Sustainability Plans for the Japan–South Korea Joint Development Agreement on the Continental Shelf, Expert Colloquium, October 14, 2022.

5. Arbitral Awards & ICJ Judgments

Continental Shelf (Libyan Arab Jarnahiriya/Malta), Judgment, I. C.J. Reports 1985.

In the Matter of an Arbitration between Guyana and Suriname, Award of the Arbitral Tribunal (The Hague, 17 September 2007).

North Sea Continental Shelf (Fed. Repub. Ger. v. Den. & Neth.), Judgment, I.C.J. Reports 1969.

Question of the Delimitation of the Continental Shelf between Nicaragua and Colombia beyond 200 Nautical Miles from the Nicaraguan Coast (Nicaragua v. Colombia), Judgment, I.C.J. Reports 2023.

6. Press Release

Ministry of Foreign Affairs, "The 6th Japan–Republic of Korea Joint Commission on the JDZ Agreement Held", Press Release, September 27, 2024.

Notes

1 *North Sea Continental Shelf (Fed. Repub. Ger. v. Den. & Neth.), Judgment, I.C.J. Reports 1969* (hereinafter referred to as the "North Sea continental shelf judgment").
2 Convention on the Continental Shelf, signed on April 29, 1958, 15 UST 471, 499 UNTS 311.
3 North Sea continental shelf judgment, para. 85.
4 Enforcement Decree of the Submarine Mineral Resources Development Act (before amendment by Presidential Decree No. 8885 on May 30, 1970) Appendix.
5 The 6th Japan-Republic of Korea Joint Commission was held on September 27, 2024, marking the first meeting in approximately 40 years, since 1985. Ministry of Foreign Affairs, "The 6th Japan-Republic of Korea Joint Commission on the JDZ Agreement Held", Press Release, September 27, 2024.
6 *Continental Shelf (Libyan Arab Jamahiriya/Malta), Judgment, I. C.J. Reports 1985* (hereinafter referred to as the "Libya-Malta judgment").
7 M. Kim, "Revisiting the ICJ's 1985 Libya/Malta case and the Primacy of the Distance Criterion under the Continental Shelf Regime: Implications and Prospects for the 1974 Korea-Japan Joint Development Agreement and the East China Sea", 65, *Korea International Law Review*, (2023), p.62.
8 Libya-Malta judgment, p.13, para. 77.
9 *Question of the Delimitation of the Continental Shelf between Nicaragua and Colombia beyond 200 Nautical Miles from the Nicaraguan Coast (Nicaragua v. Colombia), Judgment, I.C.J. Reports 2023.*
10 Art. 83, para. 3 of UNCLOS.
11 *In the Matter of an Arbitration between Guyana and Suriname, Award of the Arbitral Tribunal (The Hague, 17 September 2007)*, para. 470.
12 J. Kim, "Scope and Limitations of Exercising Jurisdiction in Areas of Overlapping Maritime Claims between Korea and Japan", 20, *Japan Space*, (2016), p.171.
13 H. Park, *[Editorial] The Termination of the Korea-Japan Continental Shelf Agreement: Urgent Need for a Response Strategy*, Korea Economic Daily, February 2, 2022.
14 National Assembly Research Service, *Implementation and Sustainability Plans for the Japan-South Korea Joint Development Agreement on the Continental Shelf*, Expert Colloquium, October 14, 2022.
15 Some hold the view that the current JDZ should be adjusted to incorporate a focus on securing marine areas that show a high potential for resource deposits; this would be a departure from solely considering area size. However, the public generally views the sea as an area where territorial sovereignty applies, much as it does on land. Even if resources have not yet been discovered, they place significant weight on the potential for both resource deposits and future profits. Thus, a significant political fallout is expected if the area is altered to Japan's advantage.
16 M. Kim, "Will the Japan-South Korea Joint Development Agreement on the Continental Shelf Be Sustainable after 2028?" in *Reading the World through International Law*, (Korean Society of International Law ed., Parkyoungsa, 2020), p.238.
17 Agreement Concerning Transboundary Hydrocarbon Reservoirs in the Gulf of

Mexico, U.S.-Mex., 2012.2.20., T.I.A.S. No.14-0718 (hereinafter referred to as the "2012 US-Mexico Agreement").

18 KEEI, Agreement between the United States of America and the United Mexican States Concerning Transboundary Hydrocarbon Reservoirs in the Gulf of Mexico, World Energy Market Insight, 2013/17, pp.10-11.

19 Constantinos Yiallourides, "Joint Development of Seabed Resources in Areas of Overlapping Maritime Claims in Areas of Overlapping Maritime Claims: An Analysis of Precedents in State Practice", 31, U.S.F. Maritime Law Journal, (2018-2019), pp.155-173.

20 Ibid., pp.169-171.

21 S. Lee, "A Legal Study on Joint Development of Shared Marine Resources", 56(2), *Pusan National University Law Studies*, (2015), p.117.

22 J. Kim, "International Legal Regime on Joint Development of Offshore Oil and Gas in Areas of Overlapping Claims: Reconsideration of the Korea-Japan Joint Development Agreement", 60(2), *Korean Journal of International Law*, (2015), p.93.

CONTEMPORARY PRACTICE AND JUDICIAL DECISIONS

Resolutions Relating to International Law Adopted by the National Assembly in 2024

Minjung CHUNG
Legislative Research Officer
National Assembly Legislative Research Service, Seoul, Republic of Korea

Abstract

As of December 31, 2024, two resolutions related to international law were adopted at the plenary session by the National Assembly in 2024. One of the characteristics of the 2024 National Assembly resolutions related to international law is a significant decrease in quantity. In 2024, there were two resolutions, compared to fourteen in 2023. Both resolutions of 2024 were cases related to condemning Japan, which Korea has historically been at odds with, and calling for Japan to correct some of its behaviors.

Key Words

Resolutions, International Law, National Assembly, Foreign Policy, Parliamentary Diplomacy, Fukushima Daiichi Nuclear Power Plant, Sado Gold Mine, World Heritage List, UNESCO

The National Assembly of the Republic of Korea ("Korea") gathers and expresses its positions regarding the government's foreign policy in the form of resolutions. Such resolutions commonly urge the Korean government, foreign governments, and the international community to implement specific measures related to Korea. To facilitate international cooperation, the resolutions use commonly accepted international communication channels, including international agreements, charters, and etc. Resolutions can be viewed as an effective tool by which the constitutional authority of the National Assembly can be protected while also guaranteeing a domestic democratic process. Given the growing importance of public diplomacy, the role of the National Assembly as a flexible form of diplomacy is also growing, and greater weight is expected to be placed on the National Assembly's resolutions.

While diplomacy, in principle, is conducted exclusively by the administration as a part of the executive power, it is becoming increasingly challenging for the administration to handle all diplomatic activities in today's diplomacy, as diplomatic issues are becoming more diverse and complex. Considering the broad scope of exchanges between countries and the transboundary nature of current issues, parliamentary diplomacy may contribute to widening the exchanges led by the administration and offer some support to resolve issues when government-driven exchanges do not work as intended. This is why parliamentary diplomacy is becoming increasingly useful and necessary in today's diplomacy.

As of December 31, 2024, two resolutions related to international law were adopted at the plenary session by the National Assembly in 2024 (Table 1). One of the characteristics of the 2024 National Assembly resolutions related to international law is a significant decrease in quantity. In 2024, there were two resolutions, compared to fourteen in 2023. Both resolutions of 2024 were cases related to condemning Japan, which Korea has historically been at odds with, and calling for Japan to correct some of its behaviors.

In 2025, it is expected that the Korean National Assembly will identify a number of agendas that reflect the universal perspective of international law such as the promotion of international peace, global environment, global economic order, and democracy, and adopt resolutions related to them. Hopefully, the National Assembly will serve as a bridge in relations between Korea and Japan by reminding the people about the strategic value and potential of the relations.

Table 1. Resolutions Related to International Law Adopted by the National Assembly in 2024

(As of December 31, 2024)

Bill Number	Bill Name	Committee responsible	Date of Adoption at the Plenary Session
2203319	Resolution Calling on the Japanese Government to Desist from Dumping Contaminated Water from the Fukushima Daiichi Nuclear Power Plant into the Ocean to Protect People and Fisheries and the Korean Government to Respond One Year Later	Agriculture, Food, Rural Affairs, Oceans and Fisheries Committee	September 25, 2024
2200467	Resolution Calling on the Japanese Government to Withdraw Its Reapplication for the Inscription of Sado Gold Mine on the World Heritage List and Implement UNESCO's Recommendations for Modern Industrial Facilities in Japan	Culture, Sports and Tourism Committee	June 18, 2024

Source: National Assembly Bill Information System (last accessed on February 24, 2025), http://likms.assembly.go.kr/bill/BillSearchResult.do.

1. Resolution Calling on the Japanese Government to Desist from Dumping Contaminated Radioactive Water from the Fukushima Daiichi Nuclear Power Plant into the Ocean to Protect People and Fisheries and the Korean Government to Respond One Year Later

On April 13, 2021, the Japanese government set forth a basic policy on releasing contaminated radioactive water stored at the Fukushima Daiichi Nuclear Power Plant. On August 24, 2023, the Japanese government began releasing contaminated radioactive water into the ocean. By the end of August 2024, a year later, Japan had released approximately 62,600 m^3 of contaminated radioactive water into the ocean in integrals (over a total of eight times). Japan is expected to continue releasing contaminated radioactive water into the ocean for the next 30 years.

In late June 2023, the International Atomic Energy Agency ("IAEA") published its final report, which claimed that Japan's measures had met international standards and that the impact of its actions on people and the environment was negligible. The Korean National Assembly has asserted that this claim fails to reflect the concerns that neighboring countries, including Korea, have raised in relation to the release of the water. Specifically, the report has inadequately addressed the long-term effects of Japan's release of contaminated radioactive water on the marine ecosystem and human health. Furthermore, the National Assembly has voiced suspicion that knowledge of this shortfall was the basis of IAEA's refusal to bear any responsibility for the content of the report. Nevertheless, Japan has appropriated the report as a key basis for its decision to release contaminated radioactive water into the ocean rather than releasing it into the air or burying it underground.

In response, the National Assembly adopted a resolution on September 25, 2024, that called on the IAEA to conduct a responsible marine survey in cooperation with marine environmental research organizations in neighboring countries, including Korea, as well as in island countries in the South Pacific region. Moreover, the National Assembly has urged the Japanese government to desist from dumping contaminated radioactive water into the ocean and to objectively verify the impact of such dumping on the marine ecosystem and human health.

Additionally, the National Assembly urged the Korean government to broaden the range of nuclides that radiation tests currently cover and to expand the radiation testing equipment used on seafood distributed via auction markets. This advice was intended to protect the safety of Korean waters and fisheries to alleviate anxiety among the people. Furthermore, the National Assembly has petitioned the Korean government to raise the issue of Japan's release of contaminated radioactive water into the ocean in the international community through the London Convention / Protocol and the Conference of the Parties or with the International Maritime Organization ("IMO").

2. Resolution Calling on the Japanese Government to Withdraw Its Reapplication for the Inscription of the Sado Gold Mine on the World Heritage List and Implement UNESCO's Recommendations for Modern Industrial Facilities in Japan

When a country's facilities are inscribed on the World Heritage List, it increases the country's cultural pride. Japan is trying to apply for the inscription of its modern Meiji industrial facilities, including the Sado Gold Mine, on the World Heritage List. These facilities, however, are the site of horrific human rights violations. During World War II, the Japanese government and corporations mobilized hundreds of thousands of Koreans, prisoners of war from Allied forces, Chinese people, and Southeast Asians into harsh forced labor at this site in violation of international law. The National Assembly is deeply concerned about Japan's efforts to inscribe such a site on the World Heritage List.

In 2015, the UNESCO World Heritage Committee ("Committee") already decided to inscribe other Japanese Meiji modern industrial facilities, such as the site of forced labor against Korean victims during the Japanese occupation, on the World Heritage List. At that time, the Committee recommended that Japan provide a commentary to visitors to understand the full historical context of the facilities, and Japan promised to follow the recommendation, which it has not yet done properly.

In July 2015, the 39th session of the Committee decided to inscribe 23 Meiji modern business facilities in Japan on the World Heritage List, including seven facilities where tens of thousands of Koreans were forced into labor during World War II, such as the Hashima (Gunkanjima) Coal Mine, Miike Coal Mine, Takashima Coal Mine, Yahata Steel Works, and three facilities in Mitsubishi Shipyard, and recommended that Japan develop an interpretive strategy to help visitors understand the full historical context of the facilities. In response to the recommendation, Kuni Sato, Permanent Delegate of Japan to UNESCO, said that Japan will set up an information center to inform visitors of the fact that many Koreans were forced into labor against their will under harsh conditions at some of the facilities in the 1940s and take appropriate measures to honor the victims to fully implement the Committee's recommendation. This statement by the Japanese delegate was included in the Committee's inscription decision (WHC Decision 39 COM 8B.14).

The subsequent progress report submitted by the Japanese government, however, did not include any information on measures to inform forced labor or honor the victims. In addition, an exhibition at the Japan Industrial Heritage Information Center in Tokyo, which was made public on June 15, 2020, did not include any measures to honor the victims of forced labor, and only offered testimonies and documents denying that Koreans were forced to labor. Japan continued to hide or cover up the forced labor of Koreans in its modern industrial facilities, and applied such sites, such as the Sado Gold Mine, on the World Heritage List in 2022. After Japan's application in 2022 was rejected for a lack of documentation, Japan filed a reapplication in January 2023.

On July 25, 2024, the National Assembly adopted a resolution calling on the Japanese government to reflect on and take responsibility for what it did in its war of aggression and withdraw its application for the UNESCO inscription of the Sado Gold Mine. The National Assembly noted that Japan's push for the inscription of Meiji modern industrial facilities on the World Heritage List while hiding the fact that the facilities were a site of forced labor directly runs counter to universal human rights norms, such as the United Nations Charter and the International Labour Organization Conventions, and international criminal law, which punishes war crimes and crimes against humanity. Appealing to international law and the universal values and conscience of humanity, the National Assembly made a resolution on the following three points: First, the National Assembly called on the Japanese government to withdraw its application for the inscription of the Sado Gold Mine on the World Heritage List. Second, the National Assembly urged the Japanese government to fully implement the Committee's recommendation and follow-up measures, which it promised to do, regarding the decision to inscribe Sites of Japan's Meiji Industrial Revolution (Iron and Steel, Shipbuilding and Coal Mining) on the World Heritage List. Finally, the National Assembly called on the Korean government to actively respond so that UNESCO would refuse to inscribe the Sado Gold Mine on the World Heritage List.

Judicial Decisions in Public International Law (2024)

Eungi HONG
Presiding Judge
Gwangju District Court (Gwangju, Korea)

Abstract

This article examines three landmark decisions rendered in 2024 in which principles of public international law were mentioned to resolve core legal issues. In the first case, the Supreme Court held that the exclusion of a same-sex partner from dependent status under the National Health Insurance system constituted unconstitutional discrimination. A concurring opinion explicitly invoked the principles of equality under international human rights treaties such as the ICCPR and ICESCR, as well as relevant foreign jurisprudence. In the second case, the Constitutional Court ruled that the legislature's failure to set interim greenhouse gas reduction targets for the period 2031 to 2049 under the Framework Act on Carbon Neutrality and Green Growth for Coping with Climate Crisis violated the State's constitutional obligation to protect environmental rights. The Court took into account the principle of progression enshrined in Article 4 of the Paris Agreement as a relevant international standard in assessing the scope of the State's constitutional obligations. In the third case, the Supreme Court recognized state liability for failing to revise administrative regulations that had long excluded persons with disabilities from access to convenience store facilities. The Court referred to the CRPD to interpret the content of the State's duty, and considered the recommendations of the UN Committee on the Rights of Persons with Disabilities in evaluating whether public officials had acted with negligence. These decisions demonstrate that the Korean judiciary is making efforts to harmonize international law with domestic law by utilizing international treaties and interpretations of international bodies as tools in the decision-making process.

Key Words

Principle of Equality, Environmental Right, Principle of the Prohibition of Insufficient Protection, Nationally Determine Contributions, Principle of Progression, United Nations Convention on the Rights of Persons with Disabilities

Supreme Court of Korea No. 2023DU36800 (En Banc Judgment) Rendered on July 18, 2024

Main Issue

The Defendant (National Health Insurance Service) grants dependent status to the spouse of an employee insured under the National Health Insurance, thereby allowing the spouse to receive health insurance coverage based on the insurance contributions paid by the insured employee without having to pay separate contributions, and includes within the term "spouse" a person in a *de facto* marital relationship, granting dependent status to such person as well.

In this case, the Defendant excluded the Plaintiff, a same-sex partner in a *de facto* marital relationship, from the category of "spouse" and did not grant dependent status. The issue is whether such disposition constitutes unlawful discrimination against same-sex partners as compared to opposite-sex partners, thereby violating the constitutional principle of equality.

Facts

1. The Plaintiff began a relationship with K, a person of the same sex, in 2013, and the two agreed to live together as partners. They held a wedding ceremony in 2019, inviting both families and friends.
2. K, the partner of the Plaintiff, became employed in 2016 and acquired the status of an insured employee under the National Health Insurance.[1]
3. In 2020, K filed a report with the Defendant for the Plaintiff to acquire dependent status. The Defendant registered the Plaintiff in its electronic system as having acquired dependent status on February 26, 2020. The Plaintiff subsequently received insurance benefits under such status.
4. On October 23, 2020, the media reported that the Plaintiff had been registered as a dependent of his same-sex partner K under the National Health Insurance. That same day, an officer of the Defendant terminated the Plaintiff's dependent status. On the basis that the Plaintiff should instead be classified as an insured self-employed under the National Health Insurance, the Defendant issued a notice to the Plaintiff on November 23, 2020, demanding the payment of insurance contributions (hereinafter "the Disposition").
5. The Plaintiff filed this lawsuit, seeking revocation of the Disposition, asserting that it is unlawful.

Reasoning

[Majority Opinion]

1. The National Health Insurance and the Dependent Coverage System

The national health insurance system under the National Health Insurance Act is a form of social security established by the State to fulfill its constitutional duty to protect the health of the people, and it constitutes the fundamental social safety net. The National Health Insurance Act mandates universal enrollment, sets insurance contributions proportionally to the economic capacity of the insured, and does not provide insurance benefits in proportion to the amount of contributions paid by the insured.

All citizens residing in the Republic of Korea become either insured persons or dependents under the national health insurance system. The dependent coverage system is a social security mechanism that allows individuals who primarily rely on an insured employee for their livelihood and lack the financial capacity to pay insurance contributions themselves to receive health insurance coverage based on the insurance contributions paid by the insured employee. Dependents covered by the national health insurance include the insured employee's spouse, lineal ascendants, lineal descendants and their spouses, and siblings, provided they primarily rely on the insured employee for their livelihood. The Defendant, as the insurer of the national health insurance, recognizes persons in a *de facto* marital relationship as equivalent to a "spouse" and grants them dependent status in accordance with its internal guidelines.

2. Framework for Assessing Violations of the Constitutional Principle of Equality

Article 11(1) of the Republic of Korea Constitution provides that all citizens shall be equal before the law and that no one shall be discriminated against in political, economic, social, or cultural life on account of sex, religion, or social status. Article 9 of the General Act on Public Administration stipulates that administrative agencies shall not discriminate against citizens without reasonable grounds.

To determine whether an administrative act constitutes discrimination without reasonable grounds and thus violates the constitutional principle of equality, it must be examined whether the act treats essentially identical cases differently. This assessment should be based on the meaning and purpose of the legal provisions underlying the act, and whether there is essential sameness between the groups subject to differential treatment. Once such treatment is identified, the legitimacy of the act must be reviewed under the principle of proportionality to determine whether it violates the constitutional principle of equality.

3. Whether the Disposition Violates the Principle of Equality

The reason the Defendant recognizes a person in a *de facto* marital relationship as a dependent is not because the person is in a heterosexual partnership, but because that person, as the partner of the insured employee, has formed an economic and domestic union. Where a person in a same-sex partnership has formed a partner relationship with an insured employee and primarily relies on the insured for livelihood, lacking the capacity to pay insurance contributions independently, such person, like one in a *de facto* heterosexual marital relationship, should be eligible to be recognized as a dependent. The requirements should not be treated differently.

Accordingly, in the context of the dependent coverage system under the national health insurance, same-sex partners who have formed an economic and domestic union with the insured employee are essentially identical to opposite-sex partners in a *de facto* marital relationship. Nevertheless, through the Disposition in this case, the Defendant is discriminating an essentially identical group based on sexual orientation.

Next, it must be examined whether there is a reasonable ground for such different treatment. In light of the nature of the dependent system, there is no reason to treat same-sex partners differently from opposite-sex partners in a *de facto* marital relationship. For an employee insured under the National Health Insurance to register a same-sex partner as a dependent, the same conditions that apply to a partner in a *de facto* marital relationship must be met-namely, that the person is in a *de facto* marital relationship with the insured, that there is a demonstrable need for health insurance benefits, that income and property requirements are satisfied, and that two guarantors submit a letter of verification affirming the couple's union. If these requirements are met, the partner should be recognized as a dependent, unless explicitly prohibited by law.

Nevertheless, excluding a same-sex partner from dependent eligibility solely because of being of the same sex partnership constitutes discrimination based on sexual orientation, for which no justifiable reason can be found. Furthermore, this amounts to denying recognition within the dependent system of the national health insurance, which is a fundamental social security system. It constitutes a discriminatory act that infringes upon human dignity and value, the right to pursue happiness, the right to privacy, and the right to equality before the law. The extent of such infringement is also significant.

4. Conclusion

The Disposition violates the constitutional principle of equality and is therefore unlawful and must be revoked. As such, the conclusion reached by the lower court is just, and the defendant's appeal, which challenges this conclusion, is without merit and shall be dismissed.

[Separate Opinion by Justices Lee Dongwon, Noh Taeak, Oh Seokjun, and Kwon Youngjun]

Under the National Health Insurance Act, the term "spouse" presupposes a marital relationship. Relevant laws pertaining to marriage,[2] as interpreted by the Supreme Court and the Constitutional Court, view marriage as a union between individuals of the opposite sex, and interpret the term "spouse" to refer to an opposite-sex partner; same-sex partners do not fall under this definition.

Accordingly, the defendant determined that the plaintiff, a same-sex partner, did not qualify as a "person in a *de facto* marital relationship" and thus was not eligible as a dependent, and rendered the Disposition. A person in a *de facto* marital relationship with a same-sex partner cannot be regarded as belonging to the same essential group as a person in such a relationship with an opposite-sex partner. Therefore, excluding same-sex partners from dependent status and classifying them as insured self-employed persons cannot be deemed arbitrary discrimination lacking reasonable grounds.

[Concurring Opinion of Justices Kim Sanghwan and Oh Kyungmi on the Majority Opinion]

The issue of discrimination against same-sex partners transcends national borders. While considering differences in history, culture, and systems among countries, it is still meaningful to consider foreign laws and practices on this matter.

The International Covenant on Civil and Political Rights (“ICCPR”) Article 2 and Article 26 and the International Covenant on Economic, Social and Cultural Rights (“ICESCR”) Article 2 prohibit all forms of discrimination based on sex and other status, while guaranteeing that all persons are equal before the law and entitled to equal protection of the law without discrimination. International organizations responsible for implementing these covenants, such as the UN committees and the European Court of Human Rights, have generally held that denying rights granted to persons in *de facto* marital relationships to same-sex partners constitutes discrimination based on sexual orientation or other status, and thus violates the principle of equality.

The German Federal Constitutional Court, in a decision on July 7, 2009, held that the refusal of a federal state pension fund to pay survivor’s benefits to same-sex partners protected under the Life Partnership Act, while granting such benefits to opposite-sex married couples, constituted discrimination based on sexual orientation, as same-sex partnerships fall within the intimate domain of personal dignity that must be respected.

Similarly, the Supreme Court of the United States, in a decision on June 26, 2015, ruled that state laws limiting marriage to opposite-sex couples violated the constitutional principle of equal protection, thereby recognizing the right of same-sex couples to marry. Based on this decision, the Respect for Marriage Act was enacted, explicitly allowing same-sex marriages.

There is a rapidly growing global consensus on providing equal legal protection to same-sex partnerships without discrimination. The majority opinion, by correcting the discriminatory treatment of same-sex partners under the operation of the health insurance dependent system in this case and implementing the constitutional principle of equality, accords with both international treaties and global trends.

Comments

This is the first ruling that recognized the legal status of same-sex partners by granting them eligibility as dependents under the national health insurance system. Following the decision, the National Health Insurance Service ("NHIS") introduced a new form of document for verifying an economic and domestic union between same-sex partners, which made available on its website as of October 31, 2024.[3]

However, upon closer examination, the scope of this decision is somewhat limited. The National Health Insurance Act includes "spouses" among eligible dependents, but it does not explicitly specify whether this includes *de facto* relationships. The NHIS has been recognizing persons in *de facto* marital relationships as equivalent to spouses for dependent eligibility based on its internally established Guidelines on Eligibility Management.

In this case, the majority opinion held that although a same-sex partner may not fall under the category of "a person in a *de facto* marital relationship" according to the NHIS guidelines, their status is equivalent in substance. Therefore, excluding them constitutes unjust discrimination.

It still remains uncertain whether courts, including the Constitutional Court, and government agencies will also begin to recognize the status of same-sex partners in other areas of social security and in the legal framework of family law in light of this decision.

Constitutional Court of Korea No.2020HUNMA389, 2021HUNMA1264, 2022HUNMA854, 2023HUNMA846 (En Banc Decision) Rendered on August 29, 2024

Main Issue

Whether the Framework Act on Carbon Neutrality and Green Growth for Coping with Climate Crisis ("the Act")'s failure to present quantitative targets for greenhouse gas reduction for the period from 2031 to 2049, despite setting carbon neutrality by 2050 as its goal under the Act, infringes upon the environmental rights of the Petitioners.

Petitioners' Argument

1. The Petitioners are members of a youth environmental organization.
2. The Act sets the goal of achieving carbon neutrality by the year 2050. Article 8(1) of the Act and Article 3(1) of its Enforcement Decree provide that the Republic of Korea aims to reduce national greenhouse gas emissions by 40% compared to 2018 levels by the year 2030. However, the Act does not present any targets or criteria for emissions reductions between 2031 and 2049, prior to the carbon neutrality goal year.
3. The Petitioners argue that Article 8(1) of the Act fails to provide the minimum level of protection necessary to address the climate crisis and regulate greenhouse gas reduction targets accordingly. Therefore, the law violates the principle of prohibition of insufficient protection and infringes upon the Petitioners' environmental rights, rendering the relevant provisions unconstitutional.

Reasoning

1. Relevant Provisions of the Act

Article 2(3) of the Act defines carbon neutrality as a state where greenhouse gas emissions emitted, released, or leaked out into the atmosphere become net-zero as they are offset by greenhouse gas absorption elsewhere.

Article 7(1) provides that the Government shall establish a national vision for the transition to a carbon-neutral society and the promotion of harmonious development of the economy and the environment, with the aim of achieving carbon neutrality by 2050.

Specifically, Article 8(1) stipulates that the Government shall set a national medium- and long-term greenhouse gas emission reduction target ("mid- to long-term reduction target") to reduce national greenhouse gas emissions by a ratio prescribed by Presidential Decree, which shall not be less than 35% compared to 2018 levels by 2030. Furthermore, Article 3(1) of the Enforcement Decree sets this mid- to long-term national greenhouse gas reduction target at 40%.

2. Legal Framework for Reviewing Infringement of Environmental Rights

Article 35(1) of the Constitution provides that all citizens shall have the right to live in a healthy and pleasant environment, and that the State and all citizens shall endeavor to protect the environment. While the content of the right to a healthy environment is concretely defined by statute pursuant to Article 35(2), if legislation for the protection of environmental rights is absent or manifestly insufficient to the extent that it infringes upon such rights, individuals may seek relief from the Constitutional Court.

The State's duty to endeavor to protect the environment includes the obligation to respond to climate change by taking measures to reduce its causes or to adjust to its consequences, in order to prevent environmental degradation that threatens the foundations of life and endangers the safety of life and body.

The question of how the State fulfills its duty to protect fundamental rights falls, in principle, within the responsibility of the legislature or the executive, who derive democratic legitimacy directly from the people, in accordance with the principles of separation of powers and democracy. The Constitutional Court may review the implementation of such a duty by the legislature or executive only in a limited manner.

Accordingly, when reviewing whether the State has failed to fulfill its duty to protect the environmental rights of citizens, the Constitutional Court must apply the principle of the prohibition of insufficient protection, examining whether the State has taken at least appropriate and effective minimum protective measures.

Whether there has been a violation of the principle of prohibition of insufficient protection is determined by whether the protective measures taken in response to a risk situation that necessitates the protection of fundamental rights possess the minimum character necessary in proportion to the nature of the risk. If the risk involves technical or scientific complexity or has an international character, the nature of the risk must be assessed objectively based on scientific facts and international standards.

3. Whether Article 8(1) of the Act Violates the Principle of the Prohibition of Insufficient Protection

To determine this, it is necessary to examine the risk situation posed by the climate crisis and the protective measure of setting national greenhouse gas reduction targets in response. This assessment must be based on the scientific analysis and projections presented in the reports of the Intergovernmental Panel on Climate Change ("IPCC"), an intergovernmental body established to address climate change, as well as the standards for international action stipulated in the Paris Agreement, a multilateral treaty that the Republic of Korea has signed and ratified.

1) The Risk Situation: The Climate Crisis

It is a well-established scientific fact, consistently emphasized in the reports of the IPCC, that greenhouse gas emissions caused by human activities are a major driver of global warming. The effects of greenhouse gas emissions on the climate system, the resulting risks of climate change, and the effectiveness of emission reductions all possess a global character. Consequently, efforts to reduce greenhouse gas emissions are guided by standards for action based on international agreements.

2) The Protective Measure: Setting Greenhouse Gas Reduction Targets

Article 2(2) of the Paris Agreement provides that each Party's responsibility to reduce greenhouse gas emissions shall be implemented "to reflect equity and the principle of common but differentiated responsibilities and respective capabilities, in the light of different national circumstances". To that end, all Parties are required to prepare, communicate, maintain, and implement their Nationally Determined Contributions (NDCs, Articles 3 and 4).

Specifically, Article 4 of the Paris Agreement states, "[e]ach Party shall prepare, communicate and maintain successive nationally determined contributions that it intends to achieve. Parties shall pursue domestic mitigation measures, with the aim of achieving the objectives of such contributions", and "[e]ach Party shall communicate a nationally determined contribution every five years … and be informed by the outcomes of the global stocktake referred to in Article 14".

Article 14 of the Paris Agreement also provides that the Conference of the Parties shall conduct a Global Stocktake every five years starting in 2023 to assess the collective progress toward achieving the purpose and long-term goals of the Agreement.

The mid- to long-term reduction target set forth in Article 8(1) of the Act and Article 3(1) of its Enforcement Decree, namely the reduction of national greenhouse gas emissions by 40% from 2018 levels by 2030, constitutes a core element of Korea's Nationally Determined Contribution as submitted and registered with the United Nations Framework Convention on Climate Change ("UNFCCC") Secretariat in December 2021, in accordance with the above standards under the Paris Agreement.

3) Unconstitutionality of the Omission of Reduction Targets Between 2031 and 2050

While Article 8(1) of the Act specifies the reduction ratio only through 2030, it does not present any quantitative targets for the period between 2031 and 2049, prior to the carbon neutrality goal year of 2050.

Meanwhile, Article 8(4) of the Act provides that the government shall review the targets every five years, considering the Paris Agreement and domestic and international conditions, and may revise or newly set the targets in accordance with the principle of progression stipulated in Article 4 of the Paris Agreement.[4] However, this merely reflects a non-binding international norm and lacks substantial enforceability. A reduction system that depends solely on the government's discretion cannot guarantee the pace of reduction or the consistency of policy.

Ultimately, even considering the other provisions of the Act, there are no effective mechanisms in place to ensure gradual and continuous reductions toward the 2050 carbon neutrality goal. This results in a regulatory structure that imposes an undue burden on future generations, and the lack of predetermined quantitative benchmarks for the post-2030 period fails to meet the minimum requirements for a protective measure corresponding to the severity of the climate crisis as a risk situation.

4. Conclusion

Article 8(1) of the Act violates the State's duty to protect fundamental rights by failing to present quantitative reduction targets for the period between 2031 and 2049, thereby infringing upon the Petitioners' environmental rights in violation of the principle of the prohibition of insufficient protection.[5]

However, the reduction target set for the year 2030 under the same provision does not constitute a violation of the principle of prohibition of insufficient protection. If the entire provision were to be invalidated, the interim target for 2030 would also be nullified, resulting in the elimination of institutional mechanisms for greenhouse gas reduction, an outcome that would be even more incompatible with the Constitution. Therefore, the Constitutional Court issues a decision of unconstitutionality with temporary application and orders the continued application of the provision until February 28, 2026, by which time corrective legislation must be enacted.

Comments

This case marks a landmark decision in which, amid growing global efforts to address the climate crisis through judicial systems, the Petitioners' claims were upheld for the first time in Asia, declaring the failure of specific climate legislation to include necessary interim reduction target as unconstitutional. The Constitutional Court closely examined both the Paris Agreement, which establishes the obligations of member states to reduce greenhouse gas emissions, and the Framework Act on Carbon Neutrality and Green Growth for Coping with Climate Crisis, which implements those obligations in domestic law, to assess whether the State had fulfilled its constitutional duty to protect fundamental rights.

Importantly, the Court emphasized that the more direct and severe impacts of climate change will be borne not by the present generation but by future generations. Since legislation to establish greenhouse gas reduction targets may restrict the rights of present citizens to ensure the rights of future ones, and since future generations have limited access to participation in the democratic process, the Court underscored that judicial review of legislative inaction in this area must be more stringent.

Going forward, legislators and policymakers should not only consider scientific, policy, and diplomatic considerations, along with competing interests, when setting reduction targets, but also recognize that these targets are now subject to increased judicial scrutiny, as affirmed in this case.

Supreme Court of Korea No.2022DA289051 Rendered on December 19, 2024 (En Banc Judgment)

Main Issue

Whether an administrative agency's failure to fulfill its duty to enact regulatory improvements to ensure the accessibility rights of persons with disabilities constitutes an unlawful omission

Plaintiffs' Argument

The Plaintiffs are persons with physical disabilities who must use wheelchairs. The Defendant (the Republic of Korea) has a legal obligation to implement corrective measures against discrimination under the relevant laws and regulations.

However, even though the laws concerning persons with disabilities and their enforcement decrees exclude most of the convenience stores from the scope of facilities required to install accessibility features, thereby severely restricting the Plaintiffs' right of access to those stores, the Defendant failed to amend the regulations for an extended period. Therefore, the Defendant is liable to compensate the Plaintiffs for damages by paying solatium for the unlawful act.

Reasoning

1. Relevant Provisions

Article 7 of the Act on Guarantee of Convenience Promotion for Persons with Disabilities, Senior Citizens, and Pregnant Women (hereinafter the "Convenience Promotion Act") provides that the scope of facilities subject to the obligation to install facilities and equipment for the convenience of persons with disabilities in daily movement ("accessibility facilities") and use of facilities shall be prescribed by Presidential Decree. Article 3, Annex 1, Paragraph 2(a)(1) of the Enforcement Decree of the Convenience Promotion Act ("the Enforcement Decree") stipulates that supermarkets and daily goods retail stores ("small-scale retail stores") with a floor area of less than 300m² shall be excluded from the category of facilities obligated to install accessibility facilities.

These provisions of the Convenience Promotion Act and its Enforcement Decree remained unchanged for more than 24 years since its implementation on April 11, 1998. However, on February 10, 2022, the Court of First Instance rendered a decision holding that the Article 3 of the Enforcement Decree, which excluded too wide a range of small-scale retail stores from the obligation to install accessibility facilities, substantially failed to guarantee the accessibility rights of persons with disabilities and thus exceeded the scope of delegation under Article 7 of the Convenience Promotion Act, rendering it invalid. In response, on April 27, 2022, the Defendant amended Article 3 of the Enforcement Decree, reducing the floor area threshold for exclusion from the obligation from 300m^2 to less than 50m^2.

2. Failure to Fulfill the Administrative Legislative Duty to Ensure Accessibility Rights of Persons with Disabilities

(1) Content of the Administrative Legislative Duty to Ensure Accessibility

The right of access refers to the right of persons with disabilities to independently access facilities and equipment used in daily life. This right is a fundamental right grounded in the constitutional principles of human dignity and the pursuit of happiness. The State is obligated to take legal and institutional measures to ensure its effective protection. In fulfillment of this duty, the National Assembly enacted the Convenience Promotion Act and the Act on the Prohibition of Discrimination against Persons with Disabilities and Remedy Against Infringement of Their Rights (hereinafter the "Disability Discrimination Prohibition Act"), which expressly provide that persons with disabilities shall have the right to use facilities and equipment on an equal basis with non-disabled persons and the right to receive reasonable accommodations. These laws impose on the State the obligation to prepare related policy measures and to take corrective action against discrimination.

Furthermore, the United Nations Convention on the Rights of Persons with Disabilities ("CRPD"), to which the Republic of Korea became a party, entered into force domestically on January 10, 2009. Article 4(1) of the CRPD provides that States Parties are obligated to guarantee the full realization of the human rights and fundamental freedoms of persons with disabilities without discrimination based on disability. Article 9(1) also requires States Parties to take appropriate measures to ensure that persons with disabilities have access, on an equal basis with others, to facilities and services open or provided to the public.

(2) Unlawful Failure to Fulfill the Duty to Amend the Enforcement Decree

According to national statistics, the proportion of convenience stores subject to the obligation to install accessibility facilities-limited under the Enforcement Decree to stores with a floor area of 300m^2 or more- was only 0.1% in 2006 and 1.8% in 2019.

Since the Convenience Promotion Act first came into force in 1998, the Disability Discrimination Prohibition Act was enacted and entered into force in 2008 to strengthen the protection of accessibility and equality rights, and the CRPD entered into force domestically in 2009, thereby imposing binding international obligations on the government to ensure accessibility. Accordingly, at least from around 2008, the Defendant bore a legislative duty to amend the Enforcement Decree to improve accessibility to small-scale retail stores for persons with disabilities. Nevertheless, the Defendant failed to fulfill this duty for a period of 14 years.

3. Existence of State Liability for Damages

(1) Elements for State Liability

When a public official, judged by the standard of an ordinary public official, neglects their duty of objective care while performing their duties, and as a result, the act in question loses its objective legitimacy, the state may be held liable for damages under Article 2 of the State Compensation Act.

Article 3 of the Enforcement Decree excluded over 95% of small-scale retail stores from the obligation to install accessibility facilities, thereby rendering the legislative purposes and contents of the Convenience Promotion Act and the Disability Discrimination Prohibition Act effectively meaningless. Even from the perspective of an average public official, it is relatively clear that the provision failed to reflect the legislative intent and substance of the relevant statutes.

On October 29, 2014, the UN Committee on the Rights of Persons with Disabilities expressed concern over South Korea's accessibility standards being limited by building size, volume, or date of construction. Additionally, on December 14, 2017, the National Human Rights Commission of Korea issued a recommendation to the Minister of Health and Welfare to revise the relevant provision to ensure access to small-scale retail stores for persons with disabilities. Given such guidance, officials of the Defendant should have been well aware, at least by the mid-2010s, that failure to amend the regulation constituted an unlawful omission in fulfilling the State's duty to guarantee accessibility for persons with disabilities.

Therefore, the Defendant's omission in failing to fulfill its legislative duty for over 14 years significantly departed from the purposes and contents of the Convenience Promotion Act and the Disability Discrimination Prohibition Act. This constitutes a loss of objective legitimacy and qualifies as an unlawful act committed by a public official through negligence in violation of law, as stipulated under Article 2(1) of the State Compensation Act.

(2) Recognition of Emotional Distress

For 24 years following the enactment of the Enforcement Decree, the National Assembly repeatedly expressed its intention to guarantee the constitutional right to access for persons with disabilities, including through the enactment of the Disability Discrimination Prohibition Act and the ratification of the CRPD. Nevertheless, the regulation restricting access to small-scale retail stores remained unchanged, resulting in prolonged suffering for persons with disabilities, whose dignity and value as human beings were routinely denied in daily life.

The amendment of the regulation on April 27, 2022, does not retroactively erase or nullify the emotional pain and difficulties endured by persons with disabilities in the intervening period. The State has a constitutional, statutory, and treaty-based obligation to protect persons with disabilities and ensure they enjoy the same dignity and worth as non-disabled persons. This is a duty incumbent on all state institutions to realize social integration by removing physical barriers to full social participation and equality.

Thus, awarding compensation for the suffering caused by the Defendant's unlawful omission is not a matter of sympathy or benevolence, but a recognition of the State's responsibility. It also serves to prompt the timely fulfillment of legislative duties and the active implementation of protective policies for persons with disabilities.

Accordingly, the Defendant is liable to pay solatium to Plaintiffs 1 and 2, who are persons with physical disabilities.

(3) Scope of Compensation for Emotional Distress

The prolonged legislative omission concerning Article 3 of the Enforcement Decree resulted in significant disadvantage to persons with physical disabilities, who were denied their right of access in daily life. Although the affected class is broad, the Defendant has since made efforts to rectify the unlawful omission, including the amendment of the regulation on April 27, 2022, and continuing further revisions.

Therefore, the appropriate amount of solatium for emotional distress suffered by Plaintiffs 1 and 2 due to the Defendant's unlawful omission shall be ₩100,000 each.

4. Conclusion

Nevertheless, the lower court ruled that the Defendant was not liable for state compensation. This constitutes a misapplication of the law that affected the outcome of the decision. Accordingly, the relevant portion of the lower court's judgment is reversed, and this Court renders a judgment.

Comments

This case was initially brought in response to the widespread lack of ramps and the presence of steps at the entrances of convenience stores, which significantly impacts the right of access for persons with disabilities in their daily lives. The Supreme Court ruling is meaningful in that it is the first decision to explicitly recognize the right of access for persons with disabilities as a constitutionally guaranteed fundamental right. It is also the first decision to acknowledge state liability for damages due to legislative inaction by administrative authorities.

The relevant laws including a Presidential Decree were enacted to guarantee access for persons with disabilities to public-use facilities to specify the scope of buildings required to install accessibility facilities. However, they failed to guarantee the right of access for the handicapped, because 98% of convenience stores nationwide were exempt from this obligation. In response, the plaintiffs filed this lawsuit in 2018 against the corporation operating the convenience stores, demanding the installation of ramps, and simultaneously filed a suit against the state seeking damages.

The Court of First Instance found that the Decree was unconstitutional and invalid, as it imposed the duty to install accessibility facilities only on a very small number of convenience stores. This, the court found, went beyond the scope of authority granted by the parent law, infringed the freedom of movement of persons with disabilities, and violated the constitutional principle of equality. The court accordingly ordered the corporation to install accessible pathways at directly managed stores. However, the court rejected the claim for damages against the state, finding that the state had not committed an unlawful act (*Seoul Central District Court Judgement 2018GAHAB524424 rendered on February 10, 2022*). The corporate defendants did not appeal this decision, while the plaintiffs appealed for the rejection of their claim against the state defendant. However, the appellate court dismissed the appeal (*Seoul High Court Judgement 2022NA2009024 rendered on October 6, 2022*).

The Supreme Court overturned the appellate decision, ruling that the conditions for recognizing state liability for damages due to administrative legislative inaction included whether the inaction had lost objective legitimacy and whether there was negligence on the part of public officials. In making this determination, the Court considered not only the parent law of the Decree (the Convenience Promotion Act) but also the Disability Discrimination Prohibition Act, the UN Convention on the Rights of Persons with Disabilities, and recommendations from the UN Committee on the Rights of Persons with Disabilities. This suggests that, in assessing whether the state has properly fulfilled its duty to protect individual fundamental rights, the Court considers not only domestic factors but also international standards, such as international instruments and the opinions of international bodies.

Notes

1 Korean nationals who reside in the Republic of Korea shall be health insurance policyholders or their dependents (National Health Insurance Act §5). The health insurance policyholders shall be divided into the insured employee and the insured self-employed. Workers and employers of all workplaces and public officials shall become the insured employee, while persons who are neither the insured employee nor their dependents shall be the insured self-employed [§6 (1), (2), (3)].

2 The Constitution §36(1) provides that "Marriage and family life shall be entered into and sustained on the basis of individual dignity and equality of the sexes, and the State shall do everything in its power to achieve that goal". The Civil Act presumes a distinction and union between the two sexes and refers to married parties as "husband" and "wife" (The Civil Act §826, §827, §847, §848, §850 and §851). It also uses the term "parents" as the counterpart to "children" (§772 and §781).

3 https://www.nhis.or.kr/nhis/minwon/wbhaba03900m01.do?mode=view&articleNo=10847140

4 Paris Agreement §4 (3) Each Party's successive nationally determined contribution will represent a progression beyond the Party's then current nationally determined contribution and reflect its highest possible ambition, reflecting its common but differentiated responsibilities and respective capabilities, in the light of different national circumstances.

5 The Constitutional Court also found that Article 8(1) of the Act violated the principle of statutory reservation, including the principle of parliamentary reservation; however, this paper, which primarily addresses the application of international public law, does not discuss that issue in detail.

KYIL

Judicial Decisions in Private International Law (2024)

Jung Hwa YOU
Judge for Cross-Border Cooperation & Coordination (CBCC) at Seoul Bankruptcy Court
Seoul, Republic of Korea

Abstract

This report analyzes three major 2024 Supreme Court decisions in Korea related to private international law. First, the Court reaffirmed the English Penalty Rule, holding that an agreed sum for nonperformance deemed extravagant and unconscionable under English law constitutes an unenforceable penalty, and that Korean Civil Act Article 398(2) on reduction of excessive liquidated damages is not an international mandatory rule (2019Da261558). Second, in determining the "place of arbitration", the Court clarified that the legal seat (place of arbitration), the physical location of hearings, and the arbitral institution's office can differ; recognition or enforcement of an award can only be refused if procedural rights were infringed to an intolerable extent (2024Ma5904). Third, the Court held that under English law, an insurer's right to claim damages from a third party after paying insurance proceeds does not automatically transfer through a letter of subrogation; instead, valid statutory or equitable assignment requirements under the UK Marine Insurance Act 1906 and UK Law of Property Act 1925 must be satisfied for enforceability (2019Da256501).

Key Words

Liquidated Damages, Penalty, Korean Civil Act Article 398(2), Place of Arbitration, Korean Arbitration Act Article 36, Korean Arbitration

Act Article 38, Subrogation, UK Marine Insurance Act 1906, Assignment

1. Applicable Law

1-1. Liquidated Damages vs. Penalty

Supreme Court Decision 2019Da261558 Decided April 25, 2024 【Damages (Etc.)】

【Main Issues and Holdings】

[1] Whether an agreed payment for nonperformance of an obligation that is extravagant and unconscionable under the law of the United Kingdom corresponds to an unenforceable penalty (affirmative).

The standard of determining whether an agreed payment for the nonperformance of an obligation corresponds to liquidated damages or a penalty and, in such a case, whether "a legitimate interest to compel the performance of contractual obligations of the other party" should be limited to compensation for the maximum amount of estimated damages resulting from a breach of contract (negative).

[2] Whether under Article 398(2) of the Civil Act, which stipulates that where the amount of damages determined in advance is unduly excessive, the court may reduce the amount to a more reasonable and appropriate sum that may be included in international mandatory provisions stipulated in Article 7 of the former Act on Private International Law that should govern the corresponding legal relations irrespective of the applicable law (negative).

Whether the application of the provisions of the law of the United Kingdom should be seen to correspond to an evident violation of good customs and other social order of the Republic of Korea stipulated in Article 10 of the former Act on Private International

Law on the grounds that the amount of damages determined in advance cannot be separately reduced as a result of the application of the law of the United Kingdom, which is the applicable law (negative).

【Summary of Decision】

[1] An agreed payment for the nonperformance of an obligation under the law of the United Kingdom is divided into liquidated damages or a penalty according to the details of the agreed payment, and if the details of the agreed payment for the nonperformance of an obligation are extravagant and unconscionable, it would correspond to a penalty and thus would be unenforceable [the so-called penalty rule; see, e.g., *Dunlop Pneumatic Tyre Co Ltd v New Garage and Motor Co Ltd* [1915] AC 79]. Whether the agreed payment for the nonperformance of an obligation corresponds to liquidated damages or a penalty, as a matter of the interpretation of a contract, should be determined on the basis of whether the agreed payment is within the scope proportionate to a legitimate interest to compel the performance of contractual obligations of the other party in consideration of the circumstances at the time of the contract and, in such a case, whether "a legitimate interest to compel the performance of contractual obligations of the other party" is not limited to compensation for the maximum amount of estimated damages resulting from a breach of contract (see *Cavendish Square Holding BV v Makdessi* [2015] UKSC 67). Furthermore, whether the agreed payment for the nonperformance of an obligation corresponds to a penalty should be determined after comprehensively considering the following matters, such as whether the details of the agreed payment for the nonperformance of an obligation require the uniform payment of a certain amount without considering the contents and degree of violation of the obligation, whether the amount of damages can be easily estimated at the time of the conclusion of the contract, whether the contract to which the agreed payment for the nonperformance of an obligation is added is

a commercial contract, and whether the parties to the contract have equal bargaining power, etc. (see the above decisions).

[2] Whether Article 398(2) of the Civil Act, which stipulates that where the amount of damages determined in advance is unduly excessive, the court may reduce the amount to a more reasonable and appropriate sum, gives the authority to the court to modify the details of the contract by intervening in the contract of the parties through a reduction by the discretion of a judge. The above provision cannot be deemed an international mandatory provision as referred to in Article 7 of the former Act on Private International Law (amended by Act No. 18670, Jan. 4, 2022) that should apply to the corresponding legal relations irrespective of the applicable law in light of the purpose, nature, and contents of legislation. Moreover, the application of the provisions of the law of the United Kingdom should be seen to correspond to "an evident violation of good customs and other social order of the Republic of Korea" stipulated in Article 10 of the former Act on Private International Law on the grounds that the amount of damages determined in advance cannot be separately reduced as a result of the application of the law of the United Kingdom, which is the applicable law.

2. Recognition and Enforcement of Foreign Judgments and Commercial Arbitral Awards

2-1. The "Place of Arbitration"

Supreme Court Order 2024Ma5904 Dated June 27, 2024 【Permission for Recognition and Enforcement of Arbitral Awards】

【Main Issues and Holdings】

[1] Meaning of the "place of arbitration"

Whether the "place of arbitration", the "location of arbitration", and the "seat of the arbitral institution" should be the same (negative).

Whether the place of arbitration may be seen to have been decided by agreement where the parties came to an arrangement designating a specific place as the place for settlement of disputes in an arbitration agreement, (affirmative in principle).

[2] Whether an infringement upon the procedural rights of the parties is noticeable in the arbitral proceedings and thus should reach an unacceptable extent to correspond to the grounds to refuse the recognition and enforcement of the arbitral awards as referred to in Articles 36(2)(1)(d) and 38(1)(a) of the Arbitration Act and Article 5(1)(d) of the United Nations Convention on the Recognition and Enforcement of Foreign Arbitral Awards (affirmative).

【Summary of Order】

[1] The "place of arbitration" refers to a legal place for an arbitration to be held, and the parties to an arbitration agreement can decide the place of arbitration freely by agreement. The place of arbitration, unless otherwise agreed, serves as a standard to establish the law applicable to the arbitral proceedings and to distinguish arbitral awards rendered in the Republic of Korea from foreign arbitral awards (Article 2 of the Arbitration Act). Meanwhile, the placc of arbitration is distinguished from the "location of arbitration" where the arbitral proceedings, including hearings, are actually made, and as the "seat of the arbitral institution" means the seat of the office of an institution managing the arbitral proceedings including the constitution of the arbitral tribunal, the place of arbitration, the location of arbitration, and the seat of the arbitral institution do not need to be the same and may be designated differently. Furthermore, where the parties came to an arrangement designating a specific place as the place for settlement of disputes in an arbitration agreement, the place of arbitration can be seen to have been decided by agreement unless there are special circumstances.

[2] Articles 36(2)(1)(d) and 38(1)(a) of the Arbitration Act and

Article 5(1)(d) of the United Nations Convention on the Recognition and Enforcement of Foreign Arbitral Awards stipulate that the recognition or enforcement of the arbitral award can be refused where the composition of the arbitral tribunal or the arbitral procedure that was the basis of an arbitral award was not in accordance with the arbitration agreement between the parties or violated the Arbitration Act or any non-mandatory provision thereof. However, it is insufficient on the sole basis of a violation of the agreement between the parties or any non-mandatory provision, and an infringement upon the procedural rights of the parties is noticeable in the arbitral proceedings and thus should reach an unacceptable extent to correspond to the grounds to refuse the recognition and enforcement of the arbitral awards stipulated in the above provisions.

3. Interpretation of Foreign Laws

3-1. The Subrogation of the Insurer

Supreme Court Decision 2019Da256501 Decided July 25, 2024 【Indemnity Amount】

【Main Issues and Holdings】

[1] Applicable law of a legal relationship surrounding whether the insurer pays insurance proceeds to the insured and acquires the right of the insured against a third party under a contract of insurance with a foreign element (held: law applicable to a contract of insurance).

[2] Method of confirming the details of a foreign law applicable to a legal relationship with a foreign element and interpreting the meaning thereof.

[3] Meaning and scope of the subrogation of the insurer in accordance with the UK Marine Insurance Act 1906 and the meaning

of the phrase "the insurer is subrogated to all the rights and remedies of the insured related to the objective of the insurance" as referred to herein; Method of the insurer being subrogated to the rights of the insured including a right to claim damages, etc. against a third party through a lawsuit under the UK Marine Insurance Act 1906.

[4] Requirements for the assignment of the claim-based right to be valid under the UK Law of Property Act 1925 and requirements for equitable assignment under the UK Law of Equity and the standard of judgment thereon.

【Summary of Decision】

[1] The legal nature of a legal relationship in which in relation to damages caused by an act committed by a third party, the insurer who paid insurance proceeds acquires the right of an insurance policyholder or an insured person against a third party corresponds to the transfer of a claim by Act.

The main text of Article 35 of the former Act on Private International Law (wholly amended by Act No. 18670, Jan. 4, 2022) prescribes that "the transfer of a claim by Act shall be governed by the applicable law of the legal relations between the old creditor and the new creditor, which are the cause of the transfer", and thus a legal relationship surrounding whether a claim may be transferred by Act should follow the applicable law of the legal relations between the old creditor and the new creditor, which are the cause of the transfer.

According to such provision of Article 35(1) of the former Act on Private International Law, a legal relationship surrounding whether the insurer who pays insurance proceeds to the insured in accordance with the insurance contract, acquires the right of the insured against a third party under a contract of insurance with a foreign element should be governed by the applicable law of the insurance contract, corresponding to the legal relations between the insured and the insurer.

[2] When confirming the details of a foreign law applicable to a legal relationship with a foreign element and interpreting the meaning thereof, the foreign law should be interpreted and applied in the same way as the foreign law has been interpreted and applied in its country.

[3] With respect of the subrogation of the insurer, Article 79 of the UK Marine Insurance Act 1906 regulates that "where the insurer pays for a total loss, either of the whole, or in the case of goods of any apportionable part, of the subject-matter insured, the insurer thereupon becomes entitled to take over the interest of the insured in whatever may remain of the subject-matter so paid for, and the insurer is thereby subrogated to all the rights and remedies of the insured in and in respect of that subject-matter as from the time of the casualty causing the loss" (Para. (1)) and "subject to the foregoing provisions, where the insurer pays for a partial loss, the insurer acquires no title to the subject-matter insured, or such part of it as may remain, but the insurer is thereupon subrogated to all rights and remedies of the insured in and in respect of the subject-matter insured as from the time of the casualty causing the loss, in so far as the insured has been indemnified, according to this Act, by such payment for the loss" (Para. (2)).

The subrogation of the insurer under the UK Marine Insurance Act 1906 means that the insurer, who compensates damages of the insured caused to the subject-matter insured on behalf of the insured, becomes entitled to take over the interest of the insured in whatever may remain of the subject-matter so paid for or is subrogated to all the rights and remedies of the insured related to the subject-matter insured. According to the legal principle of the UK Marine Insurance Act 1906, the insurer who paid insurance proceeds may be subrogated to the right of the insured to claim damages against a third party and contractual rights pursuant to Article 79 of the same Act may be subrogated to the interest that the insured recovered including the proceeds from the sale of remnants.

Herein, that the insurer is subrogated to all the rights and remedies of the insured and in respect of the subject-matter insured means that the insurer is qualified to realize the rights or remedies of the insured in the name of the insured by paying insurance proceeds to the insured but does not mean that such rights are transferred to the insurer.

According to the legal principle of the UK Marine Insurance Act 1906, for the insurer to be subrogated to the right of the insured to claim damages against a third party through a lawsuit, the insurer, in principle, should bring a lawsuit in the name of the insured after receiving the authority to bring a lawsuit in the name of the insured and cannot exercise the right in his or her own name without receiving his or her right from the insured.

[4] Article 136(1) of the Law of Property Act 1925 stipulates that the assignment of the claim-based right shall be deemed valid when fulfilling the following requirements that: any debt or other legal thing in action should be transferred; any absolute assignment should be made; notice should be given by writing under the hand of assigner; and express notice of such assignment in writing should be given to the debtor. Meanwhile, in the case of an equitable assignment as referred to in the UK Law of Equity, the intention of immediately transferring the claim-based right specified explicitly without withdrawal should be explicitly expressed and whether such intention exists should be determined objectively.

[5] In this case, Stock Company A concluded an insurance contract of marine cargo, which deems Insurance Company C and the insured as Stock Company A and the Institute Cargo Clauses A, as the terms and conditions of the contract, after requesting the transportation of a cargo to Stock Company B in the process of importing a generator, from a foreign company located in the United States. When Stock Company D verified that a cargo delivered to

Stock Company A was damaged by physical impact while transporting the cargo into the Republic of Korea after receiving a commission from a partner company of Stock Company B located in the United States, Insurance Company C, which received the Letter of Subrogation after paying insurance proceeds to Stock Company A, exercised the right of Stock Company A to claim damages against Stock Company B. The Supreme Court held that as the above insurance contract of marine cargo should be governed by UK law in accordance with the provision on the applicable law of the Institute Cargo Clauses A that the insurance policy regards as the terms and conditions of the insurance, a legal relationship surrounding whether Insurance Company C pays insurance proceeds to Stock Company A, which is the insured, and acquires a right of Stock Company A to claim damages against Stock Company B pursuant to the insurance contract of marine cargo should follow UK law, which is the law applicable to an insurance contract of marine cargo, which is the cause of the transfer of the right; according to the legal principles of the Marine Insurance Act 1906, even if Insurance Company C pays insurance proceeds to Stock Company A, the right of Stock Company A to claim damages against Stock Company B cannot be seen to be transferred to Insurance Company C; in light of the details included in the Letter of Subrogation that Stock Company A issued to Insurance Company C, Stock Company A is seen to have given the authority, etc. to bring a lawsuit against Stock Company B to Insurance Company C, but the claim-based right that is subject to assignment has not been specified, and Stock Company A cannot be seen to have absolutely expressed any intention of assigning such claim-based right or have explicitly expressed the intention of immediately transferring such right without withdrawal, and thus viewing that requirements for the assignment of the claim-based rights stipulated in Article 136(1) of the UK Law of Property Act 1925 and requirements for equitable assignment under the UK Law of Equity are satisfied on the sole basis of the details included in the above Letter of Subrogation is difficult; and, therefore, Insurance Company C cannot exercise the right of Stock Company A to claim damages against Stock Company B.

KOREAN DOMESTIC LAWS

KOREAN DOMESTIC LAWS

The Editorial Board
ILA Korean Branch

1. A list of recent Korean domestic laws is available on the online legal database of the Korea Legislation Research Institute (KLRI).

https://www.klri.re.kr/eng.do

TREATIES/AGREEMENTS CONCLUDED BY THE REPUBLIC OF KOREA

TREATIES/AGREEMENTS CONCLUDED BY THE REPUBLIC OF KOREA

The Editorial Board
ILA Korean Branch

1. BILATERAL AGREEMENTS

https://treatyweb.mofa.go.kr/usr/treaty/selectTreatyInfomationList.do

2. MULTILATERAL AGREEMENTS

https://treatyweb.mofa.go.kr/usr/treaty/selectTreatyInfomationList.do?trgtscopeCd=TRGTSCOPE_1007

INDEX

AUTHOR GUIDELINES AND STYLE SHEET

I. SUBMISSION

Manuscripts should be submitted in Microsoft Word and electronically sent to ilakoreanbranch@gmail.com

II. GENERAL TERMS AND PEER-REVIEW SYSTEM OF PUBLICATION

All manuscripts are subject to initial evaluation by the KYIL Editorial Board and subsequently sent out to independent reviewers for a peer review. The Editorial Board accepts manuscripts on a rolling basis and will consider requests for an expedited review in appropriate cases.

III. FORMATING

1. ABSTRACT

Please include an abstract (no more than 150 words) at the beginning of an article.

2. TEXT

Main Text: Times New Roman, font size 12, 1.5 spacing
Endnotes: Times New Roman, font size 12, single spacing

3. CITING REFERENCE

The KYIL requires endnotes with subsequent numbering; the initial endnote should be indicated with '*,' if it is necessary to provide explanatory information about the manuscript.

Please include a reference list for all works the are cited at the end of the manuscript.

IV. NOTES

1. BOOKS

P. Malanczuk, *Akehurst's Modern Introduction to International Law*, 7th ed. (New York: Eoutledge, 1997), p. 1.

2. ARTICLES

Chao Wang, *China's Preferential Trade Remedy Approaches: A New Haven School Perspective*, Vol.21 No.1, Asia Pacific Law Review, (2013), p. 103.

3. ARTICLES IN COLLECTIONS

J. Paulsson & Z. Douglas, *Indirect Expropriation in Investment Treaty Arbitrations, in* Arbitration Foreign Investment Disputes 148 (N. Horn & S. Kroll eds., Kluwer Law International, 2004).

4. ARTICLES IN NEWSPAPER

YI Whan-Woo, *Korea, New Zealand embrace free trade pact*, Korea Times, November 14, 2014.

5. UNPUBLISHED MATERIALS

PARK Jung-Won, *Minority Rights Constraints on a State's Power to Regulate Citizenship under International Law*, Ph.D thesis (2006), on file with author.

6. WORKING PAPERS AND REPORTS

OECD, *'Indirect Expropriation' and the 'Right to Regulate' in International Investment Law*, OECD Working Paper, 2014/09.

7. INTERNET SOURCES

C. Schreuer, The Concept of Expropriation under the ETC and Other Investment Protection Treaties (2005), http://www.univie,ac,at/intlaw/pdf/csunpuyblpaper_3pdf. [Accessed on September 22, 2015]

V. GUIDELINE FOR AUTHORS

1. ARTICLE

Manuscripts must be in the form of a regular paper including endnotes and references. The length for an articles should not exceed 10,000 words in English excluding notes and references.

2. SPECIAL REPORT

Manuscripts for Special Report must be in the form of a descriptive report which covers the international law issues related to Korea in the past 5 years. Special Report must include author's comments with less than 10 endnotes and 5 references. The length for a special report should be no more the 5,000 words.

3. RECENT DEVELOPMENT

Manuscripts must cover the trends in international law related to Korea in the preceding year. Recent Development must be in the form of a short report, including less than 5 endnotes. The length for Recent Development should be no more than 2,000 words.